The Top Shooter's Guide To
Cowboy Action Shooting

Hunter Scott Anderson

Published by

krause
publications

700 E. State Street • Iola, WI 54990-0001
Telephone: 715/445-2214

www.krause.com

Please call or write for our free catalog.
Our toll-free number to place an order or obtain a free catalog is 800-258-0929
or please use our regular business telephone 715-445-2214
for editorial comment and further information.

Library of Congress Catalog Number: 00-110081
ISBN: 0-87341-871-9

Printed in the United States of America

Dedicated to:

My wife, Donna, for taking care of our family, and the patience and understanding her special gift of love brings.

All cowboy action shooters, past, present, and those of the future.

Finally, to SASS® and the other organizations of this shooting sport that bring the Old West closer to our hearts, while supporting our freedoms and reminding us of our responsibility to protect and preserve those rights.

Bounty Hunter
1849

FOREWORD

This is one book every cowboy action shooter should read and use as a reference for shooting. It will also bring you closer to the sport. It is written by a man who has been in the trenches since the early days, and I can think of no one better suited. Bounty Hunter has done much more than his share in bringing new people to the sport. Like most of us, he has made his mistakes along the way, but has learned and taught others from them. I've butted heads with him, gotten drunk with him, traveled with him, and shot side-by-side with him. Through it all one thing has remained… I'm proud to call him my friend. No doubt, he is one to ride the river with!

Judge Roy Bean, SASS® #1

CONTENTS

INTRODUCTION

Cowboy action shooting is another one of America's unique sports. This recreational shooting sport offers much more than simply shooting the firearms associated with the time period known as the Old West or the American frontier.

As with any activity, it is the people who make cowboy action shooting what it is, and what it is seen as to the outside world. People from all walks of life populated the American frontier of the 19th century. Just as it was more than 100 years past, it is again today. There are no boundaries to participation in cowboy action shooting. This sport knows no prejudice insofar as gender, color, or religious creed. A cowboy action shooter stands as just that. Any judgment rendered is that of what you do on the range, and not who you are. Cowboy action shooting takes the best of history from times past and leaves the worst in the dust.

There can be no doubt that two of the common bonds folks find in this sport are a love of the Old West and the challenge of competition. The fact that this game is attracting so many people is not surprising. The time period represented by cowboy action shooting, from approximately 1860 to just after the turn of the century, has inspired more films, more books, and more paintings than any other period of U.S. history, perhaps more than any other like period in the history of mankind. Millions upon millions of people throughout the world have found the romance of the Old West hard to resist. Who has never, while watching their favorite Western film, put themselves in the place of the good guy standing up to evil, bringing peace, justice and happiness to the valley? It was in many ways a simple time, with simple codes of behavior. The Western spirit dwells in all of us. Perhaps the strongest bonds found among cowboy shooters every-

where are more akin to the human virtues of honesty, generosity, respect for others, and love. Combine all these different emotions with one heck of a great shooting sport, and we know now that if you build it, they will come.

This sport is primarily a three-gun sporting competition that finds competitors dressed in their personally chosen outfits of the Old West, or even the Western outfits of their favorite Hollywood characters. The firearms used are the single-action style of pistols, primarily the lever style of rifles or carbines of the period, and finally the appropriate shotguns, mainly the double-barrel or exposed-hammer pumps. It is not a "fast-draw" or "quick-draw" style of competition many are familiar with. It does however employ the use of live ammunition, and requires basic movement while shooting at mostly steel targets.

There are other books and videos on this sport that provide excellent sources of in-depth information about the clothing, leather, firearms, and other accessories available. This one will provide less about those subjects and more about the methods of improving one's performance while engaging in main stage shooting scenarios.

Although there are several other national entities, the largest governing organization of cowboy action shooting is SASS® (The Single Action Shooting Society). Today, there are more than 40,000 shooters competing as SASS® members in more than 250 SASS®-affiliated clubs. These clubs are in every state, as well as Canada, Australia, and more than one European nation. There are an estimated 100,000 participants in the cowboy action shooting sport.

While some of the largest cowboy action shooting matches are requiring entrants be SASS® members in order to compete, membership is not required in most. SASS® members are entitled to register and enjoy the use of their own alias (no one competes under their actual name). Members also receive a quarterly publication, *The Cowboy Chronicle©*, providing news, stories, upcoming matches, lists of affiliated clubs around the world, and advertising for products or services related to the sport. It is an interesting and often provocative publication that the shooters may use to contribute and be heard.

As mentioned, this book deals directly with the details of competing in this sport. It will stress at all times the importance of SAFETY, but, in itself, must not be considered a safety course for the use of firearms. ***Any person handling firearms should complete a National Safety Firearms course from an NRA-Certified Instructor. The mishandling of firearms is dangerous and can result in serious injury, even death. Neither the author of this book, the publisher, nor any other contributing party can assume any liability for any accident resulting from the actions of those using firearms or who read this book.***

Okay, now that the lawyer and legal talk is out of the way, let's go into the trenches of cowboy action shooting and talk about some serious fun.

H.S.A.

Chapter 1

THE COMPETITION WITHIN

One of the many beautiful facets of cowboy action shooting is how diversified the competition within the game truly is.

Over time, SASS® has wisely seen fit to expand the recognition of all those who compete in these events by increasing the number of different classes, thus making room for everyone. Classes (or categories) are determined by firearm choice, propellant or powder choice, by one or two-handed styles of shooting, by shooting handguns with both the left and right hands simultaneously, by centerfire cartridge handguns, and by cap and ball percussion handguns. Determination of class is also offered to women shooters, junior shooters, senior shooters and finally super senior shooters.

Whether some will admit it or not, in most of us there exists both a competitive nature and the desire to be recog-

Photo 1.0A - *Cowboy action shooting spans the gender and the generation gaps. (Left to right: Kris Hammons, a.k.a. "Calico Kris," SASS® #2416, Dave Jones, a.k.a. "Dunsmeir Red," SASS® #498, Dave Jones, Jr., a.k.a. "DJ," SASS® #11508, and Richard Adamson, a.k.a. "Avenger," SASS® #58.)*

nized in one way or another. Surely all activities considered being "sports" in nature would support this. Cowboy action shooting is no different.

What may be different to an extent is that cowboy action shooting allows you to decide how competitive you want to be, with whom you will decide to compete and on what terms. Above all else (except safety), cowboy action shooting is about having fun. The only pressure out here is that which you put on yourself.

Every shooter in this sport makes the decision of what kind of fun they want within the competition. Shooters are welcome to participate at any skill level, are not pressured to perform well (except in terms of safety), and are not judged in a negative manner for their place of finish. If just attending a match and simply being a part of the field is enough for a shooter, it is enough for everyone else. If attempting to shoot at

the highest level of skill one can acquire or improve toward that goal is a shooters' idea of fun, then that is also an option and should be no less acceptable.

It is the opinion of this author that no matter how well a shooter compares to the rest of the field; it is more fun to shoot well than it is to shoot poorly. Hitting more targets, improving one's performance (relative to one's ability), and getting through the courses of fire successfully is, without a doubt, more fun than not doing so. The look of a shooter after cleaning (meaning no misses or mistakes) a stage or scenario is one of satisfaction and that of being clearly pleased with his or her performance. Admit it or not, improving your performance among any competition is pleasurable. Even if it is only *you* that you are competing against.

Most people like to measure their performance in one way or another. Cowboy action shooting offers you the choice of doing this any way you want. I have seen shooters run to the Results Board time and time again to see

Photo 1.0B - *Part of the fun of any game is to see where you finished and to compare scores with others.*

where they stand on the list. The interest in this information is not limited to those who are closer to the top of these lists; it is more accurate to say that nearly every competitor who is interested in how they finished will be looking at the Results Board. Any shooter who says "I never want (or care) to see where I finished," or say that they never look at any of the mailed out results… well, I'll let you come to your own conclusions as to where most sentiments of that nature stem from.

Don't misunderstand. I am not saying all shooters always care about how well they have performed or where they have placed among their own class or in the overall results. What I am saying is that most shooters like to know these things and most shooters are pleased when the results show an improvement in their personal performance.

Examples of this kind are easy to relate. In the SASS® World Championship event End of Trail© 1999, a woman in the ladies Super Senior Class was 475th in the overall finishing order. By being first place in that class she was awarded a beautiful bronze trophy and received public recognition for her efforts. What mattered to her was that she had done well and found a whole lot of fun in improving her personal performance. Besides receiving the recognition of note, she was probably also pleased that her finishing position overall reflected one that was ahead of 100 other shooters. Another example might be the Duelist Class shooter (using a one-handed method of revolver shooting) who is keen to find out just how well his or her performance compared to all the competitors. Imagine the personal satisfaction felt if a Duelist Class shooter finishes not only in the top five of that class but towards the top of the two-handed shooting classes as well.

These and other kinds of competitive comparisons are done throughout the field. Shooters will measure their shooting prowess against their friends, their own class or category, top-

Shooters will measure their shooting prowess against their friends, their own class or category, top-name shooters and the whole field.

name shooters and the whole field. It is seen by most as part of the fun of this friendly sport.

As expected, the higher level of skills (and therefore higher finishes) a shooter attains through both desire and effort, the fiercer the competition becomes. This is apparent in each of the separate classes, as well as with those shooters competing for the overall or number one finishing position.

The above is not earth-shattering news to most people. Shooters will find themselves reaching different plateaus as they continue to compete and improve. This is as common to this shooting sport as to any sporting activity. The shooters who may think they have reached the top or attained the full measure of their potential will most often find how short-lived that feeling really is.

There are most often between 10 and 12 main stage shooting scenarios in a major match in cowboy action shooting. Using three and four guns in each separate stage successfully (that is hitting all the targets) is not by any means all there is to doing well, or more difficult still, to winning. Numerous situations and choices of subtle transitional moves are presented for shooters to deal with in addition to simply pulling the triggers of their firearms and hitting each target.

Political correctness aside, this shooting sport is fairly described to the layperson as "cowboy combat." Competitors are required to dress the part of a character from the Old West or that of a Hollywood Cowboy, and to use the firearms that are appropriate in kind. The shooting problems are addressed and measured in terms of time. The fastest timed runs of each stage including any additional time penalties added for misses or procedural errors, will deter-

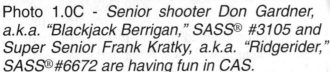

Photo 1.0C - *Senior shooter Don Gardner, a.k.a. "Blackjack Berrigan," SASS® #3105 and Super Senior Frank Kratky, a.k.a. "Ridgerider," SASS®#6672 are having fun in CAS.*

mine the shooter's initial score. Final position as to how a shooter will end up in a match is most often determined by a rank point system. Another method of scoring (though used less) is by simply adding up the total time of all the stages a shooter engages in. The competitor with the least overall amount of seconds for all the stages is the winner.

The shooters who will do well, possibly win their respective classes, or even find themselves at or near the top of a match, will all have done basically the same things (relatively speaking). Regardless of actual placement, shooters who find their finish placement improving will have prepared better, found reliability in their equipment, engaged properly with fewer mistakes, and done this at an average speed that is optimum as related to their current skill level.

This book is not simply about winning. True, it may help you place first someday, but that alone is not the point.

The real champions of this sport (as defined by their shooting successes) are not seen simply as having been first-place winners. They are fierce competitors to be sure and give 100 percent during engagement. It is their way of having fun. They do not (on a whole) have the attitude of one who must win at any cost. They are competing in what is referred to as "The Spirit of the Game" traditions of how the sport is played. These shooters of note will look to approach each stage with the seasoned eye of an expert and will attempt to figure out the best way to be as fast as they can. They will do this without breaking the rules. They will take care to adhere to the instructions as explained without stepping over the line. All shooters will (at one time or another) make mistakes that will cost them dearly in terms of added seconds to their time. The few shooters who have taken undue advantage of something a stage design calls for, thinking that this is the way to best play the game, can receive a harsh "failure to engage" penalty, and will soon come to learn what is right and what is not. There is also a fair amount of peer pressure to perform within "The Spirit of the Game."

The material presented in this book is detailed and specific to what many of the top shooters in the sport would say are the fundamentals. There is no real magic or secrets exposed here. The finer points or advanced methods are really fundamental in nature. Common sense, experience, and practical application are what you will find. How much or how little of it you may find useful will be up to you. This information provides a means to go back, check, and insure that these basic elements are being executed correctly.

It is my hope that you will gain or learn something from this book that inspires, assists, or improves your safe enjoyment of the sport. I hope to provide you with a greater understanding of the sport, allow you to shoot better and find yet another way to have more fun.

The challenge to improve will always be present. By accepting that challenge you are really challenging yourself. Know yourself as best you can. Never play someone else's game when competing. Be confident of your own skills and shoot your own game. When the match is over, and you know you did as well as you felt capable of, it will matter not nearly as much whether you won or lost or where you finished. The personal feeling of satisfaction will come from knowing that you performed well that day and met the challenge. You will know that yours was a worthy effort. Do this and you have won.

In one way or another, I hope the competition you find in cowboy action shooting brings you many personal victories.

Chapter 2

STARTING TO STUDY IN SPEED AND SAFETY

All things being somewhat relative, the speed of engagement each cowboy shooter employs during a successful stage run will also be relative to that shooters present skill level. The shooter who understands and remembers this will almost always demonstrate proper safety at the appropriate speed.

The safety requirements of cowboy action shooting are preached at every match. From the initial mandatory shooters meeting prior to the start of the day's events, to the end of the day when all firearms are safely put away, there is a general (and genuine) concern toward the safe handling of firearms. Firearm safety will often be discussed long after the shooting has stopped.

Photo 2.0A - *Dan Beale, a.k.a. "Dang It Dan," SASS® #13202 maintains safe handling techniques while moving at top speed.*

Each cowboy shooter understands the importance of maintaining safety and knows that it can never be over-emphasized. One will often hear the well-used phrase at a match that declares, "every shooter here is a Safety Officer." This is a well-founded statement and a responsibility that cannot be overlooked. It serves as a multi-task part of the sport by encouraging any shooter to question the actions of another without rebuke, providing a means by which a steady flow of safety conscious eyes see and are mindful of safety. This also assists in educating those who are new as well as providing a constant reminder to all that we may never relax our vigil. Safe to some of us is *never* feeling secure.

It is a basic rule in cowboy action shooting that the ranges are cold; that no firearm is loaded, until a shooter has reached the proper position of the loading area to do so. The unloading area will also serve as a checkpoint to insure that no shooter has come off the firing line leaving an inadvertent round in any firearm.

The rules of handling firearms in and around the areas behind the firing line or places other than the loading and unloading areas are specific as well. The shooter should be well versed in basic safety and better still, should have attended a National Firearms Safety course prior to attending these competitions. Cowboy action shooting requires that no muzzle may ever sweep or be pointed in an unsafe direction at anytime on or off the firing line. Revolvers will never be loaded with more than five rounds and hammers will always rest on an empty chamber in the cylinder. These are the very basic safety requirements.

Behind the firing line, no movement is allowed with any long gun unless the action is opened (insuring an unloaded gun) and the muzzle kept safe. Additionally, no shooter may draw or remove a revolver from leather behind the line except at a designated safe area and with the express permission of the closest Range Official at hand.

It must be the goal of every shooter to not only learn and demonstrate excellent safety habits, but also to become *instinctively* safe no matter the circumstance. The shooter who takes the time to look for the safest approach to addressing the stage will often discover this is also the fastest or most effective way to engage as well.

Maximize Speed With Planned Safety

Safety during actual engagement is of paramount concern. The firing line support personnel i.e.; the timing person, target spotters, and often a Range Officer or Posse Leader, are there to do all of those tasks *and more importantly* to insure that each shooter remains safe at all times while engaging.

No matter what happens to the shooter during a stage run or what task the shooter must perform while engaging the same, there must be present a willingness to sacrifice all else to remain safe. I have fallen and tripped during heated engagements once or twice, but have never lost sight of the need to keep the muzzle safely downrange. When you begin to engage (at any speed) this possibility exists. So, be prepared for *any* eventuality of this nature.

If a shooter looks closely there are ways to find greater speed in what might well be the safest approach. While more examples will present themselves in other chapters, the one to be described shortly is as good as any to start with.

As always, the shooter must consider safety as part of the process in approaching any stage. Safety remains constant so it is simply the application of the normal safety rules that we consider in our analysis.

Photo 2.1A - *Waiting for the signal to start, Bounty Hunter is set to draw a revolver from his cross-draw holster.*

Photo 2.1B - *Opposite view along the 180, the first revolver is seen being returned to leather after use.*

Any movement, whether standing in one place, moving laterally in either direction, moving forward, or diagonally downrange warrants serious consideration as to what will work best while remaining safe. The shooter will learn that the firing line is also the 180-degree safety plane (please refer to diagrams A and B on pages 18 and 19), and will understand what the 170 or occasional 150-degree operating areas forward of that firing line are. The shooter must also realize that the 180-degree safety plane stays constant to the zero degree heading directly downrange no matter what movement is required.

Sounding perhaps more complicated than it really is; even the new shooter will soon be able to operate safely within these limitations with relative ease. Safety is the first order of business, the second is to operate as effectively as possible. Depending on the order of firearms to be used, and direction of travel as dictated by the instructions, it is these variables that will lead you to decide how to best approach engagement.

Ready to go, the shooter is about to start a timed run. The view is from the left side of the shooter and directly along the 180-degree safety plane (initial firing line). In this example the shooter will draw his first revolver and engage one or more targets with all five rounds available. The stage instructions call for the shooter to move laterally to the right upon completion of this first revolver task. Safety dictates that the revolver must stay within the prescribed limits of the safety plane as explained by the match officials at all times, including the drawing of the gun from leather and its return to leather. This shooter is shown in the correct position to safely draw his first revolver from his left side and from what is his "cross-draw" style of holster. Safety compels the shooter to position his body in such a way that when the revolver is drawn its muzzle remains forward of the safety plane.

The reasoning behind this decision of which revolver is drawn first becomes more apparent in figure 2.1B. After firing the fifth round from the first revolver the shooter is now returning it to the cross-draw holster. You can see how the shooter is able to keep his body positioned so that the holster (and therefore the revolver) remains out front, within the limits of the safety plane. Moreover, the shooter can begin to start his lateral movement to the right at virtually the same time. This ability to "break" quickly, with little or no hesitation, begins the process of streamlining a stage engagement and reducing the time of the run.

Even though the shooter in figure 2.1B is actually taking the first step towards his next position while still in the act of returning the revolver to leather, the safety plane is being well adhered to. This is because the shooter was correct in choosing which side to draw from, and has accomplished speed and safety by his efforts. Please note the natural way the holster falls within the safety plane as the shooter turns right.

Regardless whether or not the stage instructions require the shooter to return the revolver to leather prior to foot movement towards the right, even the slight ability to turn in the desired direction will provide valuable momentum. It is even compulsory to turn in the correct direction in order to re-holster on the cross-draw side to be within the correct confines of the prescribed safety plane.

Given the opposite set of movement requirements after the first shots (a lateral movement to the left), let's look at the correct strong-side revolver move. Photo 2.1C reveals that the shooter need only turn in the direction he will now follow to safely return the revolver in the strong-side holster and automatically comply with the 180-degree safety plane. This move provides momentum towards the desired direction allowing a quick break immediately after the fifth shot is fired.

Photo 2.1D refers to a required lateral movement to the right. Choosing the strong-side revolver the shooter begins to move right while holstering. This is probably the most common of safety plane violations seen. Our view is directly along the 180 and the handgun's muzzle has broken the safety plane during its return.

If there are two similar moves during the course of fire, both requiring movement towards the same direction after separate use of each revolver, the shooter will need to choose which of those positions will allow him to stay facing correctly downrange while holstering before continuing in the same direction. Base this decision upon the elements of the engagement such as distance to move, use of another firearm and its position, and prop conditions.

Photo 2.1E shows one safe way (where the stage instructions allow movement prior to the revolver's return to leather) to obtain some motion or momentum while not breaking the safety plane, but still holstering the strong side holster. A half step sideways (as this shooter shows) is done while keeping the body facing at the zero degree heading downrange accomplishes this. The same would apply to the opposite direction providing proper care is given to the position of the cross- draw style of holster and the body position.

Photo 2.1C - *Correctly holstering into the strong-side holster while moving laterally to the shooter's left.*

Photo 2.1D - *Violating the 180-degree safety plane while holstering to the strong side and moving laterally to the right.*

It should be pointed out that the time gained by these moves is (by itself) not much. As little as two tenths of a second, to as much as eight tenths of a second are fair estimates of what the shooter can hope to get. This will depend on what the stage allows, the smoothness of the transitions, and the timing of the break.

The author understands that much of what may be offered here will not automatically be used. Many successful shooters will not always employ this method. The shooter who can simply perform a smooth transition from firing the last round to holstering without moving or starting to break can do fine. This (and other) techniques offered in this book are

Photo 2.1E - *This shooter is getting a slight break towards the next position while re-holstering to the same side safely by side-stepping to the right.*

to show what *can* be done to save time and how to remain *safe* while doing so. It is also fair to point out that some shooters will get into the habit of always starting with the same side no matter what opportunity is presented. I am not an advocate of this as it offers little opportunity to adjust to or choose a different option that may offer a more effective way to engage.

The cross-draw or cross-side holster is often associated with the phrase "doing the dance." This term describes the shooter's efforts to bring the holster into the safe confines of the safety plane when returning a revolver to leather. This can be accomplished often by either taking one step forward with the cross-draw side, or engaging with a pronounced swiveling movement of the hips in the same direction. Try to set up in such a way that does not require an additional move after the signal to start, by placing the holster within the safety plane.

Operating Within The 180-Degree Safety Plane

Diagrams 2.2A and 2.2B are plan views of what is commonly referred to as the "Shooter's Safety Plane." If the reader will keep in mind the basic rule that no muzzle must ever break the 180-degree imaginary line that extends horizontally from either side of them (as they face directly at a 0-degree heading), operating correctly and safely during stage engagement will not be difficult.

Diagram 2.2A shows the basic starting position of a shooter at the original starting point of this stage. Note how the firing line is really a 180-degree line reference point. The

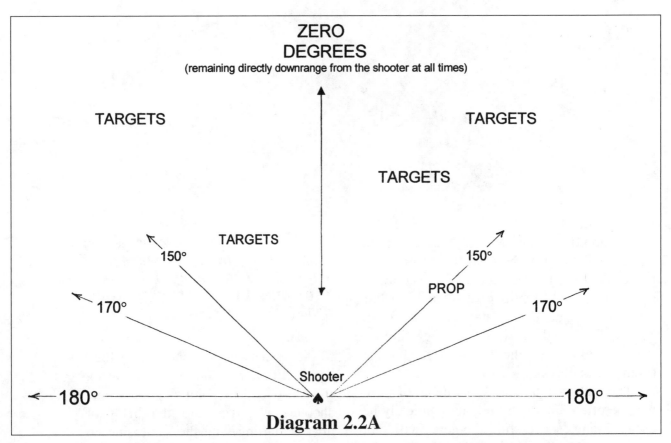

Diagram 2.2A

Illustration 2.2A - *This is the Shooter's Safety Plane at the starting position.*

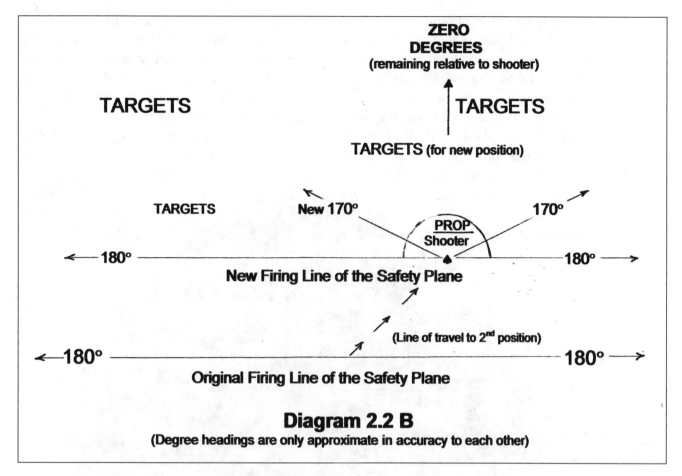

ZERO
DEGREES
(remaining relative to shooter)

TARGETS   TARGETS

TARGETS (for new position)

TARGETS   New 170°   170°

PROP
Shooter

←— 180° —————————————————————— 180° —→

New Firing Line of the Safety Plane

(Line of travel to 2nd position)

←—180° —————————————————————— 180° —→

Original Firing Line of the Safety Plane

Diagram 2.2 B
(Degree headings are only approximate in accuracy to each other)

Illustration 2.2B - *Here is the Shooter's Safety Plane, including movement.*

shooter is facing directly downrange at another point called the 0-degree heading. The two other lines extending from the shooter's body are the 170- and 150-degree headings. Each set of these headings meets the radius in front of the shooter, directly downrange.

Note the positioning of the targets downrange in this diagram. They are set in such a manner that the shooter may address each one of them and discharge each round while keeping the muzzle reasonably within the vicinity of the 170-degree radius. The 150-degree heading is shown as the optimum operating radius, and the ever-present 180-degree plane is the line of *no* absolution if violated.

Diagram 2.2B fairly represents the areas behind the shooter and in front (downrange), where the rounds will impact. It is a stage that requires little movement, and is basically a single position. The shooter may engage with one or both revolvers, a rifle and shotgun from here. The starting position of the firearms will vary, with at least one of the two long guns pre-staged on a table or leaning against a prop. The other long gun (if not pre-staged) will usually start in a "cowboy" style of port arms, held in both hands.

No matter in what sequence the firearms are used here, or to which direction the shooter will turn or move while bringing to bear or returning a firearm after use, all of the degree headings remain constant. Not violating the 180-degree safety plane, and discharging within close proximity of the 170-degree plane is clearly not too difficult a task to accomplish. Any shooter who cannot work the firearms within these confines is committing a mental lapse that is not acceptable, and should be awarded a safety penalty and stern warning for the first violation. A subsequent violation may well result in that shooter being disqualified from the match.

The second diagram (2.2B) is another plan view of a similar stage, but contains a secondary position the shooter must move forward to, at a slightly right diagonal angle.

Photo 2.2C - *View from the 0-degree heading of the shooter's correct lateral move during engagement. (EOT 2000 World Champion Joe Alesia, a.k.a. "Lefty Longridge," SASS® #9240.)*

This example clearly shows how the safety planes and 0-degree heading(s) will remain constant to both shooter and direction. At position one we will say the shooter starts with the rifle at a modified or "cowboy port arms." Both revolvers are holstered, and the shotgun will be flat, unloaded with the action open on a table in front of the shooter. A rifle stand on the right side of the table will provide a vertical (muzzle up) place to re-stage the rifle after initial use.

Minus target order, the stage engagement would be as follows: Starting at port arms, the shooter will engage the rifle targets nine times. The shooter will then set down the rifle (action open and safe) in the stand provided. Drawing the first revolver, the shooter will then engage five revolver targets. Holstering safely, the shooter will take the shotgun *with* him, and proceed safely to position two. Arriving at position two, the shooter will load and engage the four shotgun targets. Shooter sets down the shotgun (action open and safe) in the stand

provided, and draws the second revolver to engage the final five targets.

The shooter's path or direction of travel is shown from position one to position two, and the shooter is shown at the second of two firing points. The safety planes are shown as relative to the shooter's new position. Zero degrees is also shown directly downrange, in front of the shooter.

The reader must also understand during the movement from position one to position two that all the safety planes, as well as the 0-degree headings, remained constant as to directly downrange and moved *laterally* with the shooter. The shooter in photo 2.2C is moving with the shotgun, and is charged with keeping the muzzle within these prescribed limits at all times. Every shooting scenario presents a study in speed… and a study in safety.

Chapter 3

KNOW YOUR SINGLE-ACTION HANDGUNS

A Word About The Revolvers

It is often said in this sport that achieving a suitable level of consistency with the single-action revolvers (or handguns) is the biggest challenge that must be overcome to regularly score well in match conditions. There is some merit to that sentiment, considering all the attributes one must bring to bear when engaging with one or more revolvers at these speeds. Re-examining some of the basic rules of single-action revolver shooting can most often solve problems that shooters (regardless of skill levels) encounter.

The two most common revolver calibers in the sport are the .45 Colt (commonly called the .45 Long Colt) and the .38 Special. Some shooters, usually for reasons other than simply competition (or economics), choose from a myriad of other cartridges from the Old West era. While most top shooters in cowboy action shooting use the .38 Special as their handguns, it has been proven that the .45 Long Colt is hardly at much of a disadvantage when pitted against the .38 Special. The .38 Special is an excellent cartridge choice for any shooter; it's economical, easy to load, comfortable to shoot and readily avail-

Photo 3.0A - *National Champion Ross Seymour, a.k.a. "Rowdy Yates," SASS® #141 looks his part as the veteran of many a CAS gunfight.*

Photo 3.0B - *Debra LeVergne, a.k.a. "Elegant Ella," SASS® #6693 knows that heavy recoil is uncomfortable for shooters, and hard on revolvers and targets.*

able. This cartridge is one of several important reasons for such rapid growth and popularity of the sport. The SASS® organization recognizes this as well, providing rules and guidelines for the majority of enthusiasts enjoying cowboy action shooting.

Shooters understand it is easier to shoot well with revolver rounds that provide less recoil. Under the SASS® Rules of Competition handgun rounds may not exceed a muzzle velocity of 1,000 Feet Per Second (FPS). Few competitors use rounds approaching the maximum revolver FPS because of the heavy recoil. Average handloads in the .38 Specials are between 750-800 FPS. The average .45 Long Colt handloads used in the sport produce between 650-750 FPS.

More than a few ammunition manufacturers offer good lines of ammunition designed for use in cowboy action shooting. Two of the manufacturers I've had the pleasure of working closely with over several years are Black Hills Ammunition and Ten 'X' Ammunition. Both

offer a wide choice of excellent loads developed specifically for cowboy action shooting.

Power factors measured in foot pounds are not calculated in cowboy action shooting (as of today), but the average rounds as described will suffice when called upon to knock over the occasional "knockdown" target. Most major or annual events using these targets will insure they are pre-calibrated to work when hit with the average SASS® .38 Special load for revolver knockdowns, and the lighter target loads for shotgun knockdowns.

When considering which barrel length to use, understand that the longer 7-inch barrels do come with some characteristics the shooter should understand. First of all, the target distances rarely require the revolver be engaged at targets more than 12 yards distant. Most of the time the targets are

Photo 3.0C - *Donna Parker, a.k.a. "Lusty Lil," SASS® #4103 uses good sighting techniques and average target loads in her 12-gauge double for the occasional knockdown targets encountered.*

Photo 3.0D - *Barrel length choices today are much the same as they were in the real Old West. (Shown near to far are: Lynda Paul, a.k.a. "Timberline," SASS® #3855, Dennis Martinez, a.k.a. "Flint Westwood," SASS® #94, Careen Furstenberg, a.k.a. "Wild Daisy," SASS® #24418, and Pat Myers, a.k.a. "Blue Eyes," SASS®#92.)*

between 7 and 10 yards. At these distances there is no significant accuracy gained with a longer barrel. Secondly, the longer barrel does take slightly more time to remove from and return to the holster. There is also agreement that sight and target acquisition with a longer barreled revolver is not as quick and easy as it is with the shorter barrels. There is less barrel rise or muzzle flip associated with the shorter barreled revolvers as well. Lastly, with the added length and weight of the long barrel revolver, most shooters find it more difficult to shoot at the speeds this sport of fantasy will most often beckon.

The most popular barrel lengths are the 4-3/4 inches and the 5-1/2 inches. Perhaps chosen for some of the same reasons as those above, many gunmen of the Old West felt these shorter barreled guns were quicker and easier to wield than their longer barreled brethren.

Basic Nomenclature And Sixth-Round Reloading Techniques

Cowboy action shooting requires that single-action revolvers be used for main match competition. "Single-action" refers simply to the mechanics of the handgun; meaning that the shooter (in order to advance the cylinder) must physically cock the hammer *each* time a round is to be fired. In order to fire, the hammer must be brought all the way to the rear of its travel, to the *"fully cocked"* position. It is in this fully cocked position that the hammer will fall forward, striking the primer (or cap) after the trigger has been engaged. Each round requires the same action for each subsequent discharge.

While capable of holding six rounds in the six chambers of the cylinder, there

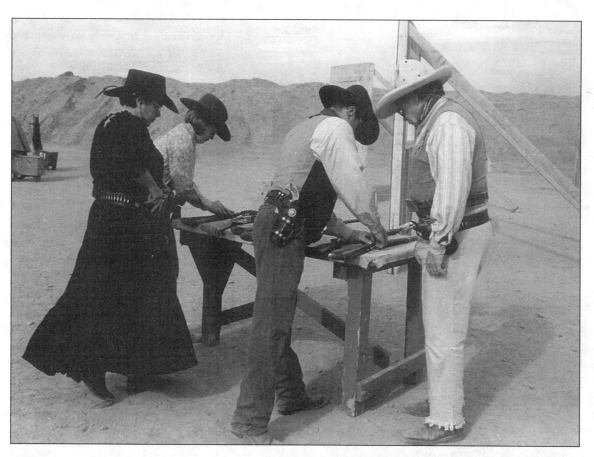

Photo 3.1A - *Jerry Meyer, a.k.a. "Wolfbait," SASS® #5227, provides a watchful eye as Ken Amorosano, a.k.a. "Chisler," SASS® #392, loads before engagement.*

is a hard and fast rule in cowboy action shooting that *no more than five rounds will be loaded*. With only a very few exceptions (like when special instructions for a particular stage are issued), this rule will always be followed. To assist shooters, and to insure safety at the loading tables, a Range Officer or other support person will be assigned to supervise this operation.

The empty (or sixth) chamber of each loaded handgun will *always* remain directly in the position known as "under the hammer" prior to engagement. One common technique used when loading the revolver to insure the hammer will rest on the empty chamber is called the "load one, skip one" method. Besides this method, the shooter should *always* visually inspect the cylinder's final rotation, and confirm the empty chamber is correctly aligned so when the hammer is in its fully down (forward) position it is on top of an *empty chamber*. All these actions are performed while keeping the muzzle in a *safe* direction.

Photo 3.1B - *This Ruger Vaquero correctly shows where the empty chamber is directly under where the hammer rests in the "fully forward" position. See where the live rounds are in relationship to the empty chamber that is under the hammer.*

Photo 3.1C - *The same revolver is shown loaded incorrectly. Note that there is a live round in the chamber directly aligned with the hammer in the down position.*

The reason for this is the same today as it was in the Old West. A fully depressed hammer resting over a live round can be struck accidentally and may cause the firing pin to ignite the primer of that round. While some modern, single-action revolvers are equipped with transfer bars instead of firing pins to eliminate this problem, *all* handguns used in cowboy action shooting are subject to this strict rule. *There are no exceptions.*

The "load one, skip one" method of loading is accomplished in this manner for a Colt style of revolver: Placing the hammer on the "half-cock" or "midway" point, the loading gate is opened, and the cylinder will turn freely. Place the first round in one empty chamber, and then turn the cylinder clockwise allowing one *empty* chamber to go past the loading area. The next (second) round is then placed in the next empty chamber, or the third chamber exposed. The third, fourth, and fifth rounds are placed in the next three empty chambers as the cylinder is turned to accept each one.

As the fifth and *final* round is loaded, the cylinder is *not* turned. The loading gate is *closed* at this time. The hammer is then brought directly back to the "fully cocked" position. The shooter must then *safely* allow the hammer to go to the "fully depressed" or down position. This is accomplished by keeping the thumb on the hammer and depressing the trigger. This is done *slowly*. The shooter must *always* keep the muzzle pointed in a safe direction at all times.

As the hammer is being brought back to the fully cocked position, the cylinder is automatically being advanced, with the *empty* chamber going into the desired position "under the hammer" when the hammer is again lowered.

Stage designs will sometimes require shooters to load one or both revolvers with a final or sixth round. This is done only when on the firing line, and is part of the engagement itself. This task may require the shooter to load this sixth round either before firing the initial five rounds, or (more often) will require the shooter to load the sixth round after one or more of the first five rounds are fired. In either case, with either the traditional

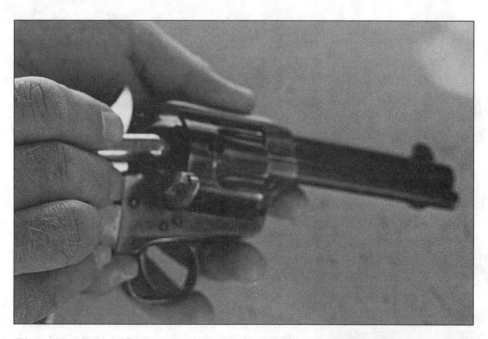

Photo 3.1D - *A Colt-style revolver with its hammer in the "half-cock" position, loading gate open and ready to be loaded with the first of five rounds.*

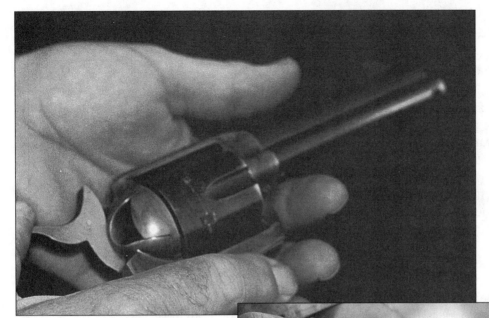

Photo 3.1E - *Bringing the hammer to the half-cock position before loading requires safe muzzle direction. This must always be adhered to during any of these (and other) operations.*

Photo 3.1F - *Loading the sixth round on the firing line during engagement is not unusual.*

Photo 3.1G - *This shooter has loaded the sixth round, closed the loading gate, and is turning the cylinder four times or "clicks." Note that this Colt-style revolver's hammer is still in the half-cock position.*

Colt style or transfer bar style of revolvers, the method of loading is basically the same. Loading the sixth round after the first five rounds are fired will require the cylinder to be turned in order for the sixth round to be the next one under the hammer (ready to be fired) when the hammer is brought to full cock. One other thing to understand is that the Ruger transfer bar style revolvers will not require the hammer to be at the half-cock position in order to begin the process. Simply opening the loading gate unlocks the cylinder on a Ruger.

Loading the sixth round after the stage engagement has begun but prior to firing the first five rounds in the revolver eliminates the need to advance or turn the cylinder after insertion of the sixth round. With the first five chambers filled with live rounds, the shooter will simply load that sixth round, close the loading gate, bring the hammer to the fully cocked (ready to fire) position and fire all six rounds. This does however present a possible safety hazard, and has become a less used part of stage design.

Sixth round reloads will most often occur after the shooter has fired the first five rounds, thus requiring the shooter to load the sixth round into the empty chamber and then position the sixth round to be the next round fired by turning the cylinder correctly. Let's go through the process of loading and firing the sixth round step by step.

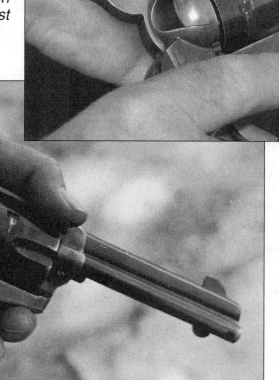

Photo 3.1H - *Step One: Firing the fifth and final round from the revolver, the shooter brings the revolver down, transferring it safely to the weak hand, and to a position that is best to begin loading the sixth round. Most often this position is about waist high.*

Photo 3.1I - *Step Two: Keeping the muzzle safely down-range, the shooter (if the revolver requires it) will use the strong hand to bring the hammer to the half-cock position. Transfer bar revolvers eliminate the half-cock part of this step.*

Photo 3.1J - *Step Three: The shooter must open the loading gate in order to turn the cylinder until the empty chamber is exposed at the mouth of the loading gate. In this case, the weak or "off" hand serves to support the revolver as needed. The shooter's off hand will remain on the cylinder at this point, and (if needed) will keep the exposed empty chamber correctly aligned to accept the round.*

Photo 3.1K - *Step Four: The shooter will then retrieve a round from either his or her body or (if the stage design calls for it) from some other pre-determined place.*

Photo 3.1L - *Step Five: The shooter inserts the sixth round into the empty chamber and is ready to begin advancing the loaded chamber as desired.*

Photo 3.1M - *Step Six: Upon closing the loading gate of this Colt-style single-action pistol, the shooter will advance the cylinder clockwise until the sixth round is the next one in the "under the hammer" position. This advancing of the cylinder is done by the off hand, by feel or listening to the "clicks" as the cylinder turns, or by both. Turning the cylinder clockwise requires four of the six possible clicks in one complete rotation to occur. A "single turn" means that each one of the six chambers has moved one position in the rotation. Most of the single-action revolvers used in the sport will click each time the cylinder advances one chamber. This "click" is felt and/or heard by the shooter. To complete step six, the shooter must advance the cylinder four single turns or clicks and (when it is applicable) while the hammer remains in the half-cock position.*

Photo 3.1N - *Step Seven: Completing the rotation, the shooter is ready to bring the revolver to bear. The hammer is brought directly to the full cock (ready to fire) position, and the sixth round (if in the correct position) can be discharged.*

Photo 3.1O - Shown is *another position or angle of the pistol that may be used during the act of advancing the cylinder after reloading.*

Additional Notes On Sixth Round Reloads

Shooters using Colt-style revolvers that require the hammer be brought to half-cock position (see step one), should understand that this move must be done without undue haste. There can occur a total lock-up of the cylinder (an inability to freely rotate) if this is done improperly. This will require the shooter to bring the hammer to full cock, lower to the fully depressed position, and start the maneuver over again. Practicing this technique with an *empty* and *safe*

revolver is highly recommended. Practicing the entire process using live rounds at a range, under the supervision of a certified instructor, is also recommended.

Incorrect advancing or rotating of the cylinder usually results in one of two conditions. If the cylinder rotation is short, meaning only three single turns occurred instead of four , the shooter will find the hammer has fallen on one of the expended rounds, and no discharge will occur. In this instance, the live round will be the very *next* round fired upon re-cocking of the hammer. If the cylinder rotation is one turn (or click) too many, the shooter will find that

Photo 3.1P - *Judy Bleek, a.k.a. "Maggie Grace," SASS® #9402 is proceeding with the stage engagement after handing off a revolver (correctly held) with an unexpended round to the attending Range Officer Dennis Davenport, a.k.a. "High Country," SASS® #1068. As a result, she has gotten past the failure correctly. Ron Stein, a.k.a. "Tupelo Flash," SASS® #27453 supports as target spotter.*

the next *five* attempts to fire the round will fall on empty or expended rounds. Continued attempts to fire the sixth round unsuccessfully are most often a result of not having a round under the hammer, but may also be caused by a light tap on a primer, or the possibility of the revolver having a timing problem. This condition has important implications the shooter must understand and deal with properly. Under the SASS® current Rules of Engagement, a "shooter may not return a handgun to leather with a live round in the cylinder." The shooter must either set the handgun down *safely* with the hammer in the fully depressed position, or (again with the hammer in the fully depressed position) hand it off in a *safe* manner to Range Officer or the assisting Firing Line Support Officer. The other important factor to consider here is to continue the engagement of the stage, and to realize the least amount of lost time due to this failure.

Understanding the possibilities of what can happen during stage engagement is important to every shooter's success. The shooter who has considered unforeseen conditions or problems that may arise, and how best to deal with them, will find far less difficulty in getting past each problem. In this instance, don't waste any more time or attempt additional actions that serve simply to hinder your stage run and don't be dumbfounded or confused. Set the revolver down *safely* or hand it off *safely* to the R.O. and *continue executing the stage at your normal pace.* Put the problem behind you as best you can, and don't let it create any more problems.

The Ruger Vaquero single-action revolver is a good example of the transfer bar system. Not only does this revolver *not* require the hammer to be at the half-cock position to open the loading gate and free the cylinder for rotation, the pawl can be modified to allow the cylinder to turn freely in *either* direction. If this is done as part of an action job (certain modifications to enhance a firearm's performance) the shooter may learn to simply rotate the cylinder counter-clockwise a shorter distance to the correct position than the clockwise rotation would otherwise denote. There is not a lot of time

saved here, and this modification may make it easier to rotate the cylinder incorrectly under stage conditions.

Reloading Five Revolver Rounds During Engagement

Reloading all five revolver rounds during a stage run is a valid scenario one may encounter occasionally at a cowboy action shooting match. If the shooter is prepared and has had proper opportunity to learn how this is best accomplished; it

Photo 3.2A - *Actually in motion, "High Country" is wasting no time proceeding to another firing position while dumping expended revolver cases on the way.*

is one of those areas of "transition" in a stage where significant time is gained. The shooter who has not prepared may find reloading five revolver rounds a long and laborious task, fraught with difficulties and costly added seconds.

An excellent run from when the shooter has fired the fifth (or final) round out of a revolver, dumped all the required empty cases, re-loaded five new rounds from the body (or other place), and fires the first round of these next five is around *10* seconds. The average top shooter will complete this task in about 12 seconds. The average shooter will take between 20 and 30 seconds, and below average shooters will take up to a full minute.

This is a *non-shooting* task, one that simply takes some basic understanding, reasonably smooth

actions, correct set-up and a little practice. It is not one of those things that requires "youth" or "raw talent." *Any* shooter can improve this task with a little effort. Shooters who go from below average to average times will find an extra *20* seconds cut from their stage runs requiring this task. Even the average shooter, whose skill level is such that cutting time off a run is more and more difficult as he improves, can find significant time in this area.

Granted, large matches will not often employ this design because of the additional time constraints it places on getting shooters through the course of fire, but it does happen at smaller matches with regularity. Moreover, shooters may find other situations similar to this. Some include starting with an empty revolver and loading "on the clock." Top Gun Shoot-Offs, side matches, and just becoming familiar with the sixth

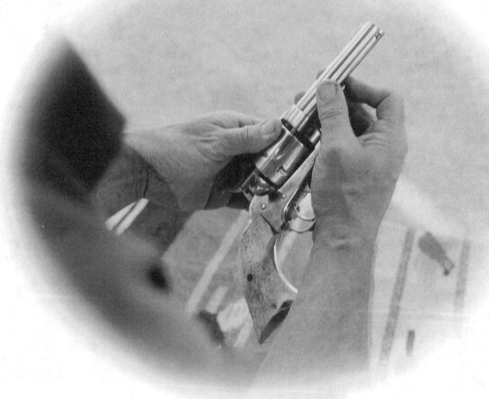

Photo 3.2B - *Empty cases can be tough to remove. Honing and polishing each chamber can help this problem.*

round reload are all good reasons to get better acquainted with proper reloading techniques.

Action jobs, or the "slicking up" of a cowboy action shooter's revolver will be looked at in more depth later, but one of the elements of a good action job relates directly to successful reloading. In order to reload five new rounds, the operation starts with the quickest way to dump the first empty (or spent) cases. There is more than one reason that allows empty cases to be extracted with relative ease by the shooter. Honing and polishing each chamber correctly is an easy first step. These surfaces come into direct contact with each round, causing some friction. The friction is increased dramatically when the round is fired, and the empty case actually expands to some degree. The less friction between the walls of the chambers and the sides of the empty cases, the easier it is to remove those cases.

The initial powder charge of the round is an area of consideration for reloading as well. The high-velocity, factory specs, or "hot" loads are more than just uncomfortable for shooters in terms of recoil or being hard on the revolver and targets. High-velocity rounds will cause greater case expansion from the higher pressures exerted at discharge, and will therefore not allow the subsequent case extraction process to be as easy (or quick) as it might

Photo 3.2C - *World Champion and winner of End Of Trail 2000, Joe Alesia, a.k.a. "Lefty Longridge," SASS® #9240, quickly runs a patch through the chambers of his revolver at the loading table prior to a stage requiring reloading. Eric Carlstedt, a.k.a. "Magnum Quigley," SASS® #1021, loads his lever gun.*

otherwise be. The medium or lower powder charges producing medium to light case expansion will serve the shooter much better. One other item to remember when faced with a revolver reloading task is to carry a short rod and cleaning end of some kind. Just prior to loading the revolver(s), give each chamber a quick, dry swipe to clean and remove any loose debris.

Cowboy action shooters seem to enjoy the challenges of figuring out different ways of doing things in their attempts to find a way to shorten their timed runs. With few exceptions, they do this not as "gamers" (a derogatory term of invalid origins), nor do they do these things to "win at any cost." The thought process behind shooters who look to figure out ways that will legally improve their run is a constant challenge. From the most rudimentary rules of correct engagement to the finest techniques used saving only tenths, even hundredths, of a second it is a compelling and never-ending challenge. It is as fun as it is frustrating at times. Less frustration comes from greater understanding. A direct violation of the sport's rules of engagement or the specific instructions of a stage scenario should result in the appropriate penalty being assessed to the shooter. Good shooters (let alone those considered "top" shooters) will rarely attempt to go outside the rules to improve their times. These shooters do, however, go as far "inside" the rules as safety will allow in their desire to meet the challenge.

Here are three ways commonly used by shooters to extract empty cases from the chambers of the handgun. Photo 3.2D shows the method seen most often; holding the revolver in the off hand, on half-cock and the loading gate opened. The strong hand is working the ejector rod and providing some stability to the revolver as the off hand turns the cylinder, bringing each chamber into position for case extraction.

Photo 3.2E shows a slightly unusual way of how the off hand can actually do the work of two hands. Notice the strong hand merely holds and steadies the revolver at the grip. The revolver is held slightly upwards as the off hand rolls the cylinder with the palm of the hand, and the finger works the ejector rod when needed.

Photo 3.2F shows the revolver being held at an upward angle, providing the best opportunity for the cases to simply fall out of each chamber as the

Photo 3.2D - *This is the basic technique for removing spent cases from the chambers of a single-action revolver.*

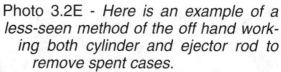

Photo 3.2E - *Here is an example of a less-seen method of the off hand working both cylinder and ejector rod to remove spent cases.*

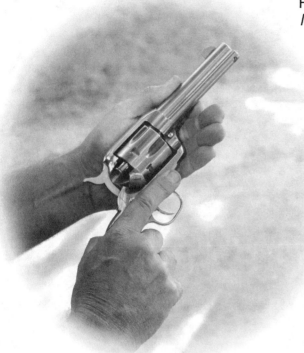

Photo 3.2F - *High Country holds the revolver at the optimum angle to allow gravity to help the extraction process.*

cylinder turns. It is advisable (though not shown here) to have the strong hand poised in such a manner that the ejection rod can be instantly used if a case does not fall out on its own.

Besides the basic elements described for sixth-round or five-round reloading during stage engagements, there are other key elements to learn about reloading. Part of preparing for any stage run includes equipment set-up. Reloading is no different. The shooter must know beforehand exactly where those needed rounds will come from, and that the placement provides optimum opportunity for success. The successful run will appear smooth, without any added actions or undue movement. There will be little or no hesitation or fumbling, and no apparent hang-ups or other "glitches."

For example, reloading rounds from the body is usually done from the loops on the gun belt or another belt (like a shotgun belt) that has additional loops for revolver or rifle rounds. Reloading from a vest pocket or other pocket when a belt could be used is hardly what the gunfighter of the Old West would have done, given a choice.

Beyond having the right gear for the job, there are some other initial set-up considerations. If the stage will require the shooter to move rapidly from one position to another prior to taking rounds out of the loops to reload a firearm, those rounds need to be retained (not subject to falling out) during this movement. The shooter who understands that there is a difference in how deep the rounds must be in the loops for

Photo 3.2G - *Up in the loops, rounds should be in front and easily accessible.*

both required retention *and* the least amount of drag when they are to be withdrawn and used, will fair better than one who has no clue. This is especially important with shotgun rounds.

The shooter, who knows he will remain in a single stationary position from the start of the stage run until any additional rounds for reloading are needed, will find that he or she can set the rounds up higher in the loops without fear of losing them. Experience will aid the shooter to make the correct adjustments for each situation.

Setting up to reload with rounds off the body should also include some thought about checking that the clothing we wear in cowboy action shooting is ready for action, and *not* ready to get

caught up in our cloths. The comfortable, loose-fitting shirts and suspenders that are as much a part of the sport as the firearms themselves, will never be eliminated to gain advantage. Therefore (as it should be), the shooter must learn to deal with this potential problem as a normal course of action. Loose clothing can interfere with the clean execution of taking rounds off the body easily. Grab a round or two along with a piece of your shirt, and see how far you'll get. Loose suspenders also pose avoidable hazards. A thumb that somehow gets inside the suspender on one side will cause only frustration to the shooter. It takes little time and even less thought to prevent these almost silly-sounding problems. Tuck that shirt in a little more after making ready that belt holding those rounds. Take a little more care in where you may place the belt loops holding the

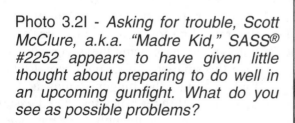

Photo 3.2H - *Neatness can count in the shooter's set-up.*

Photo 3.2I - *Asking for trouble, Scott McClure, a.k.a. "Madre Kid," SASS® #2252 appears to have given little thought about preparing to do well in an upcoming gunfight. What do you see as possible problems?*

desired rounds in relationship to where your suspender is bound to have a slight sag. Get set to have fun. You are about to do battle in the make believe places of today's O.K. Corral or Dodge City. The gunmen of yesteryear stayed alive by using their wits. It is natural for us to use ours as well.

Another technique to consider is that of placing the rounds in such a manner that any adjacent rounds do not hamper or delay the shooter's initial grab. Spacing an empty loop in between live rounds may help avoid a miscue here. Another common technique is to always carry and place two or three more rounds than is called for. Most match rules will not allow a shooter to retrieve a round that has fallen to the ground (called a "dead" round), and unless an additional round is available from the body, this will result in a five-second penalty just as if it were a missed target. It becomes important here (as in almost all areas of engagement) that the shooter know beforehand how to best handle that little glitch or mistake. A mishandled round that slips and drops should not cause any action on the shooter's part other than the automatic act of going to the next available round. Any other motion is without value, costing only more time and will often propel the shooter into a series of mistakes caused by increased haste. When this happens (and it *will* happen) try to understand that increasing the speed of your run past what you are capable of running (at your current skill level) to make up for one mistake already made will almost always end up in disaster.

To attempt great hand speed when grabbing rounds off the body and loading them in kind is a mistake. It does not take great speed to move the hand mere inches one way and then another. What it will do is serve to create conditions that will promote fumbling, dropping rounds, and end up as slow loads that appear forced. Strive toward a quick and controlled movement that is accurate. A deliberate motion, designed to pick the desired round (or rounds) smoothly from the belt, followed by the same deliberate, controlled delivery to the firearm will produce the desired results.

These techniques relate to both rifle and shotgun reloading as well. If the shooter is too hasty in the attempt to be fast, and has one glitch or problem while grabbing rounds off the belt, it will totally negate whatever time was to be gained from the increased speed. Additionally, the run will now end up slower than that of the shooter's average effort.

Most of the revolvers I have used for main stage engagement are chambered for the .45 Long Colt caliber. There are few reasons for this other than years of use, becoming comfortable with some of the associated attributes like revolver weight, and recoil or pressure wave. I do not see the .45s as more "manly" or subscribe wholly to its reputation of being more "authentic." Now the reader might wonder if I had ever basked in the light of a campfire listening to those shooters praising the .45. I'd be a liar to say no, I never did that, but this is cowboy action shooting and it wouldn't be cool to look a gift horse like that in the mouth. The truth is this: it's not easy to deliver great performances with any caliber handgun.

If I thought shooting a smaller caliber handgun like the .38 would have made that big a difference in this sport (one that requires a shooter to perform well in so many areas), I would have changed many years ago. I hope the reader won't misunderstand this personal philosophy, surely there *are* differences that have merit, and these differences are no doubt more significant to some shooters than others.

A final note with regard to these reloading techniques. I find myself smiling a little inside when the stage calls for any reload problem. The reason, you ask? To me, there is little doubt that the extraction of empty cases and the reloading of new rounds are performed with greater ease using the larger caliber rather than the smaller caliber revolvers. I happen to find handling the bigger rounds and putting them in the bigger holes faster and easier than the same movements with the small ones.

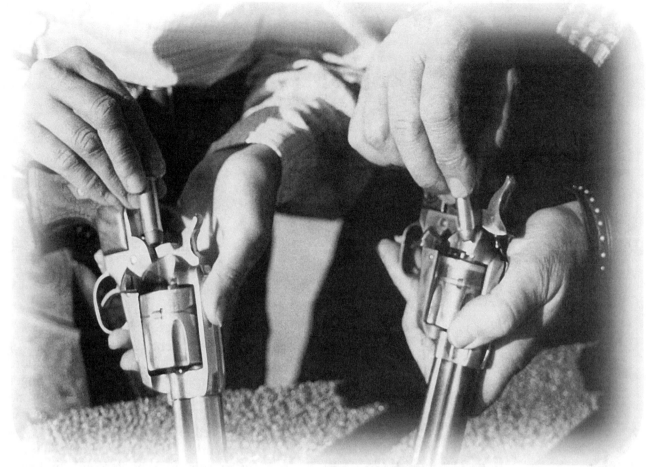

Photo 3.2J - *Which one looks easiest to work with to you?*

I have purposely not addressed the issue of adjustable or fixed sights on revolvers. Both styles of revolvers are used with enough success that neither is the wrong choice. If adjustable-sight revolvers like the Ruger Blackhawk were truly advantageous over the fixed-sight models, the record of competition *and* competitors would spell that out clearly… and it does *not*.

Trigger Control

The trigger "press" or "squeeze" as often described to shooters means essentially the same thing. It is the way in which the shooter exercises correct trigger control. One of the easiest ways to understand this in terms almost any shooter can instantly grasp, is to think of how one puts on the brakes while driving an automobile. A hard jerking motion or uneven application when braking produces poor results. An even, constant press produces desired results. It is a reasonable comparison. Good trigger control is best accomplished with the latter of the two techniques.

Whatever you call it, trigger control is the correct pressure applied on the trigger to produce as true a *rearward* direction as possible. Pressure applied by the finger that is slightly angled one way or another can transfer even the slightest amount of incorrect angle to the muzzle as the round goes off, causing the flight of the projectile to act accordingly. It is universally accepted that the index finger of the strong hand (the strong hand is the one holding the revolver) placed with the fleshy part (directly opposite of the fingernail) of the finger on the trigger produces the

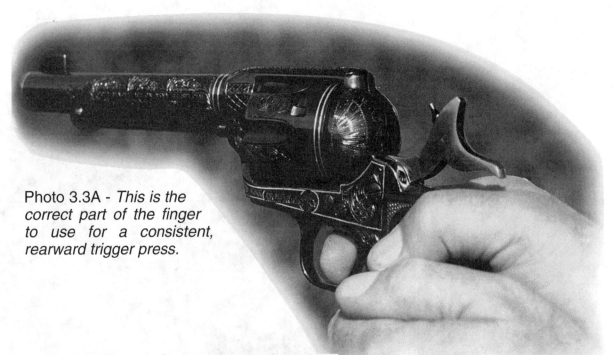

Photo 3.3A - *This is the correct part of the finger to use for a consistent, rearward trigger press.*

Photo 3.3C - *Magnum Quigley shows where not to position the trigger finger. This will not allow you to obtain the best rearward motion.*

most consistent results. Placement of the very tip of one's finger or (more common) the first joint of the finger will often induce a slight angle to one side or another as the trigger is squeezed to the rear.

While there are exceptions to every rule, few shooters will find success using the incorrect methods shown. Accepting this, the task becomes one of consistent execution in order to produce the same desired results. To do this, we must back up and begin with the initial grip of the strong hand on the revolver. This is called the "master grip."

Find Your Master Grip

The shooter should find a master grip that becomes as much of a true extension of their hand and arm as is possible. What may feel a little awkward at first, with a little time and a growing appreciation of the results, will be well worth the effort. Photo 3.4A shows excellent alignment of the revolver in the hand, and how it appears as an extension of the shooter's arm. It is accomplished by rolling (or moving) the right hand (in this example) slightly

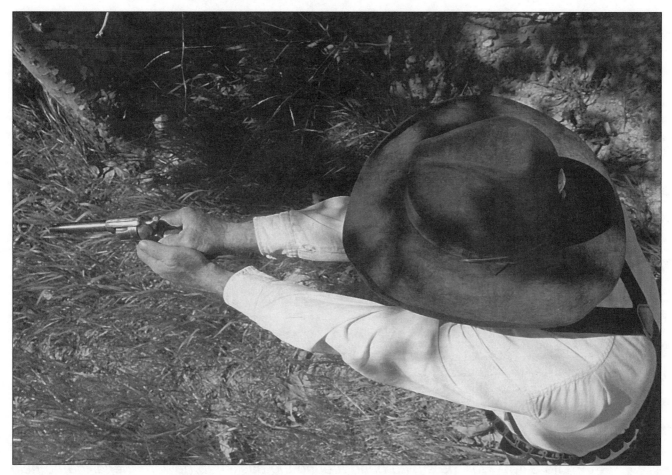

Photo 3.4A - *The most effective master grips are those that have made the revolver as much of a natural extension of the arm as is possible.*

to the shooter's left, or inside. Holding an empty gun with the muzzle in a safe direction, hold the barrel with the off-hand and roll (or move) the strong hand into a position that is similar to photo 3.4A. Find the point where the index or trigger finger falls on the trigger correctly as shown in photo 3.3A. The amount of pressure or how hard the revolver is gripped should only be enough to retain a firm, unchanging master grip. Too much pressure or too hard a grip creates tension, a loss of stability, and unwanted motion transferred to the handgun's muzzle. Don't overdue the amount of how far you roll the hand over in order to get the perfect extension. Each shooter is different. Remember that what you want here is for the trigger finger to fall on the trigger correctly each time you grip the revolver, with little or no conscious effort made.

The height of the strong hand on the back strap of the revolver is another consideration when developing your master grip. The size of the shooter's hand will play a part in this, but it really only matters that the shooter find the most comfortable, most reliable, and easiest way to maintain effective control of the revolver.

It is fair to point out that a shooter who (because of hand size or personal preference) does *not* place the little finger of the strong hand under the revolver butt may experience a gradual shifting of the hand upwards along the back strap of the revolver. This (when it does occur) actually moves the top (or web) of the hand closer to the hammer, and at some point the shooter may find the

Photo 3.4B - *Roll the strong hand around the backstrap (toward the inside) to help find the best position for your own master grip with an empty gun pointed in a safe direction.*

hammer touching the top (or web) of the hand when the hammer is in the fully cocked position. This condition is far more likely to occur if the shooter is using more powerful revolver rounds. During a string of five shots, the recoil caused by each discharge can cause the hand to rise slightly each time the revolver recoils.

The method of gripping the revolver with the strong hand's little finger under the revolver's butt can serve to reduce this. Again, the positioning of the strong hand on the revolver is to achieve an effective, stable master grip. Look to establish a permanent grip that will provide a platform of stability, correct placement of the finger on the trigger, and correct alignment and extension of

revolver and body. Finally, the shooter's goal should be to produce these same attributes each time the revolver is brought to bear.

Photo 3.4F shows how a slender hand with long fingers may not be able to use the finger under the revolver butt effectively. The size of the hand does not (in this case) encompass a large portion of the revolver's grip, and therefore is not able to exercise good control when the little finger is placed under the butt of the revolver (not shown).

There are differences in the angles or shapes of different grips for revolvers, as photo 3.4H shows. The same can be said for some of the revolvers as well. No single firearm can be said to be the best for all shooters, there are plenty of choices in deciding which configuration may work best for each shooter.

Photo 3.4C & 3.4D - *Two lady champions, Linda Patton, a.k.a. "Running Bare," SASS® #2323 (left) and Jeanie Ming, a.k.a. "Prairie Weet," SASS® #778 show strong hand grips with and without the little finger under the revolver butt.*

Photo 3.4E - *Candy Johnson, a.k.a. "Calamity Candy," SASS® #23367 shows how the hot or more powerful loads commonly cause the hand to rise on the revolver's back strap, to end up interfering with fully cocking the hammer.*

Photo 3.4F - *A slender hand with long fingers may not always use this type of grip successfully.*

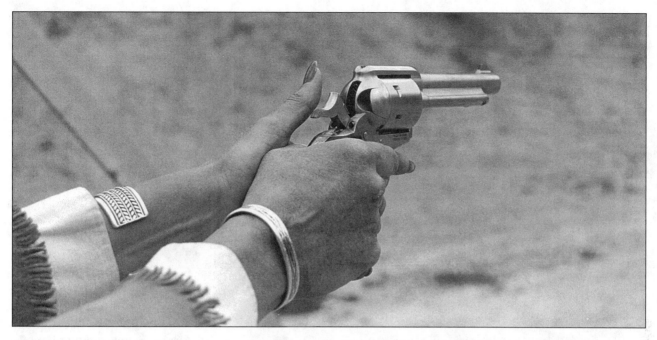

Photo 3.4G - *Lighter loads and raising the hand on the same revolver may produce dramatic improvements for this shooter.*

Shooters should not think that just because one grip or another feels best to them, that the revolver's performance is going to automatically provide them with the best overall results. Often, one compromise or another is involved. Adaptation, experimentation, and analysis after field use are the best way. The proof (as it is often said) is in the pudding. Master grips as they relate to the one-handed shooter or "Duelist" will be addressed in Chapter 4.

Using The Weak Or Off-Hand

Commonly referred to as the weak or off-hand, this is, of course, the hand opposite of the one holding the revolver in the strong or master grip. Cowboy action shooters competing in any class permitting the use of two hands to operate the revolver should come to understand, and use to their advantage, what the off-hand brings. Proper application of this second point of contact to the revolver can be much more than just a stable platform from which to engage. The off-hand is the key element to the successful manual cocking of the single-action at the speeds seen in today's events. The off-hand goes further in allowing

Photo 3.4H - *Jerry Koch, a.k.a. "Texas Jack Morales," SASS® #5026, beside some of the different grip sizes, angles and shapes available for single-action revolvers.*

Photo 3.5A - *Caught working the off-hand in a mid-stride cocking stroke, Todd Heywood, a.k.a. "Dog Soldier," SASS® #3823 is right on target with his method.*

Once again it is up to the shooter to decide which way of holding the handgun with the weak hand works best. Try not to decide based on simply what may feel right, look first at what you want to accomplish. Again, what may feel awkward at first can often provide the desired results with a little work. Moreover, most new techniques will probably soon feel as comfortable as any used before.

this rapid cocking of the single-action's hammer by allowing the cocking to take place *without* any interruption or change in positioning of the strong hand as it maintains the fixed hold of the master grip.

As you experiment and develop your off-hand positioning, think in terms of isolating the rest of the body from the movements of the weak hand as it operates the hammer again and again. If your elbow, upper arm or shoulders are moving at the same time, you are adding to

Photo 3.5B - *On the left, Miranda Dalton, a.k.a. "Dead Eye Dalton," SASS® #17551, shows her hold with one finger of the off-hand around the front of the trigger guard, and Diane Miller, a.k.a. "Dixie Bell," SASS® #3565, shows how two fingers can also be used.*

Photo 3.5C - *Noted World and National Champion Dennis Ming, a.k.a. "China Camp," SASS® #649, demonstrates how the other fingers of the off-hand are wrapped on or around the fingers of the strong hand.*

(instead of reducing) the overall motions. This, in turn, simply increases the chances of this motion affecting the firearm's muzzle.

Looking at the last few photos, these points of contact are where the off-hand is anchored to the revolver, and from which the rest of the off-hand must perform the important task of cocking the single-action revolver's hammer. The shooter will immediately recognize that there must be slight movement of the broadest part of the hand in order to move the thumb back and forth over the distance required to cock the handgun. Note the difference in photo 3.5Das the thumb is on top of the hammer (starting the rearward cock), to the position shown in 3.5C when the thumb has brought the hammer all the way back to the fully cocked position.

In effect, there is an axis or pivot point near the center of the palm of the

Photo 3.5D - *Manipulation of the revolver's hammer requires slight movement of the off-hand for each shot.*

off-hand to some degree. The contact point of this part of the off-hand is usually on the thumb of the strong hand. The shooter will feel the off-hand pivoting on this point as the hammer is cocked and re-cocked. Allowing for the right amount of freedom of movement around this pivot point of sorts will soon be smooth, and part of the shooter's subconscious actions. Even the average cowboy action shooter will cock and fire five times in less than five seconds. With a little work this can easily be done in just over three. It is routinely done in the low two-second area by many top shooters. If it was not made clear, these times are including hits on targets!

Thumb Cocking The Revolver

It is the job of the thumb of the off-hand to cock the hammer during engagement. This should be accomplished with the appropriate amount of speed as related to the individual's current skill level, hopefully insuring no "glitches," such as missing the hammer, will occur. Each shooter will (through trial and error) find which of the two positions shown in photos 3.6A and 3.6B will work best for their own thumbs to rest after cocking the hammer. Photo 3.6A reveals the thumb has been brought back to an upright position, slightly to the left of the hammer, and is poised to re-cock at the instant the hammer has fallen to the fully depressed position and fired a round. This does require the shooter to move the thumb into this

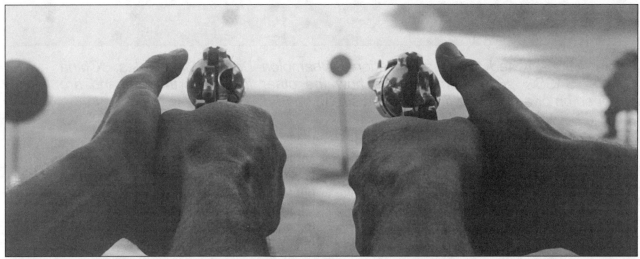

Photo 3.6A & 3.6B - *Common positions for the thumb to rest when not performing its important task of cocking the hammer for each shot.*

position *after* bringing the hammer to its fully cocked position.

The photo in 3.6B shows another successful method. After cocking the hammer, the thumb rests directly behind the fully cocked hammer, close to, most often touching, the web of the shooter's strong hand. Upon firing the round, the thumb follows the falling hammer to re-cock for each ensuing shot.

It is fair to say that the "thumb up" position shown in photo 3.6A is the more common of the two. The "thumb down" position is nevertheless an effective alternative some shooters may come to prefer. There are some problems that the shooter should be aware of that can occur during either cocking method.

Photo 3.6C shows the thumb returning to a position too far away from the spur of the hammer in the fully depressed position. This position will take additional time for the thumb to reach the hammer spur. Worse still, is that the distance from the hammer will promote both unwanted side movement imparted to the equa-

tion and increase dramatically the chances of a slight miss hit on the hammer. A miss hit by the thumb can result in the miss indexing or short stroking of the revolver's correct cylinder advancement. This is a serious loss of time, causing the shooter to often advance the cylinder's empty chambers all the way around in order to find and fire the fifth or final shot. It is also one of many slight miscues that hinder the normal focus and therefore success of the subsequent tasks the shooter must complete.

The problem shown in photo 3.6D is that of the thumb being brought back to a spot that is too low to effectively re-cock the hammer after it falls. After the hammer falls, this thumb will have to move further upward in order to perform the next cocking action. Again, this adds distance and movement that is unnecessary and increases the chances of one miscue or another.

Photo 3.6C - *The thumb is up, but its proximity to the hammer is too far away.*

Photo 3.6D - *The thumb is not held high enough.*

Photo 3.6E - *The thumb is not far enough behind the fully cocked hammer.*

A problem more common than most would guess, is the way an incorrectly placed (or moved) thumb behind the hammer can actually interrupt the motion of the hammer as it falls from the fully cocked position to fire a round. Most often, it is not even recognized by shooters doing this, because it is rarely felt. The mere brush of the hammer's spur against the shooter's thumb as it falls, will cause motion that transfers instantly to the muzzle. This will almost always result in a missed target. Photo 3.6E shows the most common error of this kind, the thumb has not been brought back to a position far enough behind of the fully cocked hammer. Another similar mistake is the premature, hasty forward movement of the thumb in anticipation of re-cocking the hammer.

Both of the techniques offered to prevent this are considered the most effective ones currently used. The key in using either of them successfully is to build a solid foundation from the start. Do not try to go as fast as some other

shooters you will see when starting out. Make sure your basic mechanics are sound first, and that you are achieving clean (error free) movements. The speed will come automatically. Remember also that the smoothest method of cocking the hammer for you will be the one that you learn to do without thinking. You want it to become effective, easy, and smooth in a very personal way. Whatever way this may be, remember that the least amount of motion transferred to the revolver during use is the most desirable. Jerky movements, hard or overly forceful motions will not improve your game.

One more technique used with success is shown in photo 3.6F. The off-hand's thumb has come to rest on the left side of the revolver's frame after bringing the hammer to the fully cocked position. This can offer increased stabil-

Photo 3.6F - *Ken Thornton, a.k.a. "Cletus Starr," SASS® #22081 shows how resting the off-hand thumb in this position after cocking the revolver may offer greater stability when needed.*

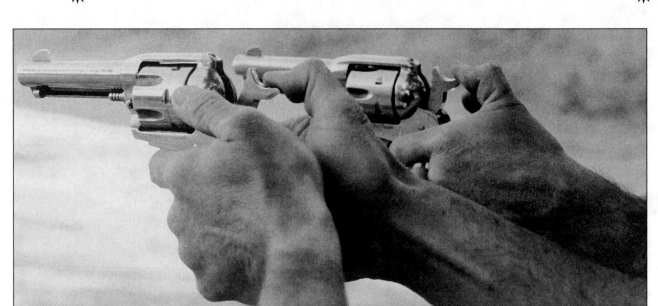

Photo 3.6G - *Left- or right-handed, cocking the hammer with the strong hand's thumb will never provide improved performance in two-handed revolver shooting.*

ity. One example where this may assist the shooter is a stage where the targets are smaller and/or at greater distances than normally set. Anytime you want another anchoring point this will work well. Brand new shooters may find this intermediate position a good place to begin as they develop their skills with the revolver.

The worst method of re-cocking the single-action revolver when using a two-handed hold is shown in photo 3.6G. Using the thumb of the strong hand (used for the master grip) to cock and re-cock the single-action revolver denies any chance of real improvement in your revolver shooting. Not only is the master grip broken each time the thumb of the strong hand is raised to perform the cocking motion, the master grip must be *re-acquired* to some degree prior to re-engaging the trigger. Bringing the thumb of the strong hand up to engage the hammer spur is also a movement that is so contrary to the basics of what practical movement would dictate, that miscues resulting in multiple problems would be the rule, not the exception. This method will adversely affect both

the strong hand and the off-hand's ability to control the revolver. You will see it done from time to time, but not by any shooter who attains much success.

Completing The Two-Handed Revolver Address

The shooter in photo 3.7A is in an effective, "at the ready" position to engage with the revolver. To begin with, the wrists are correctly aligned, firm and straight. The arms are forming part of the address known as an isosceles or triangular style. The reason for keeping the arms out as straight as possible, referred to in this book as "extended and locked," is to achieve the most forward (and therefore stable) platform from which to absorb the revolver's energy. Understand that this extension and lock is not one that the shooter should over-emphasize by thrusting farther forward than would seem comfortable, it should be just enough extension so the arms are at their natural length and straight. The extended arms assist locking the revolver into a position with fewer tendencies to shift. The wrists are also part of this. Realize too, that this extension and lock is not done with a tightening or flexing of the shoulder or arm muscles. Rigidity will cause tension to transfer to the farthest point of extension,

Photo 3.7A - *Terry Miller, a.k.a. "T.L.," SASS® #3566, shows excellent form in his address.*

namely the muzzle. To hold firmly, or to even increase the stability of this position, the shooter will learn that this requires only a slight turning of each elbow inward (towards one another).

The figures in photo 3.7B shows what a full isosceles shooting stance looks like from a few different angles. The outstretched arms create the sides of the triangle, while the angle of the shoulders and feet would be the bottom of the back line connecting the sides. The distance of the feet are much the same for any good address, about hip-width apart, but can be adjusted to the shooter's need or preference.

This address may or may not require lateral movement to one side or the other after revolver use. It offers the shooter an ability to shift the upper part of the body in either direction along the radius of targets with the least amount of strain or tension at either end of the radius. As does any address, it does require the shooter to be aware of the need to shift correctly and stay within the 180-degree safety plane if the cross-draw side comes into play.

The tailoring or modifying of this stance will serve as an advantage to the shooter. Note how the shooter in photo 3.7C has modified the position of the lower torso, with one foot slightly forward of the other. The shooter's upper torso is still turned downrange, remaining in the basic triangular angles of the isosceles. Some shooters may feel comfortable with this set-up all the time. In this case it shows how best to set up for subsequent actions with the least amount of movement. The right-handed shooter in this case must first draw one revolver and engage the five targets from left to right. The next move will be to return the handgun to leather, and retrieve the rifle from the vertical stand it is pre-staged in.

There is a series of problems presented here that the shooter must look to when making the initial approach. Recognizing these (and other problems presented) in the same way will become automatic with time, practice, and a good pre-stage routine. The problem or challenge presented is in three parts. The shooter wants to effectively solve all three tasks without *any* unnecessary movement that may hinder the potential of a fast time. The shooter understands that all anticipated actions must always take *safety* into consideration first. Here is an effective way to approach this challenge.

KNOW YOUR SINGLE-ACTION HANDGUNS   55

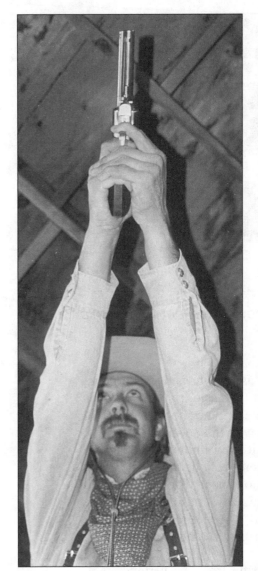

Photos 3.7B - *Magnum Quigley (above), Gene Pearcey (top right), a.k.a. "Evil Roy," SASS®#2883, and former World Champion Dennis Martinez (bottom right), a.k.a. "Flint Westwood," SASS® #94 show some different views of the widely advocated isosceles shooting address.*

Photo 3.7C - *Shooters can tailor the Isosceles to work perfectly for them.*

Photo 3.7D - *This shooter is on the firing line, ready to engage.*

The shooter in photos 3.7C and D is correctly set up for the stage run. The first problem was to set up in a position that would require no movement of the feet, but would allow enough free radius of the upper torso to address both revolver and rifle targets comfortably. The shooter's front foot is the key here. Setting the front foot at a point slightly left of the center of the target radius allows the torso to turn more comfortably to the left side of the radius, which is the direction more restricted by having the left foot forward. The second problem is solved because turning toward the right side is less restricted in kind, and provides more freedom of movement to quickly pickup the staged rifle on the shooter's right and bring it to bear with no lower body movement. The third problem is solved by itself when the shooter makes the correct choice of which revolver to use first. With the left foot forward, the strong side holster is within the safe confines of the 180-degree safety plane and may be safely drawn. As the shooter turns to the right when sweeping the first five revolver targets, the torso carries the hip even further into the safety plane. As the fifth shot is fired, the shooter is in excellent position to re-holster safely and, with a slight turn, pick up the rifle.

Where the shooter chooses to stand in relationship to the staged firearm is important. Set up so the turn to pick up the rifle is comfortable, and avoids stretching. If this is not possible, set up for one easy step rather than a long reach. Again, think of the front foot as an axis point. A point that takes into consideration how far the shooter will be required to turn in the restricted direction as opposed to the less restricted or natural direction. It is common to see shooters setting up and taking address with empty, outstretched arms along the radius of targets before they engage. Not a lot of time can be taken here, but the shooter will soon find this takes only a few seconds if they have studied the problem prior to going to the line.

Photo 3.7E - *Flint Westwood is one of many fine shooters still using this stance, but too many potential problems have made this stance obsolete for most new shooters to learn.*

The reader may wonder why the stance known as the "Weaver" or "Modified Weaver" is not mentioned in detail. While some may argue otherwise, there are several reasons which have led to the Modified Weaver address becoming somewhat outdated. Not only is this stance no longer taught by most law enforcement agencies, it is said to promote problems for all but the most highly skilled and constantly trained special units. It is a stance and hold that uses a "push and pull" system where the off-hand is applying rearward pressure at the same time the strong hand applies forward pressure. This in itself is not conducive to the cocking and re-cocking duties performed by the weak hand when using a single-action revolver. In addition, the tilt, or bend of the off-hand's arm offers an angled platform that can easily change position in one way or another during engagement, causing denial of the more stable, geometrically even position found in the isosceles stance. It is said, that when placed in conditions of high stress, or when an armed threat may present itself, the natural position to assume is that of a protective one, with arms extended straight out. The isosceles most resembles this automatic defensive move and serves best in an aggressive mode as well.

I had better be clear here in stating the fact that many fine shooters use the Weaver with success. I do not presume to tell anyone this position of address is worthless, for certainly it is not. I do believe, however, that many more shooters who do use the Weaver may find more success by using the isosceles. Success is just as hard to argue with here as failure would be.

The shooter's posture of address is another important key to success. Like any athlete preparing for action, the body assumes an attitude to allow flexibility rather than rigidity. The shooter in photo 3.7F is a good example. With the knees slightly bent for flexibility, this promotes the shooter's forward attitude towards the targets. The forward attitude is not outside the shooter's natural center of gravity, or so exaggerated it might upset the natural balance. This position is almost one of slight aggression. It can aid the shooter in focusing on each target. It is a stance or platform from which the shooter can traverse along the target acquisition line with stability and speed. It also is one that allows the shooter to absorb recoil much more effectively than one who is upright.

It is important the shooter learn to keep his head straight and shoulders as parallel with the ground as possible when engaging with the revolver. Cocking the head over to one side or another during engagement adds tension and reduces freedom of motion. The same is true for the shoulders. Assuming a starting position on the firing line that does not take into consideration what range of motion and which direction(s) this motion must follow, may well cause the shooter to compensate by angling the head and shoulders unnaturally. Incorrect angling of the head and the shoulders will also have an adverse affect on revolver sighting and target acquisition.

The most effective position of address will allow the shooter to begin engaging with the least amount of

Photo 3.7F - *Eric Carlstedt, a.k.a. "Magnum Quigley," SASS® #1021 shows a well-balanced position with revolver up and ready from two views.*

movement. Yes, you have already heard this and will probably hear it yet again. The instance I'll discuss right now, is one more part of the initial address. Whenever possible, the shooter should set up in such a way that engagement can begin without changing the line of sight. If the shooter has only the single task of attaining the master grip, bringing the revolver out and up as the off-hand comes into position to support and begin the cocking process, then that should be the *only* motion. If, for some reason, the shooter must be looking at a revolver (that is pre-staged on a table) in order to perform a quick and clean pick-up, then the *only* added movement would be the head tilting upwards as the revolver is brought up.

Without going on and on here, the point I want to make clear is that to move or change any position without good reason has no merit. The shooter should be set, ready to go and listening for the timer's signal while in the *best* possible position. If the shooter changes the position of his body, the shoulders, legs and head position also change. There is now a new line of sight to the first target, a new angle from which the address is presented and, finally, the shooter had to move and adjust in order to accomplish this task. *don't* do this unless it is absolutely necessary. It may cause the shooter to regress into bad habits of stance, sighting and other problems. It also adds to what the shooter's mind must focus on. It serves no good purpose by itself. If all the shooter has to do is move the hands and arms, then that is the *only* part of the body that should move.

The upright stance shown in photo *3.7G* is a good example of what *not* to do. The shooter has little flexibility when any tasks or transitions are to be made, will probably be adversely affected by recoil and will never improve without some drastic changes. A shooter whose stance resembles this will waste time bending or moving awkwardly, trying to transition one way or another, and will then often rise up to the same rigid, upright position *again*. Using this stance it is much more difficult to obtain a fast break or complete a quick movement to another required position. Shooters who use this stance in their approach are often fighting their nerves and cannot relax. No doubt that these poor souls could use a little help from one who can offer this basic training in a gentle and friendly manner. Maybe you could be the one to help someone like this to relax and shoot better.

Photo 3.7G - *An upright stance will hinder the shooter's chances for success in more than one way.*

Each round fired is producing a certain amount of recoil that must be absorbed to some extent by the shooter. The rigid, upright stance does not absorb well, nor does a shooter using this stance recover in large part from the shock of the recoil as it is sent through the hands, along the arms and into the shoulders. This inability to recover also serves to create an increasing, overall imbalance that can begin to rock the shooter rearward onto the heels of the feet. All the same forces a well-balanced stance will absorb and distribute evenly will have the opposite effect on one that is not as well balanced. The rigid, upright stance will also compel the shooter to use greater strength in order to control the forces working against the body. Exerting greater strength in order to compensate here only creates increased muscle tension and strain.

Even though we are talking about the revolver in this chapter, don't lose sight of the fact that lever guns and especially the shotgun are adversely affected by the rigid, upright stance described.

Sighting The Revolver

The ideal sight picture through most shooter's eyes is very close to that seen in photo 3.8A. It is seemingly a simple task, one that is easily comprehended and executed under expectations of hitting targets with relative ease. Unfortunately, it does not usually work that way.

There are (as we have gone over) too many other attributes of handling the revolver that can change the impact point at the time of discharge. Most instructors agree that shooters have to see the front sight on the target with the top of the front sight's blade filling the rear sight notch correctly in order to achieve consistent hits.

One way of focusing on the front sight is to remember to *lay* the sight on the target, not place the target behind the front sight. Try to pick up the front sight blade as the revolver comes up to the forward firing position, and (again) *lay* that front sight on the target. As the point of focus is the front sight only, both the rear sight and the target will appear blurred when sighting is done correctly.

While dry fire (UN-loaded firing) practicing is not very exciting (even kind of boring), improved sight acquisition is one of many reasons to do this regularly. Bringing the revolver up and obtaining the front sight on any target begins to program the shooter's muscle memory. Soon (with as little as

Photo 3.8A - *The front sight blade fills the rear sight's notch perfectly.*

ten minutes a day practice for one week), the repetition of bringing the revolver up, focusing on the front sight (as it is laid on a target) will become part of the shooter's muscle memory. There will be more offered on this topic as we go on to other chapters.

The Shooter's Dominant Eye

Another subject related to sighting is the dominant eye. Most shooters will use their dominant eye for focusing automatically. Some shooters may not know which to use, let alone which eye is the dominant eye. Some shooters may not even have a dominant eye. To find out is easy. With your arm straight out in front of you, hold the index finger up. Find a suitably small object to use as a target of sorts, and hold the index finger so it covers most of this object. Do this first with *both* eyes open. Keeping the arm and finger on the selected object, first close one eye and check to see if the object has moved to one side or the other. Open both eyes again and then close the opposite eye to see what happens. The eye that sees no change in the object's position (no apparent movement) while the other one is closed, is the dominant eye. If the object remains behind the finger regardless of whether one eye is open or closed, then there is no one dominant eye. Most right-handed people are right-eye dominant, while most left-handed people are left-eye dominant. There are exceptions, of course. Not only will some people find that they are neither left or right eye dominant, some left-handed people may be right-eye dominant and some right-handed people left-eye dominant. I happen to be right-handed and left-eye dominant. The only thing in the world (that I am aware of) that I do left-handed as a result of this, is to shoot all long guns from my left shoulder. There is relevance in understanding this. Many cowboy action shooters are new and inexperienced, often without any prior knowledge of handling firearms. The shooter who may be exhibiting extreme difficulty in sighting their rifle or shotgun may be attempting to sight with their dominant eye from the *wrong* side. Revolver shooting is not usually affected in this manner.

Using One Or Two Eyes While Sighting

Shooting (or sighting) with both eyes open may not be absolutely necessary for success, but there are some very good reasons to do so. One reason is the additional peripheral vision and increased light. This (while perhaps arguable) may allow quicker acquisition from target to target. More importantly and without question is the advantage of less strain being put on the eyes in general. A long day of match shooting will produce a certain amount of eyestrain on all shooters. Those shooting with both eyes open are most likely to experience less strain than those shooting with one eye shut. Again, shooting with one eye closed is not necessarily a recipe for failure, but is widely seen as the least desirable or effective method to use.

Training a new or junior shooter to keep both eyes open when sighting is often easier than it is to train an experienced shooter. Not knowing the difference or not being ingrained with the habit of using only one eye may be the advantage.

The eye that does the work of focusing on the front sight blade must be trained so that it is not distracted by what the other eye sees. A shooter having trouble becoming comfortable with this technique may find that to squint or narrow the non-sighting eye will help. Another method used is placing a piece of transparent or "frosty" scotch tape over the safety glass lens of the non-shooting eye. The trick is to simply reduce the ability of the non-shooting eye to focus and interfere with the shooter.

There are many shooters (including myself) who have never learned to shoot with both eyes totally open. My other, non-sighting eye is (at best) kept at a narrow squint. Aware of the possible eye strain this condition can induce during extended match play, I will take care to relax and rest my eyes several times during a match.

Photo 3.8B - *Trained correctly, this young shooter keeps both eyes open during sighting. (Alexis Masterson, a.k.a. "Idie Clair," SASS® #6846.)*

Sighting In Your Revolver

The actual sighting-in of the revolver, or what some may know as zeroing the firearm, is addressed here with basic information only. The shooter should understand that the point of impact made by the projectile or bullet is affected by several different conditions. Different applications of bullet weight, powder charge and barrel length can all cause the impact point to change.

The average revolver target in cowboy action shooting is about 10 yards away from the shooter. Shooting from the most stable position available, the shooter must remember to aim at the same identical point on a paper target each time that a round is fired as they begin to dial in their handguns. While there are three basic aiming points shooters will use to insure the bullet will hit the center of the target, the most common is called "point of aim" or "dead center." This means the bullet will strike that exact point (or very close) where the top of the front sight is laid on the target. The correct alignment of the front sight blade in relation to the rear sight's notch must also be correctly applied. The other impact points referred to are the 6 o'clock and the 12 o'clock hold. Picturing the target as a clock, if the shooter prefers a 6 o'clock hold, the revolver will be sighted in so that the round strikes dead center of the target when the sights are aligned to the 6 o'clock (bottom center point) position of the target. The 12 o'clock hold is exactly the opposite. Of these two, the 6 o'clock hold is used more often.

Moving the round impact for elevation (straight up or down) is sometimes done with bullet weight. A heavier bullet will raise the impact point and a lighter one will lower the impact point. Powder charges will also come into play here. The few revolvers that supposedly come "pre-sighted" from the factory will usually require a round that is a factory-produced, standard round for general civilian use in terms of bullet weight and velocity. One example to look at is the .45 Long Colt. The civilian version of this round has most always been a 250-grain bullet with an average of between 850 and 1,000 FPS (feet per second). As discussed, this particular configuration is not very comfortable for the shooter, nor is it best suited for this style of competition. Moreover, most of these firearms were *never* truly designed to take the abuse of what thousands of factory rounds would have on them.

Adjustable rear sights are one answer, but are not as popular as the more "traditional" look of the fixed rear sight revolvers used in the Old West. If or when the shooter decides that a lighter bullet weight is the way to go, a fixed rear sight revolver will most often need modification done to the front sight. Larger caliber revolvers perhaps more than smaller caliber revolvers. The front sight will usually need to be lower than is standard in order to raise the impact of the lighter projectile to the desired point. One common method (although sometimes frowned upon by some owning expensive revolvers) is to file down the front sight. Many original revolvers of old will have had this modification done prior to use in this sport. So it's not a new idea or one exclusive to cowboy action shooting.

Windage or impact points along the horizontal plane of the target may also need to be addressed if not centered after correct elevation sighting is completed. A competent gunsmith can take a paper target and compute the amount a barrel must be turned one way or the other in order to correct this problem. Tweaking or bending the front sight to change windage is not recommended except under the most special of circumstances.

Fixed rear sights can be modified somewhat to allow the shooter pick-up or to see the front sight a little better. This modification is usually just widening the rear notch with a file. Still, it is best to consult with a gunsmith prior to attempting to do it yourself.

Action Jobs

It is normal for single-action revolvers purchased through distributors or factories to have a stiff action. To what degree the action is stiff (even rough) can vary, but there is little doubt among cowboy action shooters that using a revolver with a smooth action is more fun than not. An action job of merit will not only provide the shooter with handling characteristics that are greatly enhanced over a stock revolver, it can also mean less wear and tear on the equipment too.

Inquiries made to fellow shooters regarding the who, what and where of a good gunsmith will usually provide several choices. Obtaining a consensus of opinion is best. The reader should understand that no gunsmith's reputation is perfect, and that they may hear an occasional horror story. The ones with solid reputations will be spoken of much more positively than not, and will stand behind their work.

Over the past 10 seasons of cowboy action shooting events, my personal gunsmith has been Lee Fisher of Lee's Gunsmithing in Orange, California. Choose a gunsmith in (or close to) your area that has participated in the sport, understands the needs of those competing in cowboy action shooting and will stand behind his work. Bob James of James & Guns in Phoenix, Arizona is another outstanding gunsmith in the western United States. Don't be surprised when the gunsmith you have chosen to do your work informs you of a rather long backlog. The gunsmith on top of his workload will be quite honest about the turnaround time, and will usually be within one week or so of that estimate. Sadly, the author cannot mention all the fine gunsmiths in this sport, but will list some more of them in the Directory.

The following is largely information gathered by Dennis Ming, a.k.a. "China Camp," SASS® #649, and Lee Fisher, a.k.a., "Ringo," SASS® #257. Hopefully, the reader will better understand what it is they want out of a competent action job after reading this information.

Photo 3.9A - *Above is Lee Fisher, a.k.a. "Ringo," SASS® #257. His action work for the firearms used by "China Camp" (at right) and many other top shooters has earned him some serious bragging rights over the years.*

Smooth Hammer Action

Single-action revolvers usually come from the factory with a heavy exterior hammer pull. In the heat of engagement this heavy pull can often result in a half-cocked (or miss-cocked) hammer. When the shooter re-cocks the hammer after this initial error, the loaded chamber skips ahead, ultimately causing the shooter to re-cock the revolver an additional five times to bring the skipped round back under the hammer. Even though this can happen after an action job, it is far more likely to happen without one. The bottom line is that you need a smooth hammer. Buying an after-market spring kit that will lessen the drag and having a competent gunsmith install it to ensure reliability is key.

Polishing the Chambers

Worthy of repeating, there are engagements in a match that require the shooter to reload. Simple polishing of the cylinder's chambers using a chamber-polishing tool specific to the caliber will facilitate the extraction of spent cases, enhancing the insertion of fresh cartridges. The edges of the chambers may be chamfered to further assist the reloading process. These two improvements do not affect the overall functioning of the revolver, and remain within the Single-Action Shooting Society (SASS®) Rules of Engagement.

Open The Forcing Cone

It is a well known fact among revolver shooters that opening the forcing cone improves accuracy and decreases the amount of leading at the throat of the barrel. The angle by which the forcing cone is opened depends upon the gunsmith's experience and what he sees as most reliable. Get your gunsmith's opinion on this one.

Custom Tune the Springs

Correct and careful balancing of the action to improve reliability and ensure smooth functioning often requires replacing and/or tuning the factory springs. Experienced shooters will often attest that custom springs last longer and provide greater consistency in the overall functioning of the revolver. Your gunsmith should find the proper balance between spring tension and reliability.

Setting An Appropriate Trigger Pull

Ask your gunsmith what trigger poundage (pull weight) he intends to set on the action of your gun. Experienced gunsmiths will usually inquire about the shooter's level of experience prior to setting the trigger pull. Too light a trigger pull will promote accidental discharges. An average trigger pull for cowboy action shooters is around 1-1/2 pounds or 24 ounces. Compare that to the average hunting rifle with a 4-pound trigger pull and you see that it doesn't take much pressure to set off a round from a revolver set up for cowboy action shooting. Avoid "home gunsmithing" when it comes to trigger jobs. Leave it to the professionals and you won't be sorry.

Polish The Internal Parts

One of the marks of an excellent action job is one where all the internal parts, including the ejector, have been polished. Part of this may include adjusting the ejector spring for ease of use.

Check The Rear Barrel Face

Your gunsmith should check and set the right amount of gap between the cylinder face and the rear of the barrel.

Final Notes On Action Jobs For Revolvers, Rifles And Shotguns

Essentially, the action jobs on the firearms used by today's cowboy action shooters provide the same ease of handling, increased reliability and, finally, make the revolver more "user friendly." The cost of similar work will vary from gunsmith to gunsmith. Be informed when making a decision about who will work on your firearms, and what you will get for your money. The average action job is about $200, although some may cost several hundred. Most of the top shooters I know have spent the lesser of the two amounts. It may cost a few dollars to enhance your guns, but the enjoyment and improved performance you will experience is well worth the money in the long run!

A Few Afterthoughts To Consider

The reader will find information sprinkled about this book about shooting tactics for the firearms used in CAS. At this particular moment, I am going over a manuscript that is basically completed, changing this, adding that, etc. Here are a couple of items I didn't want to leave out, and are (to be honest) afterthoughts.

Shooting between the bars can (for some) be one of the more difficult props to manage well in CAS. What the shooter faces in each instance is pretty much the same and may well be the answer or direction in which to look for improvement.

What I'm talking about is the distance of swing along the target line. Normally, there is nothing to interfere with a shooter's ability to traverse across the line of three or more targets. We do this without much thought, focusing more on our position of address, getting that front sight on each target and other aspects of good approach. To move along any target radius with impunity from any object that may limit this freedom of movement permits us to bring to bear our best techniques.

The stage designs that present bars, windows, individual window lights, knotholes, doors, or other similar problems are fair and honest stage traps. In this instance, the freedom of movement may be restricted to as little as four inches across. Past that distance on either side is a bar. Crossing over a fixed object like this with the front sight while focusing *does* produce a significant distraction. To address each target through the same four-inch opening requires that there is first an opportunity to acquire each target, and that the shooter can adjust, shift or perform any number of little moves that are not required in normal situations.

Often, the shooter cannot make this one space work for all five rounds, and must shift to another opening within the span of bars (or position within a window, etc.) to resume tar-

get acquisition and engagement. Here are some of the things to do, and *not* to do, in this type of engagement.

- **DO realize you will engage from a less than optimum position, one that requires your best control.**

Photo 3.9B - *Brent Meinhart, a.k.a. "Doc Holiday," SASS® #419, engages a bank of revolver targets from behind bars.*

- **DO NOT** address this position at your normal speed or rhythm of engagement.

- **DO** address the targets through the bars prior to shooting if at all possible.

- **DO NOT** decide which area or areas you will engage through after the stage run starts.

- **DO** consider the possibility of engaging through one opening, but consider, too, the other adjustments that might have to be made in order to do this.

- **DO NOT** thrust the revolver barrel through the opening unless this is part of the plan to address all the targets.

- **DO** find a spot on the ground (or another landmark) that permits optimum sighting and target acquisition prior to the run. If transitioning, it is this spot you must hit to address and engage from as planned.

- **DO NOT** go in and out of the bars to re-address each target unless it is required.

- **DO** decide which targets will be engaged from which clear space, whether it is one or more spaces.

- **DO NOT** lose sight of each primary target during movement; this is a loss of focus due to distraction.

- **DO** insure you can swing both the revolver and yourself along the target line at full extension by allowing enough distance between you and the prop. Do this when the plan calls for the need to do so, and not automatically.

- **DO NOT** risk or attempt to perform an unfamiliar technique unless you understand the probable outcome.

- **DO** plan, focus and execute the moves you are most confident will produce reasonable success.

- **DO** think and reason what will be a reasonable engagement speed within your current skill level that will produce hits, and visualize each shot to be made.

Okay, having said all that in the hopes of providing improvement in this area (and others), there is one more important thing to say. Remember always to do as I *say*… and *not* as I may sometimes *do*.

Photo 3.9C - *Mark Effle, a.k.a. "Midway," SASS® #449, demonstrates the right… and the wrong way to make revolver shots from a rest.*

Photo 3.9D - Thanks Midway, we just ended the revolver chapter with a rifle tip….

If a decision is made to shoot the revolver from a position of rest, don't make the mistake of resting the butt of the revolver (or the bottom of the hands) on the prop. As Midway shows, the best way to achieve maximum stability is from an area less subject to the motions produced around the revolver itself (like the arms).

The rifle can be used in a number of different positions of "rest" to improve the shooter's platform. As it is with the revolver, the best results will be seen when the shooter has not allowed the firearm to rest directly upon the prop. Whatever the reason; small targets, bonus targets, or other conditions that may warrant a shooter's decision to sacrifice a little speed for the increased reliability a rest offers, it is a basic tool that may come in handy someday.

Chapter 4

DUELIST, BLACKPOWDER & GUNFIGHTER CLASS

The Duelist Class Shooter

First introduced in SASS® competition around 1991 or '92, the "Duelist" class has become very popular among men and women shooters. So much so that it has become the second largest class of competitors in the sport, surpassed only by "Men's Traditional." Seen by many as a more authentic style of shooting a single-action revolver, this is arguable and a moot point, at best.

What *is* more important is the challenge presented and the skill required for a shooter to become successful (let alone a top shooter) in this class. There are usually separate duelist classes for both men and women.

Though not considered an acceptable design for main stages today, several seasons ago all shooters might have found themselves at a stage that required the revolver to be engaged with the strong hand only. While ladies and juniors were permitted to cock the

Photo 4.0A - *Bill Hill, a.k.a. "Dub," SASS® #1487, takes classic aim with his "ghost gun," an early Colt Bisley. Bill found this gun in 1991, (or, as Dub says, did it find him?) and discovered the initials W. Hill had been engraved on it by an owner long since passed away. Who says CAS isn't haunted?*

Photo 4.01A - *End Of Trail 2000 Duelist Champion Matt Stolle, a.k.a. "Buckskin Frank Leslie," SASS® #215, and Ladies World and National Champion Jeanie Ming, a.k.a. "Prairie Weet," SASS® #778.*

revolver with their off-hands as needed, this little "fly in the ointment" presented an interesting problem to many of those not used to it.

The Duelist Class is not recommended for the inexperienced or new shooter. It requires the shooter to draw, cock and bring to bear the single-action revolver with one hand only. All subsequent actions are also performed with the strong hand alone during engagement with the revolver, save that of a possible reload. There is a definite fatigue factor to consider here, as well as the unquestioned and paramount responsibility of safety the shooter must continually exercise.

Competing for a full season as a duelist in 1994, I found out for myself just how challenging and enjoyable this class is. The decision having been made to enter and compete in this class, I was intent on finishing at or near the top and I began to prepare in earnest. That season was a memorable one for me as it was my good fortune to be first "Duelist" at every major event I entered, except one, that year. The highlight of that season for me was

to win the national duelist title at Winter Range, finishing eighth overall out of some 240 shooters. The only event I did not compete as a duelist in that year was End of Trail, where I finished second overall, competing in Men's Traditional. I mention this because it was my best finish at an EOT (End of Trail) to date, and one I attribute directly to having been shooting all the other events that year as a duelist. I will tell you why later.

The Duelist Style Of Shooting Requires Adaptation

Once you have decided to adopt this class as your own, there are many areas you will need to understand and become accustomed to. I highly recommend that an immediate effort is made to strengthen the strong hand and wrist. If not by using one of the many squeezing devices we all know of, then by some other way. While the requirement of sufficient strength will certainly affect some more than others, the duelist shooter who finds the afternoon's stages more difficult to shoot clean than those engaged earlier in the day is likely to be failing in hand, wrist and arm strength. Boring as it may be, don't overlook this ingredient in your preparation.

Mentioned a moment ago was perhaps the single most important task a duelist shooter must look to achieve. That is to shoot *clean*, with the absolute least number of missed targets possible. This is, of course, true for any shooter in any class, but it is all the *more* so to the duelist. The duelist cannot address and engage targets nearly as quickly as can the shooters in the two-handed classes. The recognized trait of a good duelist is how clean they shoot and how fast they shoot clean. Whatever it takes to see that front sight on each target before the round is squeezed off is the duelist's number one priority.

The shooter who adapts to these ways will learn discipline in their revolver shooting, if nothing else. Speaking in average terms, it requires more discipline to shoot with one hand than it does with two. As I said, in 1994 I decided to compete again in the two-handed Men's Traditional Class at End of Trail World Championships of Cowboy Action Shooting®. Two things stand out as vivid memories when I began to shoot with two hands a few weeks prior to EOT. First, it was that my left thumb had forgotten how to cock the revolver's hammer like it once did. What stood out even more to me at the time was that I had become a better revolver shooter. One hand or two hands, it did not matter. The fact was that shooting duelist for one season had increased dramatically my discipline in engaging with the revolver. I saw the front sight faster. I brought the revolvers

to bear more effectively, and I hit more targets faster than ever before. A decided improvement had materialized. To this day, I am convinced that much of that improvement is owed to the time spent shooting as a duelist.

Adopting A Duelist Master Grip

While some duelists are starting to engage using either hand, it is still most common to see the strong hand used to engage with the revolver(s) as a duelist. Unlike the two-handed master grip, the duelist shooter's hand must perform all required tasks alone. The master grip itself is no longer a permanent, stationary grip as it was when the off-hand was there to assist. Each time the revolver is cocked, the grip is altered significantly. The strong hand's thumb must come off the revolver, cock and re-cock the hammer. Each time this occurs, a mul-

Photo 4.0B - *Shooters may need to develop a different, more effective master grip as duelists. (National Champions Mike Latterborn, a.k.a. "Handsome Valentine," SASS® #4752, and Cathie Ringler, a.k.a. "Renegade Rene," SASS® #4751.)*

Photo 4.0C, 4.0D & 4.0E - *Here is a look at the complete process; from initial discharge... to re-cocking the revolver... to being ready to fire again.*

titude of potential problems are presented. The trigger finger's position on the trigger may change. The shooter's overall hand placement on the revolver may also change. The recoil of the revolver in one hand is not as controllable, making each subsequent acquisition of both target and front sight more difficult. The important task of obtaining good arm extension and full "lock-out" is further hindered.

Understanding these problems, the shooter can now work on his or her own personal adaptations of methods used to find success. The photo 4.0C shows a shooter gripping the revolver much higher than might have been used for two-handed shooting by this shooter. Average size (and certainly smaller) hands will find that by raising the hand on the revolver's back strap, it will increase overall control. It also allows the thumb to be raised up with greater ease in which to cock the hammer as needed. Note how high the web of the hand is, and that in this position the hammer may actually be touching the web of the hand in the full cocked position. This condition is not as detrimental to the duelist as it is to the shooter using the two-handed grip. The duelist's motion of bringing the thumb up to cock the hammer also causes the web of the hand to move. As the hammer reaches the fully cocked position, the web of the hand follows the returning movement of the thumb, as the full grip is re-acquired. So, it is the hand that accommodates

or adapts to the hammer's position. The master grip of the two-handed shooter remains firm, in one position during engagement, meaning that bringing the hammer to full cock with the off-hand's thumb can possibly be adversely affected by the strong hand's stationary position on the revolver if held too high.

It cannot be over emphasized that there still needs to be a properly aligned master grip, one that aids the shooter in correct overall alignment and, therefore, where the trigger finger falls on the trigger.

The photos: 4.0C, D, and E illustrate how the master grip changes, and how the hand moves back into the original master grip position to fire the follow-up shot. Note how the web of the hand must move into position below an already fully cocked hammer. This eliminates any of the problems related to the height of the hand on the backstrap that the two-handed shooter should be aware of.

These illustrations cannot really show well how this revolver (with a 4-3/4-inch barrel) reacts during discharge. Simply put, the gun's reaction is largely a result of the recoil causing a certain amount of muzzle flip and shock that will vary from both revolver barrel length and caliber. Frame characteristics and actual weight of the revolver affects this motion as

Photo 4.0F & 4.0G - *Frank Holder, a.k.a. "Bull," SASS® #1081, a top duelist competitor, shows the two positions for the thumb to rest after re-cocking duelist style.*

well. The shooter will become accustomed to how his particular revolver reacts during discharge, and will adjust accordingly in finding the right "feel" of how to best re-cock while this motion occurs.

The photos in 4.0F and 4.0G show two positions at which the thumb can rest during a full duelist master grip as the trigger is engaged. Both are secure providing good stability. One may provide some shooters with an added amount of stability if needed, but may be somewhat slower. Notice in photo 4.0G how the thumb is returned to the part of the frame directly next to the hammer, as opposed to the lower position back on the revolver's grip. This can aid in reducing some of the slight muzzle movement or wavering experienced when shooting with one hand. The reader may remember it may also be used at such times when more precision is needed due to target size and distance.

The stance of the duelist is similar to that of the two-handed stance in terms of posture and flexibility, but does require some adjustment and understanding of what may be best for each shooter. Note that photo 4.0H depicts a shooter who has taken a classic stance with a forward (almost aggressive) attitude of the upper body to absorb recoil and turn easily through the target radius presented.

Photo 4.0H - *End Of Trail 2000 Junior Champion Luke Bradbrook, a.k.a. "Captain Moonlight," SASS® #22905, from Australia shows us his excellent duelist stance.*

Another important factor shown is the position of the off-hand. It has anchored itself (in this case) on the weak side, near or partially on the holster. An anchor point of some kind on this weak side provides yet additional stability to the duelist shooter. While not all duelists employ this technique, a loose hanging arm and hand during engagement with no fixed anchor point can add unwanted movement that works against the shooter.

Finally, the duelist is faced with one more important factor to consider. This is adopting the most comfortable and advantageous positioning of the feet. Like the two-handed

Photo 4.0l - *Wolfbait shows one way to correctly set up for the right-handed duelist engaging with two revolvers and a rifle. (Note his off-hand anchor point).*

shooter, consider what tasks lie ahead. Drawing, shooting and re-holstering both revolvers within the safety plane without moving is one consideration. Drawing, shooting and re-holstering one revolver with lateral movement to one side or another is also a consideration. Engaging with one or both revolvers from the same position and then adding one or even two of the long guns with as little movement as possible is yet another.

Just as you would look for in most any other problem like this, look at direction of travel, range of movement required to comfortably address the targets along their radius, and consideration of the safety plane at all times. Also, check the distances for the most effective means of pick-up and re-staging a rifle, shotgun or both (as it applies).

Some matches may allow the duelist to hold onto one of the long guns while engaging. This may be of value when the shooter can eliminate the act of securing a long gun before engaging with a handgun.

Competing With Black Powder

Another shooting class that presents an interesting challenge for shooters is the Black Powder Cartridge Class. This class requires that the powder (or propellant) used for all rounds be black powder or an acceptable substitute thereof. The revolver address used in this class is the two-handed style.

The obvious and most significant factor about this class is the smoke. Vast amounts of smoke and haze are created during stage engagement. Many of Mother Nature's conditions, such as wind direction, wind velocity, damp or

Photo 4.1A - *National Champion Ross Seymour, a.k.a. "Rowdy Yates," SASS® #141, is reminded here that the smoke and haze of black powder often requires patience, and even a little extra imagination on the shooter's part.*

wet weather, sunlight and even time of day play an important role in what these shooters face on any given day. Additionally, the stage designs themselves, such as required target orders, required sweep directions of targets and the prop presentations are other factors to take note of.

Regardless of what other attributes some may say are needed to be a successful or consistent black powder shooter, experienced hands agree that *patience* is definitely a virtue. That's because you can't *hit* what you can't *see.* This last sentiment is probably 90 percent correct, with only a 10 percent chance left to the shooter who employs divine visualization on occasion to hit a target that's known only to be in the general vicinity. It is more accurately described (in this case) as a good guess and it requires a fair amount of luck to hit a blind target. The patience a good black powder shooter exhibits is diffi-

cult at best, it is hard enough to slow down and hit those targets when you *can* see them, and in the heat of a cowboy *action* shooting scenario, to slow down is to die (figuratively speaking, of course).

There are at least two ways that will perhaps assist the shooter in gaining some measure of patience while shooting in this (and any other) class. The shooter who becomes fed up with too many misses, and who knows (but is not implementing) that slowing down is the only way to improve, can consider these two tricks.

During practice or at a practice match, insist that during each stage run any miss will cause you to stop dead in your tracks. At that point (in front of everyone there) count out loud, "one thousand one, one thousand two, one thousand three, one thousand four, one thousand five." This of course, is the equivalent of the five-second penalty awarded for that miss, and you will *still* get the five second penalty from the person scoring. It *will* impress upon you and demonstrate just how much time you really wasted in being too hasty. Most often only one second or less is needed to re-acquire and hit that target. If employed, this method will either temper the shooter with a little more patience, or (if still unsuccessful) will probably send them directly back to the smokeless classes. This training method can assist any shooter in many areas of speed and control, no matter which class or category is competed in. Except for the laughs one may get after the first time others see it used, it becomes real old real fast to miss and stop to count out loud. By the way, this is not for the shooter whose skill levels are producing more than one or two misses per stage; other problems need to be addressed there.

Another method (although not nearly as dramatic) that may help is to refrain from cocking the revolver or levering the rifle after each shot *until* the next target is clearly in the shooter's sights. This (in my opinion) is not nearly as effective as the "counting in public" method, but may work for some.

Getting past this basic patience principle, the shooter will now begin to define just *how much* patience to use. He will also know when, why and how to use it. This is where most of the other current conditions, both natural and man-made, come into play. For the black powder shooter, it becomes necessary to understand what the particular condition will likely produce, anticipate this and act accordingly. Here are several examples of what one might encounter at an average match.

- **Stage directions that compel the shooter to engage revolver, rifle or shotgun targets (or all three) from a left-to-right direction or a right-to-left direction. Stage directions in which target sweep directions vary, target orders that go back and forth, double- or triple-tap, or otherwise dictate how the shooter will engage.**

- **A slight to moderate breeze blowing in the same direction as the target order sweep may well offer obscured target sight to one degree or another. Observation on the part of the shooter as others engage may assist readiness. If the target distance and size is large and close, this may allow the shooter to engage at a faster pace (within personal skill levels), and (if conditions allow) actually stay ahead of the smoke caused by the prior discharge. If the shooter knows the smoke will impair subsequent shots during the transition(s), preparing to engage at the correct pace will enhance the chances of success.**

- **A moderate to stiff wind blowing along the line of the target order sweep may (depending on the exact speed of both wind and skill of the shooter) allow engagement to occur with little or no lingering haze or smoke. Prepare to correctly engage , for target size and distance only.**

- **A slight breeze blowing from the shooter's zero degree heading (directly into the shooter's face) may cause the smoke to go straight out and then directly back at the shooter, or even linger in front of the shooter. Prepare to engage more slowly, observe prior runs.**

- **A moderate to stiff breeze blowing in the same direction as above (at the shooter) may cause the smoke to go instantly from the muzzle towards the shooter. If the wind is strong, there may be only a brief sensation of envelopment causing minimal impairment. Prepare to engage for target size and distance only.**

- **Slight to stiff wind velocities blowing directly downrange (from behind the shooter) will require similar decisions about which course of action to take.**

- **No wind or little wind in a protected shooting area is one of the toughest conditions presented. The addition** of damp weather or even rain can add to a black powder shooter's nightmare. Prepare for the worst. Large targets may allow some visualization. Full extension and lock out are crucial for blind shots when the risk is taken. Reinforce the decision to allow smoke dissipation and subsequent target acquisition to occur. Remember how long each five-second miss feels, and how much dissipation occurs in half that time. Remember also that the other black powder shooters must face this dilemma as well.

There are many other wind and climate conditions besides the ones just described. Besides the recommended approaches the shooter has another tool with varied increments of adjustment to bring to bear in these situations. This tool is movement. The shooter may find that shifting the address vertically and horizontally may outweigh the normal technique of remaining stationary. Bobbing up or down, a half or full step to one side or the other can bring an otherwise almost blind target into view. Remaining disciplined, insofar as the other aspects of address, while doing so may find this beneficial at times. Movement like this does have its price and the problem of having to reacquire the target and sights can be a costly choice.

Props should not be forgotten when considering how to best engage a stage. Moving through a makeshift house or room with walls (even a ceiling) while shooting black powder is high on the list of tough conditions. Acquiring targets through a wall of smoke is one thing, breathing it and taking it in the eyes is not usually pleasant either. Again, observe other runs. Work the stage and prepare for your own engagement with first-hand knowledge. Knowing what to expect in all scenarios goes a long way toward understanding what it will take to be successful.

It is fair to say that while competing within the black powder classes a great deal of effort must be directed toward the maintenance of both firearms and components. In contrast, the smokeless loads enjoy a minimum of effort in comparison.

Many competitors in this class look to SASS® to find a better way to monitor or maintain a more level playing field insofar as reasonable equity in the different amounts of smoke produced by different loads.

Photo 4.1B - *Rowdy Yates changing height to find the target.*

Photo 4.1C - *Forewarned is forearmed when facing obstacles such as facing the sun through a smoke filled adobe.*

Finally, while I am not personally an avid competitor in these classes, I have engaged stages using the blackpowder firearms as provided by friends. There is a lot of fun to be had facing the challenges of blackpowder shooting in the three-gun combat format of cowboy action shooting. It really makes one wonder and respect those whose lives hung in the balance of these battles. One interesting anecdote regarding the use of these guns in the Old West stems from an old saying most of us would recognize as "the night the lights went out." This saying came from gunplay. Vicious and without warning, many shootings occurred in saloons, at night and often with alcohol affecting men's judgments. The saloons were often lit with gas, lanterns or candles. Imagine for a moment the terror experienced in the confines of a dimly lit saloon or gambling hall as the loud concussions of fire-belching revolvers caused the lights

Photo 4.1D - *Imagine for a moment...*

to extinguish themselves, leaving only momentary glimpses as lit by the long flames and sparks belching out of those firearms. Even more terrifying perhaps was that such close-quarters use of these firearms often also produced smoldering clothing on the victims of this gunplay.

The Gunfighter Class

This more recently introduced class in cowboy action shooting requires the shooter use both revolvers, often holding one in each hand while shooting. Some stage instructions will find the shooter bringing to bear only one revolver at a time, but the shooter will fire with both the weak and the strong hand alone. It is a decidedly challenging, one-handed revolver class. So much so that there remains a certain amount of

controversy in today's implementation of much that surrounds it.

The general rules of Gunfighter Class engagements are not fully developed at the time of this writing, so I will not be too specific in that regard.

I will, however, point out the fact that the attributes a shooter must display to engage safely (let alone effectively) with both revolvers out, alternating shots between each one, drawing and holstering safely are formidable. It requires great skill in becoming an adequate shooter here, and a greater skill to master the art.

Many local clubs require shooters to demonstrate they can safely compete in this manner. Some of these clubs provide a certification of sorts to those who qualify. While more and more major match officials are offering this class for shooters, there are many officials and shooters who are not ready. Properly designed stages, Range Officer enforcement, and other elements require some clear insight and in-depth knowledge of this class in order to offer shooters the "real deal." I have engaged stages, competed in top gun shoot-offs and experimented in this style of shooting on many an occasion, and would agree with those who believe that there needs to be a structured program of real merit in the qualifications to compete, and even a club's offer of a Gunfighter Class.

For those of you who do shoot this way, or plan on trying your hand at it, here are some things to think about.

Practice is an absolute necessity. Drawing and holstering each revolver at the same time and obtaining a good master grip takes work. Cocking the revolvers either one at a time or simultaneously takes strength and dexterity. So, even if your strong hand is able to do the job without a problem, make sure you bring the weak hand up to an acceptable level as well.

Photo 4.2A - *Don Ormond, a.k.a. "Tex," SASS® #4, knows this class is not for the weak or faint of heart, as it takes a lot of work and skill to become good at (let alone master of) the gunfighter style of shooting.*

Photo 4.2B - *Tex keeps both muzzles within the correct distance behind one or the other during discharge and cocking tasks.*

The Gunfighter needs to maintain good arm extension and remain locked out as much as possible. One requirement sure to become a permanent rule will be that no muzzle of either revolver will be allowed to be brought back to a position that is to the rear of the other revolver's cylinder during use. It has been common to see a cocked revolver well behind the other revolver (and the hand holding it) when engaging. This presents a serious safety hazard.

While some Gunfighters are reputed to be able to discharge a round out of each gun at the same time on one target

Photo 4.2C - *Dirk Rash, a.k.a. "Capt. John Sutter," SASS® #3822, demonstrates the potential for danger using two revolvers at once.*

Photo 4.2D - *A top Gunfighter, H.G. Mavlar, a.k.a. "H.G. Wells," SASS® #3511, cleans up both sides of a dusty street in a scenario from today's Old West shooting competition.*

(as in the case of double tapping), I know of none who can do this with a high degree of consistency in both hits and speed. Regardless of what the rules may sometime require or allow, most Gunfighters will fire one revolver and then the other, aligning each revolver's sights on the target in kind.

The act of cocking each revolver is done either separately or both at the same time. It is best to cock each one separately when first learning; time will tell whether cocking both at the same time will be an advantage for the individual.

Basically, all the techniques a good Duelist shooter exhibits are the same for the Gunfighter. The only real differences are that the Gunfighter uses both hands, with both guns out while engaging, and must use two strong-side holsters. These are differences not to be taken lightly!

Chapter 5

HANDGUN, SHOTGUN & RIFLE LEATHER

The personal choices concerning which holsters and belts today's cowboy shooters may use are many. There are scores of leather makers offering dozens of different holsters, belts and other related items. The shooter will usually decide on which to purchase based upon looks, price and even availability. Performance is another area to understand before laying out those hard-earned bucks.

As it should be, the majority of shooters in this sport want holsters that really look great, and are (within reason) historically accurate. As long as you are happy, and the look of your rig lends itself to an Old West theme, it works.

Choosing a period holster that has a great look does not mean a sacrifice must be made in the effectiveness of

Photo 5.0A - *The legendary China Camp and Top Modern shooter Dave Patton, a.k.a. "Dasterdly Dave," SASS® #2324, stand tall with two different styles of strong-side holsters.*

Photo 5.0B - *Robert and Terry Hall, a.k.a. "Hoss," SASS® #15689, and "Claremore Calli," SASS® #18709, enjoy performance, style, and a personal touch with their matching rigs.*

the holster during stage engagement. Not only were many of the authentic holsters made (or modified) to better accommodate an easy and quick removal of a revolver when it was needed, they were also worn in many different positions to provide similar advantages.

There is no real advantage in wearing a cross-draw holster that has a high degree of cant (or slant) often seen around a match. Not only are these holsters no more effective than one that is not canted, there is often an increased risk that the revolver may fall out during stage engagement. There is also an

increased chance that the safety plane may be violated during the initial draw or the return of the revolver to leather. Understand that there are many perfectly acceptable cross-draw holsters that have a less pronounced amount of cant or angle. The ones that may have too much cant are so angled that they will often approach a position that is almost parallel to the ground.

Many shooters (including myself) have found that using a straight, strong-side style of holster that is worn as a cross-draw is both safe and effective in cowboy action shooting.

It will come to the attention of anyone who is looking at the various styles of holsters that some will appear to be quite low cut around the

Photo 5.0C - *Someday many good-looking rigs may need new or modified cross-draw holsters made for them if a limit for the cant or angle is imposed.*

West. A holster that offers enough exposure of the revolver for an effective draw can be found in many configurations.

The holster should be made and shaped in such a manner that it is made for the type or style of revolver to be used. It should be mentioned that a longer holster (one designed for revolvers of longer barrel length) is often fine for revolvers with shorter barrels. This not withstanding, it is the way in which the leather holster molds itself around the revolver's shape that is key. Retention during movement must be reliable, but not so much so that the draw cannot be reasonably smooth or that the revolver is so tight in the holster it can cause the holster itself to move radically upwards during the draw, hindering the shooter's efforts.

One commonly seen method used for additional retention is an added piece of leather tied to the holster and looped at one end. This loop will fit tightly over the handgun's depressed hammer and assist in keeping the revolver securely in the holster. Referred to as a "thumb break," the leather loop is adjustable. At such time the shooter wants to draw the handgun, this "thumb break" must be removed. This is not an optimum condition, but if using the thumb break means

top of the holster. This design is done to increase or enhance a shooter's ability to make clean contact with the revolver during the initial draw.

There are as many different opinions as to what works best and why as there are holsters. For what it's worth, I like holsters that offer both performance and the look of the Old

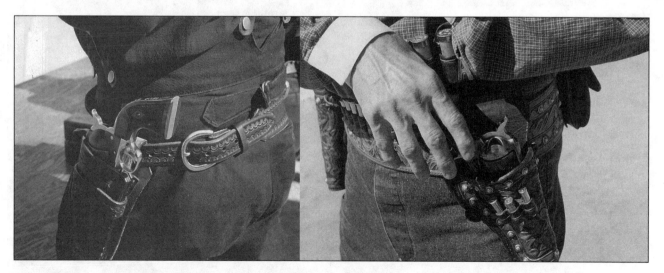

Photo 5.0D - *Not without style, these holsters reflect those cut to expose a large portion of revolver.*

Photo 5.0E - *Shannon Dalton, a.k.a. "Squatzta Shoot," SASS® #15070, shows off her great looking rig that is also built to perform.*

Photo 5.0F - *Thomas Jacobs, a.k.a. "Solicitor General," SASS® #9800, wearing his Mexican "double loop" holster.*

keeping control of that revolver, do it. An ill-fitting holster, one that has lost most of its original fit due to age, or a cross-draw holster thats steep angle of cant threatens the loss (falling) of a revolver, might well be a prime candidate for a thumb break. Retention during any stage run is important, let alone those done with all-out effort. I have lost revolvers at two major matches in recent years, and while the consequences of these errors are harsh (a stage or a match disqualification), they are also fair. In all fairness, I should point out that both incidents were because of a lapse in my judgment, and not a holster failure.

Photo 5.0G - *Cindy Ebbert, a.k.a. "Bodie Rose," SASS® #18621, demonstrates a condition that can cause more than just one problem.*

The shooter shown in photo 5.0G is experiencing some difficulty while attempting a clean draw. Not only can this distract the shooter; it can result in the holster becoming re-positioned and adversely affecting the way the revolver is re-holstered as well. Several areas can be checked to reduce the chances that this will occur.

A new holster, made correctly, will seem a little tight until it is somewhat broken in, so don't jump the gun on this one. Working the gun in the leather, making some practice draws (safely, with an un-loaded revolver) will often solve this problem. If the shooter has shoved the revolver down into the holster too forcefully, the retention may well increase. This in itself is not all bad, and depending on stage movement prior to the revolver's use, is advisable at times. If the holster retention is always considered rock solid, so much so that the revolver never comes out without a real tug that upsets the holster, it may be too tightly formed. If this condition does not change with a little wear, contact the holster maker. If the holster's loop is not correctly fitted for the gun belt worn by the shooter, even the correct amount of resistance or retention will cause the holster to move up and down more than it should.

Look to wear a belt that is wide enough to permit the holsters to be adjusted horizontally but that has enough width to also aid in keeping the holsters stationary when drawing and/or moving. Simply wearing the gun belt itself tightly around the shooter's waist will help this. If the slack is still more than desired, another option is to secure and modify the holster on your own. Get the holster in place on the belt where it will serve best and punch a small hole through the holster's loops just below where the bottom of the belt rests within the loop. Using one or more positions to secure the holster in this fashion, just run a small piece of leather through the cant angle on a cross-draw holster. It is not recommended to make this alteration so tight that the holster cannot shift horizontally along the belt when needed.

Returning a revolver to leather is an important part of making effective transitions. The reader can easily see which holster of those shown on the next page is good and ready to receive a returning revolver. Holsters that lose their shape as they age or are crushed during storage into a semi-closed position may not work the way you want. Learning to care properly for your rig may keep you out of some pretty ugly situations.

Leather is a natural product. Its properties are subject to time and the conditions to which it is exposed. What I am going to tell you here is what I have done occasionally to my holsters and why. I am not advising anyone to do this… but I think it is worth knowing about.

What I'm speaking about is the soaking of holsters in water to tighten (however briefly) a holster's fit and to reform the original, overall shape to that of the revolver. It has been my experience that after a while the leather will begin to break down and lose some of the original shape. The revolver can feel a little loose in the holster and the mouth of the holster may tend to close at different points. Even though the procedure I will describe may ultimately lead to the further breakdown of the leather (as I understand it), it has worked for me well enough to continue using this method on occasion.

When such problems as above are perceived, I fill the sink with warm water, put the holsters in the water and let them soak for about 15 to 20 minutes. I then take the holsters out of the water, lightly towel off the excess water and take them outside. I then make sure the holster's opening (mouth) is at the position I want it to dry to. At that point it is simply a matter of letting the sun dry the holster. If it is winter or there is no sun, I have let the drying occur indoors. The age of the leather seems to be a factor in how long each re-shaping will last.

Photo 5.0H - *Matching the belt width with the holster's loop will help improve stability.*

these holes, make a small knot, and (done right) this will reduce the holster's ability to move up and down. The same principle can be used to reduce or limit

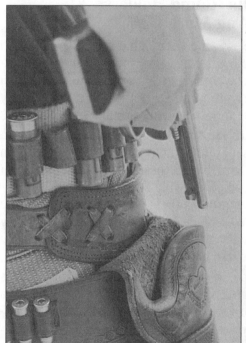

Photo 5.0I, J & K - *The Good, the Bad and the Ugly of a holster's mouth.*

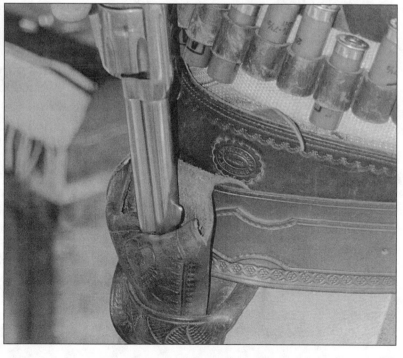

Do not even think about using a microwave or other such oven to dry a holster. If you do, you're on your own. Some of the holsters I have owned for long periods have needed to dry with a gun inside them in order for the leather to reform correctly. What I've done with these is taken a non-gun prop, wrapped it up in plastic and stuck it in the holster. While the old leather does not keep this new shape for a long time, it does bring temporary relief and life to an otherwise worthless piece of equipment. When doing this to my current main match holsters, I do not find it necessary to let them dry with a revolver (or equivalent) in them.

Again, I am not saying this method is not without its faults or that the reader should immediately soak the leather. All I am saying is that it has worked for me when I needed to regain some of the original shape and tighter fit in some leather gear. By the way, when the loops in my shotgun belt seem to be getting a little loose, and the rounds will not stay at the height I want them to, guess what I do to fix that little problem?

Shotgun Round Holders, Belts And More...

One of the best (and easiest) ways to improve one's stage times when using the shotgun in cowboy action shooting is to start with a shotgun ammunition holder that will really assist the shooter and not one that simply works.

There are few top shooters seen without a totally separate belt worn to carry their shotgun rounds into battle these days. That does not mean a shooter with a shotgun round holder that goes around their revolver belt cannot be effective or place high at any match, it simply shows what the most successful shooters have found works best.

Made in canvas configurations as well as leather, the shotgun belt holds its rounds by a series of loops or pouches. It is only the imagination of a cowboy shooter (and the SASS® Handbook) that limits what may be used. Like any gunfighter worth his salt, I would sit and ponder over what might be a better (or quicker) way to get those rounds off my person and into my shotgun. Of all the different configurations I've tried, in the end it was the single-loop system on a separate belt that provided me with the most reliable and effective service.

Some shooters prefer a single-loop system that is, in fact, a single pouch system. In other words, each of the round loops is closed at the bottom, rather than open. Many of the open-loop systems will have some kind of continuous leather piece that acts as a stop and runs along the full length of the belt. Not unlike the

Photo 5.1A - *Top shooter Hunter Anderson, a.k.a. "Lefty Longridge," SASS® finds it "easy pickings" to get out two shotgun rounds while moving rapidly to the next firing position.*

Photo 5.1B - *From left to right, Rick Miguel, a.k.a. "Washoe Kid," SASS® #8270, Mike Wallace, a.k.a. "Mustang Mike," SASS® #4105, Andy Cauble, a.k.a. "Nasty Nick," SASS® #1320, and Ron Stein, a.k.a. "Tupelo Flash," SASS® #27453 are ready to rock and roll.*

pouch system, this is to insure that the rounds will go only so far down in the loop, and not present an extraction problem.

These shotgun belts are defined in the SASS® Rulebook and are limited in some respects. Construction may not include steel or plastic liners. The belts must conform to the natural contour of the shooter's body (i.e., may not be made to tilt an unreasonable distance away from the body). SASS® has also seen fit to require the belt be worn at or below the belly button as some have complained that wearing it any higher is unfair. Personally, I do not understand this concept, but SASS® is subject to many such complaints and does its best to act fairly. My personal beliefs are more akin to the notion that if a gun-toting hombre in the Old West could have thought of an idea, and either built it in the bunkhouse or hired someone to

build it for him, then it should be legal. It should also be noted that no round holders on the wrist or the shotgun itself are acceptable under the SASS® Rules of Engagement at this time.

Getting more to the heart of the matter, it is this piece of equipment's purpose to provide a shooter a reliable means of rapid round retrieval. One additional advantage this belt offers is room to include several loops for revolver or rifle round reloading off the body. Another advantage is that rounds can be placed with space between them to promote a cleaner pick-up by not touching others right next to them.

There is also the added ability to hold 20 or more shotgun rounds. This can come in handy at times. The average

Photo 5.1C - *Choctaw knows that a separate shotgun belt offers some distinct benefits.*

some that will carry 10 rounds, but a more common number is eight. This (as mentioned) may lead to a slight problem… like being out of ammunition too soon. Another reason is the addition of a piece of equipment along the primary belt that is already holding two revolvers. Slight adjustments from side to side may become harder to accomplish and may even be ignored thanks to the presence of the round holder. This type of round holder may well impede a shooter's ability to make a clean draw or return to leather with either revolver. The revolver butts may also present yet another obstacle in cleanly picking the shotgun rounds off the round holder. Finally, there is a height

main stage will usually not require more than eight rounds from the shotgun, but shooters should take note that SASS® Rules clearly and rightly state that dropped rounds hitting the ground are considered "dead" and may not be picked up. In view of that, shooters should always carry more rounds than are called for in the stage instructions. This is easily done with a separate shotgun belt.

Looking at the shotgun round holders that are placed over the shooter's normal gun belt, there are some things to consider before opting to use one. The first thing is the limited amount of rounds that can be carried. I've seen

Photo 5.1D - *Bob Sheppard, a.k.a. "Pinkerton," SASS® #2351, wearing a snap-on round holder over the main gun belt.*

Photo 5.2A - *Many find that wrapping the lever with leather makes it more comfortable and a better fit.*

The required racking of a rifle's lever to bring a new round into the chamber can be an uncomfortable, even painful task. Many shooters will remedy this situation somewhat by wrapping leather around the lower portion of the lever. The size of the fingers will most often determine the thickness or amount of leather used. It may be seen as a more effective way in which the three fingers engage the lever as well, eliminating what some shooters may consider slop or too much space in the lever.

consideration worth mentioning. The hand will have to go farther away from the shotgun to retrieve the rounds. Many shooters will lose time because they cannot see those rounds, and must always make a blind move to remove one or more.

I must point out that some shooters using the snap-on round holders described will often do very well. I used one with relative success for at least three seasons before switching. Even if you now fall into this category of shooter, consider the time and effectiveness you may find with an even better system.

There is a possible solution to consider without investing in a new shotgun round belt if a shooter already has the snap-on style. Dig around among all that unused leather or go out and find a belt that will fit the waist (across that belly) and simply snap the round holder on that belt. The width of the belt should be such a size that the round holder will be held securely. Adding another snap-on round holder will double the round capacity, and is economic.

The last bit of leather one may see and consider using with a shotgun is a kind of leather boot placed over the rear (or butt) of the stock. Insignificant in large part, it can disguise an unsightly (but legal) recoil pad, and may serve to prevent the butt from slipping. One bit of advice to those who may try this: make sure the leather fits, is not loose, and will not hinder correct placement of the butt stock in the shoulder.

Photo 5.2B - *Ed Lucas, a.k.a. "Rusty Gun," SASS®, #5005, shown with a canvas shotgun belt.*

Chapter 6

TRANSITIONS FOR SUCCESS

Fast trigger time is not the most important factor when it comes to good overall times during engagements. There is far more time lost or gained on correct and thoughtful transitions during a stage run than that of simply fast trigger time. In fact, even the transition to each new target (target acquisition) must first be accomplished correctly before the shooter should engage the trigger. That is only the tip of the iceberg.

Photo 6.0 - *Top shooter Dan Beale, a.k.a. "Dang it Dan," SASS® #13202, demonstrates how effective transitions between trigger times is the key to faster stage runs.*

Any competitor in cowboy action shooting (excluding the top 10-percent) can dramatically improve his or her stage times by applying more effective methods of moving without increasing the normal speed at which they currently engage. Comparing any two shooters of equal delivery speed and accuracy, the one that will invariably produce superior stage runs will have executed the more efficient maneuvers in non-shooting transitions.

Simply put, the goal is the overall reduction of all movement that is not absolutely required to complete the engagement or stage scenario. Less simple (but hardly unattainable) is the thought process, the practice, and practical application of these methods. Seen often as the "tricks of the trade" by others, these moves are not secret, do not require above average or special skill and are not really difficult to learn. The reader should understand that effective transitions in cowboy action shooting stems more from common sense than any other trait or quality.

From Stop To Go

There can be no start without a position from which to begin. Before we get to the "go" of this lesson, let's touch upon how we may begin. There are several starting positions a shooter can expect to begin the actual stage engagement. Effective transitions from each is crucial in obtaining many things, not the least of which is the confidence of having made a good start at the beginning of the stage.

Stage instructions should provide shooters with a clear understanding of how (and where) their hands, feet or body can be prior to the signal starting the run. In turn, the shooter must know how he can best accomplish the task of applying the most effective movement(s) in order to bring each firearm to bear on the target(s) in the quickest and most effective manner as dictated by the position. As the reader continues to go over this material, some of the information/techniques may well appear more effective for some shooters than others. Keeping this in mind, remember that choosing what method or technique to employ can be dictated by the situation, and is also related to the shooter's ability to recognize his or her own strengths and weaknesses on the firing line. Understanding (or admitting as the case may be) one's limitations will often be the key to success. It's easy to be excellent at what you're good at, but it's much more difficult to be good at what you struggle with.

One basic rule of competition in this sport, insofar as correct transitions, is going from the ready (or start) position to engagement. This transition of "stop-to-go" applies to all tasks performed directly after the signal to start. This, of course, includes both shooting and non-shooting tasks. Once the shooter is fully set, the focus should be on the start signal. This may not seem overly important, but reaction time to the "beep" of a timer can be as little as 1/10th of a second to as much as 1-1/2 seconds.

Since we are talking about improving the time of a shooter's stage run, it must start here. More importantly, this is an easy one to start with, requiring only the shooter's complete attention. For those who remember playing "Red Light, Green Light," the childhood game of drinking milk on the "Engineer Bill" television program, it's an easy comparison of anticipatory reaction to an audible command. For those who do not remember this little game (it helped a child drink his milk) it was

an early drill for focusing on an upcoming start signal. By the way, it was a *lot* of fun to drink milk this way!

The Range Officer's commands will include "Is the shooter ready?" and will then be followed with "Stand by." Acknowledging the ready command, the shooter should be focused on reacting to the signal and nothing else. My personal goal of reaction is to be well into the first transition (no matter what that is)

Photo 6.0A - *Gary Ladd, a.k.a. "Cat Cummins," SASS® #1870, has milk, and is ready to play an old-fashioned game of "Red Light, Green Light."*

before the beep of the timer has fallen silent. The length of this "beep" or buzz of the timer's signal is around one second, so I feel that if I am well into my initial move before the beep is over, I've gotten off to a good start.

Now don't think that overreacting to a starting signal is the point of this lesson, for it is not. A shooter may notn and should not, attempt to jump the timer's signal. Anticipate… yes, but only that the signal is coming. To jump the clock, or move prior to the actual signal… no way man, that is *not* how to play. Just focus on moving at the exact moment the signal goes off. A shooter who demonstrates continual pre-beep movement (creeps before the beep) is most often made to start all over again requiring at least the steps for another final set-up, and is forced to regain mental focus.

Another point to remember about anticipating or reacting to the starting signal is that you do have some control. This is for those times when, for some reason, a less experienced timer operator fails to give you a second or more after a "stand-by" command. If the timer gives a series of commands that are not correct before the beep goes off, you can back off, and ask for another start. Really, sometimes you'll get such a rapid set of commands, it'll blow you away. If you *do* go on a command, *any* command, understand you cannot come back after the run is over and petition for a re-shoot because you didn't like the starting commands. You went for it, Bubba, too late now.

If the timer instrument is set on "instant," an operator can press the start button manually. As indicated, if this is done without any time in between that last command, it may cause the shooter to feel somehow "jumped" or (as it is called in baseball), "quick pitched." Another occasional way this kind of thing will happen is if the timing operator omits part of a normal starting command in the initial countdown. As stated, the normal countdown sequence should include "Does the shooter understand the course of fire?" (affirmative response), "Is the shooter ready?" and, after an affirmative nod or verbal response to the last question, the command should be "Stand by." There should then occur a short but definite delay before the actual beep. This is the time to be focused, set and anticipating a signal to begin. If the timer asks "Is the shooter ready? "(and you nod yes), there should be at least a one- to three-second interval prior to the beep. It is fair to point out that there may not be a "stand by" command given at all times.

If you do not begin to engage, you may tell the timing operator you were not ready, and ask for both another start and correct commands. It is within the rules and perfectly reasonable to do so. To receive a poor start and then to react and begin the engagement can upset the shooter's focus and cause problems that could have been avoided.

A knowledgeable timing operator will rarely make an error of this kind. Even a timing operator who is new will find little instruction is needed (maybe a reminder) to get it right. Many matches will find timers set on the "delay" function in order to provide between one and three seconds of time to pass after the start button is hit. Do not start to over-anticipate the starter set on delay; just go through your normal set-up, focus and anticipation of that beep. We'll go over a little more about the beep later on when we discuss the pressure that some feel is attached to the actual signal and how it may be intimidating.

Revolver Transitions

The shooters in photo 6.1A are shown ready to start a stage run with their revolvers out, and at an approximate muzzle angle of 45 degrees downrange. There are two key elements in correct transition here that are often overlooked.

As photo 6.1B shows us, one shooter is better prepared to move and engage than the other. Let's look closer. The better prepared shooter has the thumb right on the hammer, ready to

Photo 6.1A - *Rowdy Yates and Choctaw demonstrate two positions of starting used with the revolver out at approximately 45 degrees downrange.*

Photo 6.1B - *Brad and Pat Myers, a.k.a. "Hipshot," SASS® #7, and "Blue Eyes," SASS® #92, show the good and the bad of preparing to move into action.*

Photo 6.1C - *Paul Reed, a.k.a. "Captain John B. Armstrong," SASS® #6221, brings his handgun to bear with Jerry Meyer, a.k.a. "Wolfbait," SASS® #5227, looking on.*

bring it to the fully cocked position, and the index finger inside the trigger guard ready to execute the trigger press. The other shooter has neither thumb nor trigger finger in these positions. Why? Is it unsafe? Is it illegal? What are the advantages?

First of all, let's answer the "why". Those two little positions of the thumb and index finger *on* the hammer and *in* the trigger guard are transitions accomplished prior to the timed run. The shooter does not have to move after the beep, and has therefore eliminated some movement. Even more significant is that the possibility of missing the hammer with the thumb, or improper positioning of the index finger on the trigger after the beep has started the run, is now eliminated.

Is it unsafe to practice this method? Is it illegal? No. According to the SASS® Rules of Engagement, neither of these actions is unsafe. The only one that is worthy of addressing here is the index or trigger finger. SASS® requires that the muzzle of a handgun be out and downrange at an approximate angle of 45 degrees before the finger is in the trigger guard. This position fits within that scope of requirements. The shooter has only to concentrate on the beep, raise the arms and revolver to the target, obtain good front sight picture on the target and squeeze that first round off. The shooter will not have had to make contact with the hammer and get the index finger in the trigger guard on the way up. Again, while little time is saved here in terms of seconds, it is the elimination of two possible errors that is of value.

Regardless of what position the handgun starts from (whether it is gun out at a 45-degree angle, staged on a table, in the holster with the hand off or on), the motions made bringing the handgun to bear should be smooth and effectively quick. Effectively quick in that a shooter can raise the handgun up too fast, finding target

Photo 6.1D - *Choctaw is ready to engage, final position is set.*

Photo 6.1E - *Ready to fire, he has raised the handgun only.*

Photo 6.1F - *He has not remained stationary; notice the height change compared to photo 6.1D.*

acquisition more difficult (and slower) than if the motion had simply been smooth, quick, but more controlled. Understanding the importance (and benefits) of what should be happening as the revolver comes out and up toward the target(s) will assist the shooter as he becomes more competent in this area. Shooters will find that attempts at raising the handgun too quickly will result in going above or over the desired point of aim. At best the shooter must adjust and re-position the revolver's sight to acquire the target. At worst the shooter will find the first round missing well high, over the target. Don't fool yourself with the notion that bringing a revolver up to bear in a quick, controlled reaction is any more than a few hundredths of a second slower compared to one raised up with simply the greatest speed possible.

To effectively bring the handgun to bear can be understood and implemented by following the prescribed flow of actions determined by what is safe and makes sense. As the revolver is brought out, and reaches the minimum muzzle angle of 45 degrees, the shooter should be automatically cocking the hammer and have the index (or trigger finger) in a ready position. Too many shooters lose time, focus and, therefore, effectiveness by *not* making this happen correctly. Waiting until the revolver is up and pointed at the first target to then cock the hammer and/or move the trigger finger inside the guard is additional motion that adds time to the run. Initiating one or both of these actions at the wrong time also promotes distraction. Once the revolver is up, it should be fully ready to fire and the shooter should be totally focused on seeing that front sight on the target.

If this method sounds too simple or insignificant to you, try it both ways with a timer. At the range have someone time that first shot by bringing the revolver up and cocking it after reaching the target. When you have done this, go ahead and fire the shot.

See what that time is, and recall the slight distraction of being on the target while cocking the gun. Then do the same thing, only this time cock and ready the revolver for firing on the way *up*. Experience how natural this is; how you can better focus on the target and get the first shot off far more quickly.

As the shooter sets up to engage, several factors determine what body position will promote the best results. One thing that should not change (unless stage props compel change) is the height of the shooter once set. Many shooters can be seen at the start of a stage with body set, ready to draw or engage with the gun out, their legs slightly bent, seemingly in an optimum position. Nodding an affirmative to the Range Officer's "Is the shooter ready?" command, the shooter is frozen and focused, as he should be. Reacting to the timer's beep or signal to start, the shooter begins the move to bring the revolver out and up to bear on the target. Close observation will reveal a correct, effective move by some, and an incorrect, less effective way by others.

The most effective action is shown in photos 6.1D and E. Notice the height of the shooter has *not* changed during the initial move. Movement is restricted to the parts of the body that *must* be used to bring the gun up, namely the hands, arms and shoulders. The shooter's head remains in the same position as much as possible, focused and ready to combine target with front sight as smoothly as possible.

The least effective action (one that is totally without benefit) is shown in photo 6.1F. Here, the shooter has made the move with the revolver and is raising (therefore changing) the position of the body. Why would a shooter do this unless compelled to do so? The revolver is moving up to a stationary position from which to engage. The shooter's head (and eyes) must be stationary as they direct where the revolver (and subsequent bullet) is going. If the shooter raises his body up, the head goes with it. The

Photo 6.1G - *Louise Hill, a.k.a. "TNT Tilly," SASS® #807, readies for a "snatch & grab" transition.*

stationary platform from which to engage is now moving for *no* reason and takes more time to re-position to a fixed spot.

This action is done almost automatically by some shooters; they may not even know it occurs. Check yourself on this one, it is an important part of how smooth you transition into your firing positions.

It is not uncommon for the shooter to find a stage that requires the pre-positioning of one or both handguns in various positions in or around props. Photo 6.1G shows the revolver out, on top of a table. This transition, from hands flat on the table to grabbing the revolver and finally bringing it to bear on the target, is critical. The execution must be managed in a smooth motion, and one that results with both hands having found their normal, correct positions. That means the strong hand has found its master grip correctly, and the weak hand has found its optimum support (stability) position as well.

Done correctly, the shooter will have also accomplished the cocking of the hammer and will have his or her index or trigger finger ready to engage prior to the revolver's final sight alignment position. But you knew that already, right?

Too hasty a pick-up here will often result in a myriad of problems that can snowball. A poor master grip that has the index finger too far into the trigger guard or that finds itself holding the revolver in an unfamiliar, even uncomfortable position, is one of the first problems. The weak or support hand that has fallen victim to too hasty a grab may wind up holding the revolver in a similarly unfamiliar manner. This may result in the shooter's thumb being in such a position as to cause a miscue in cocking.

TRANSITIONS FOR SUCCESS   101

Photo 6.1H - *Wolfbait at the "hands flat" starting position, ready to make a smooth sweep at the beep.*

revolver's muzzle and result in missed targets. The shooter's rhythm will be disturbed by all of this, and the one missed target may well turn into more. The entire stage run, including the use of two or three more firearms during that run, can be adversely affected by one seemingly small error like this.

Somewhat misleading in name, this "snatch and grab" technique is really more of a "smooth, sweep and up" operation. The shooter should be willing to practice this method to the extent needed to produce the correct grip by both hands, a "ready to engage" position for both the hammer and the index or trigger finger, and, finally, the confidence to execute the move smoothly, with no thought of error.

The shooter will instantly feel these problems, but will very often *not* stop to re-adjust prior to getting off the first round, let alone subsequent rounds. As the reader has been informed, these particular mistakes in positioning will often cause unwanted motion to transfer the

Again, the shooter should be set so that no movement other than the hands, arms and shoulders will occur. Focus on the revolver, not downrange. The head will have to tilt upwards

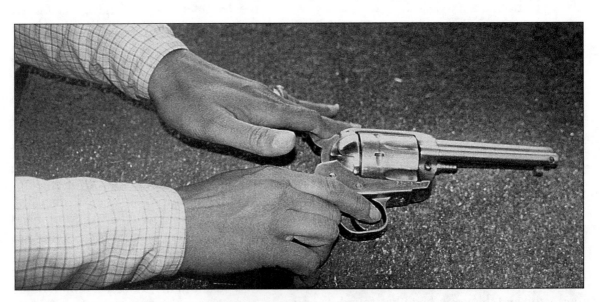

Photo 6.1I - *The strong hand picks and lifts, while the weak hand tilts the revolver into shooting position.*

as the revolver comes up, but should *not* change in initial height. The shooter will have the stage run committed to memory of course, and will be completely focused on making the move required at the exact moment of the starting signal or beep. A smooth motion that picks or sweeps the revolver up easily, with deliberate, firm points of attachment made by the hands is what you want to achieve. Make sure you can execute this method well before you try to make the pick-up without eye-balling the revolver.

The crucial point is getting the revolver off the flat surface and obtaining the desired grip on the gun at the same time. Photo 6.1I shows the strong hand moving to begin a pick and lift motion while the weak hand is actually tilting the revolver upwards giving the strong hand support in its effort. At speed, one might perceive the weak hand as "flipping" the revolver into the strong hand. As the strong hand settles into the master grip, the weak hand will find its final support hold on the revolver as it comes off the table. This is the most common method used by the top shooters in the sport today, although it is not the only one in use.

While I have not found this method best (at least for me), it is worth describing and may work for some shooters. The weak hand will do the lifting of the revolver off the table while the strong hand meets the revolver and obtains the desired gripping position. Just as with both methods, the hands are meeting in the middle and producing an upward sweeping motion.

If the reader will look closely at photo 6.1G, the shooter has the arms extended while waiting to begin. This is one of two ways the arms may work well. With the arms fully (or close to) extended, the shooter will raise the arms straight up to the firing position.

Looking at photo 6.1H, the shooter has the arms closer in to the body, extending only partially outwards. This will allow the shooter to raise and *push* outward, towards the target if they so desire. Many shooters have been

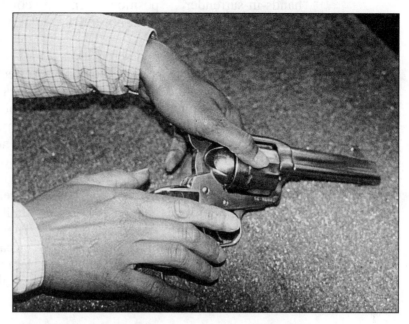

Photo 6.1J - *Another method of getting the revolver off the table uses the weak hand to pick up and lift at contact.*

trained to engage in this manner, acquiring the target and front sight as the revolver travels forward.

You must practice these moves to become competent, and, moreover, confident in the application of them. It is easily done at home; insuring the handgun is safe and un-loaded, start out slowly, even at slow motion speed to get the right points of contact. Look to obtain a smooth pick-up, resulting in the revolver cocked at the top and on target. Develop the memory that lurks in the mind controlling your muscles. Don't worry about how fast you do this. Concentrate more on correct technique in the beginning. To be quick you must first be smooth. The smoother your actions are, the quicker they get.

The three shooters in photo 6.1K are demonstrating three of the four most common starting positions from which the handgun will be drawn from leather. They are (from left to right): the "hand-on-gun" position, the "Gabby Hayes" or "hands-in-surrender" position, and, finally, the "hand-close, but-not-touching" position.

Most difficult is the middle position. Holding both hands up (usually the minimum height is at the shoulders) finds the shooter with some distance to move downwards before contact can be made with the handgun, and a smooth draw can be started.

The position shown on the right (with the hand close to the revolver but *not* touching it), reveals that the shooter has far less distance to travel, although still must make the initial contact after the starting signal. The position shown on the left of photo 6.1K is the most

conducive to achieving the quickest, error-free draw. Let's look at each of these positions a little more closely.

As with each maneuver, an accurate and effective outcome will require some practice on the shooter's part. A later chapter will explain establishing muscle memory by repetition and how these moves can become part of the array of subconscious tools or automatic actions a shooter may develop.

Both of the shooters in photo 6.1L are excellent gunhands, and for this example we shall say they are equally skilled and trained. There appears to be a big difference, however, in each of their initial approach to this problem. All things staying the same, it is fair to say that clean draws will be forthcoming, and

Photo 6.1K - *Shown from left to right: Cal Elrich, a.k.a. "Quick Cal," SASS® #2707, Gene Pearcey, a.k.a. "Evil Roy," SASS®#2883, and Gil Guerra Jr., a.k.a. "Cisco," SASS® #7590, demonstrate the most common starting positions.*

Photo 6.1L - *"Which one is better for me to focus on, the target or the revolver?"* *The 1999 End Of Trail Champion Paul Miller, a.k.a. "San Juan," SASS® #1776, and Southeast Regional Champion Spencer Davis, a.k.a. "Marshal Harlan Wolf," SASS® #5019, show that different approaches can be used to achieve the same outcome.*

will be within hundredths of a second of one another. Why? Because one has drilled one way, finding the same amount of comfort and success as the other has done in another way. The shooter who is focused downrange (presumably at the first target to be engaged), has found that he is comfortable (and effective) without focusing on his revolver as the hand drops to make the contact. It has become part of his array of developed tools and (unless there is a change in his success rate) he will most likely stay with this method. The other shooter (equally skilled in this example) has found that "eyeballing" the revolver as the hand drops to make contact works best for him. Many fine shooters can perform either way, but most will favor one or the other.

For the shooter looking directly downrange, his "edge" or confidence factor is having a direct line of sight on the target as the revolver comes up. For him, not having to acquire the target during the motions of down, grab, raise, cock and fire is the perceived advantage or his "edge."

The other shooter finds the same perceived advantages with the opposite action. His "mind's eye" has the target direction and position fixed. His focus before the signal to start is on that revolver. He, too, will make an accurate grab with his strong hand (producing his master grip), be cocking the gun and acquiring both target and front sight at the right moment.

The differences and lesson to understand here is that the confidence of a shooter does not always reside in one particular technique or another to insure equal success. There are, of course, some basic techniques that the better shooters adhere to, but there are many choices one can make. Whatever works well for you

Photo 6.1L1 - *End Of Trail International Class World Title holder, Bob Dunkley, a.k.a. "Bad Ass Bob," SASS® #3814, is set for a blind draw with his hands up.*

is what counts. In time I'm sure you will develop and use whatever techniques you are confident will promote the chances of making successful draws.

Just as it is simply common sense to know we must walk before we can run, *all* shooters should first perform the draw with visual aid as they first begin to practice and become familiar with the move. I'm not saying you can't learn unless you do this, but you will find that fewer mistakes will be made if you have mastered the draw while first looking at the revolver.

There is significant risk to the blind draw here, as well as the significant risk attached to this starting position whether you are looking or not. Too hasty a move to the handgun may well produce a poor grip. At the very least it will compel the shooter to re-adjust, causing time loss. At worst it can lead to missing one target or more. At five seconds a pop (some matches may be 10!) for each missed target, it pays to be deliberate, accurate and move at the speed at which *you* can execute these moves correctly.

The shooter on the right of photo 6.1K has his hand poised, very nearly on but *not* touching the handgun. This is correct. Unless the instructions are specifically written or changed otherwise, get the hand down and really close to the revolver. Shooters who start with the hand farther away from the handgun than is allowable are placing an increased risk factor on themselves for no reason. With playful humor in mind, I would warn the reader of those that do not agree or preach otherwise, they probably believe real cowboys or gunfighters waited for their adversary to draw first and never cared if the sun were at their backs as they faced their opponents. Yeah… right! To these gunfighters I would only smile, and say "Go ahead pards, play it your way… but you'll be pushing up daises if you do… and on this very day."

The last shooter to look at (on the left side of photo 6.1K) is in the ready position with his hand firmly on the revolver while still in leather. This is the easiest draw, creates the fewest mistakes and is most often the fastest draw as well. When the instructions call for you to start with the hand on the revolver, be sure your hand is really ON that handgun. Not just touching or resting on it. Have as much of your master grip completed as possible. There is added confidence in attaining your familiar, solid master grip before the start. You can direct your focus past that important task now completed. The one part that is not recommended for this move is to have the trigger finger in the guard while the revolver is still holstered. The rules are more specific as to where the revolver must be before it is cocked, and for us here, I think it better to leave it at that.

Photo 6.1M - *From left to right: Larry Mudgett, a.k.a. "Marshal Gun," SASS® #9232, Mike Hallack, a.k.a. "Hoss 2," SASS® #3381, Sheri Wah, a.k.a. "Wee-Wah," SASS® #22923, and Paul Loverne, a.k.a. "Hopsing," SASS® #2021, show us a strong-side holster line up.*

Years of experience has shown that cowboy action shooters find the most effective way to wear their holsters is on their hips, level or close to level. The low-slung or traditional look of a fast-draw style of holster will be less effective in at least two ways. A holster riding on the thigh instead of the hip may end up bouncing or moving about. If tied down to the thigh (as is common with these holsters), the holster angle becomes the same as the leg. Any action to or from a sitting, kneeling or other similar position serves more to inhibit a shooter's draw or return to leather. Additionally, there is an added probability of losing a revolver from a holster that is (at times) more parallel than perpendicular with level ground. The reader can simply see from the many examples shown by the shooters in this book what works best.

Most shooters decide that transferring the revolver to the weak hand to be returned to leather after the fifth round is discharged does not save enough time for the effort involved in learning movement. This does not mean it cannot be used by some with a great deal of success. I personally do not use this method, although many shooters do. Several seasons ago I experimented with the weak-hand transfer to a reasonable extent and found that ultimately it did not improve my effectiveness or speed, nor did it seem natural in feel, at least for my particular style. Since we are all different, and since this method does work very well for a few of the sport's top shooters, it certainly merits consideration.

Photo 6.1M1 - *Good shooters having fun, the first two might find working the Buscadero rigs a bit more awkward than the more traditional ones. (Near to far: Jay Price, a.k.a. "Hyatt Earp," SASS® #239, Chris Arnold, a.k.a. "Cimarron Kid," SASS® #264, Frank Sinclair, a.k.a. "Friendly Frank," SASS® #10676, and Herb Lyman, a.k.a. "Lawyer Daggett," SASS® #6515.)*

Photos 6.1N1,2 and 3 show the three positions of this transfer. In step one, the shooter has just finished firing the fifth (final) round, and is turning the revolver over as the weak hand takes control, beginning to return it to leather. The next step shows the revolver about half-way down towards the holster as the strong hand goes for the other handgun. The two items to notice here are that the revolver is upside down as it is held by the weak hand, and that the strong hand has gone directly to the next revolver to initiate its draw. If the stage instructions had called for the use of a long gun, and the positioning of that long gun permit-

ted the shooter to remain safe while doing so, the strong hand could be making the same move towards the long gun instead of the second revolver. The possibility of making an error during these maneuvers increases dramatically for all but the most skilled shooters.

The last step shows the revolver's muzzle is entering the leather, ending the return transfer. The shooter will have "eyeballed" the revolver to this position, and the second revolver is out, on the way up.

Now realize that there is more to consider here than just what meets the eye. First of all, the safety of this move must not be overlooked. Keeping the muzzle within the prescribed limits of the safety plane (as described in Chapter 2) is paramount. Consider, too, that the weak hand must insure the return is solid, one that insures the revolver is totally secure in the holster. I mean that the handgun is down and in hard, not able to wriggle loose (and possibly pop out) during subsequent moves.

Understand as well, that while the weak hand is charged with this maneuver, the strong hand must be making the correct draw (good master grip) on the next revolver. So, while both of these tasks can be done, they require precision, leaving little or no room for error. The safety factor not withstanding, a little bobble in the re-holstering of one revolver or a poor grab with the strong hand on the other will render this method useless in terms of time. Admittedly, when it's done well it appears impressive. Does it really save time? I remain unconvinced that this is the best idea for most shooters, feeling that far too much time and effort is needed to become truly competent.

The most common re-holstering method is simply returning the revolver to the holster with the same hand that started the draw. A shooter who is prepared and reasonably practiced can re-holster and draw the second handgun just as quickly as the weak-hand transfer method. Moreover, this method is the more reliable of the two, and provides less opportunity for error.

Photos 6.1N1, 2 and 3 - National Champion Greg Nevitt, a.k.a. "Blackjack McGinnis," SASS® #2041, shows the three steps of a weak-hand revolver transfer.

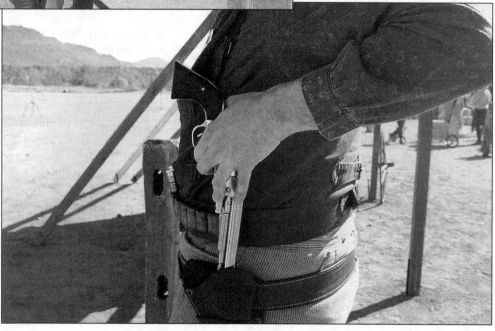

The important parts of these transitions are in the outcome. Did the shooter manage to return the revolver to the holster in one quick and accurate move? Did the revolver find a secured place in the holster? Finally, did the shooter make a good draw with the second handgun or a good move to another firearm without any problems?

When I have prepared properly for a match, that is, when I've worked on my returns and draws so that they are fluid and done with accuracy, the muscle memory takes over. The strong hand will return the revolver (to either holster) without my having to "eyeball" it in. While focusing on the downrange targets or a move to another position, the strong hand will make that correct contact and subsequent draw with the next firearm. Even if I feel I cannot re-holster blind (and must look the revolver into the holster) that day, there still can be found a high degree of performance and success just by being deliberate. Walk before you run. And, if you know you can run, but happen to be a little tired that day and realize you can't go quite as fast as usual, try jogging at a comfortable pace!

It pays to know your options when a choice is presented during a stage. Plan your transitions ahead of time to help you save valuable seconds. Stage designers will sometimes provide the shooter with an opportunity to choose when some of the firearms may be used on a stage. Given a choice to engage with a revolver that must be holstered after use can be of some significance. Do you use the revolver during the middle of the run or at the end of the run? The revolver used at the end of a run does *not* require re-holstering under the clock. This is significant. The savvy gunfighter is more than happy to eliminate one whole transition this way.

The return position is best explained by a stage with two handguns starting flat on the table. Either the stage instruc-

tions are vague (which is too often the case), or they are specific in the way a revolver is to be secured after use. Specific instructions can be either to return each handgun to leather after use, *not* to return to leather (meaning leave it on the table), or the rules can allow you to do either. It is much faster to return that revolver to the flat position on the table than to return it to leather. Don't miss this move, it is not only faster, it is the no-drip, hassle-free method to use in this situation.

Rifle Transitions

Several conditions can dictate the shooter's most beneficial movements during a stage run. The key to success is to recognize how they are related to your skill level. Understanding which direction the shooter will head before or after the use of the lever gun, the position in which the lever gun is pre-staged and where the lever gun will go after it's used are all important elements of a successful run. You may be required to add movement with a lever gun during the stage, kick a door open along the way and shoot targets in a specific order. This list could go on. Yet all these conditions are simply engagement instructions and can be performed safely by any competent shooter. We will address the transition of the lever gun specifically here, but I hope it offers some insight as to some other choices that shooters challenge themselves with. You've got to plan ahead.

Engagement must follow the stage instructions as written and with reasonable intent to do so (see the SASS® Rulebook). How a shooter will attack the problem is up to the shooter. Keeping in mind that you should not violate the "Spirit of the Game." yYou can find all kinds of ways to innovate, adapt, and overcome the age-old battle waged against the clock. So, as we look into these transitions with the lever guns, remember that part of these lessons is technique… another part is theory of address.

The shooter in photo 6.2A shows how to position himself correctly to transition easily, without undue movement, to a lever gun leaning in a pre-staged position. Before the start of the stage, the shooter makes sure he is in such a

Photo 6.2A - *Lefty Longridge is ready to make the right moves from the best position.*

start signal and then place the lever gun down before moving or going on to another firearm during the run.

There are at least three other elements to consider as the shooter sets up. The positioning of the feet should be just right to engage without altering after the start signal. Also consider the target positioning as it relates to the shooter's position. To one extent or another the shooter will most often have to turn the body's torso from one side to another to engage the targets. Sometimes this movement will be repeated (as in more than one sweep). The desired position will allow the shooter to pick up the lever gun, bring it up smoothly on the first target, and acquire subsequent targets without any strain or uncomfortable twisting of the upper body. Unless there is a prop or other condition that requires some re-positioning during this address, additional movement will only increase the time it takes to acquire the target picture. A position that finds the torso stretched or strained to make the acquisition of a particular target increases the chances of missing the target.

Another element to consider is when to use which revolver; before or after bringing the lever gun to action. If the right-handed shooter prefers the left foot forward while engaging with the rifle, then it may be the revolver on the left side (most often a cross-draw) that will be best to use. With the right foot to the rear, the strong side holster will be on (or most likely slightly behind) the 180-degree safety plane. This positioning will place the left side holster forward, within the safety plane's confines and will require no body movement in order to draw safely. The opposite applies to a left-handed shooter.

position that retrieving the lever gun will not require an extra step or even force him to lean over too far when picking up the gun. At the correct moment the shooter should be able to pick up and ready the lever gun by simply reaching with his hands. The same applies to the shooter who must start with the lever gun in the cowboy port arms position, engage at the

The last item we will address here is the shooter's movement after initial engagement. Any movement in any direction becomes significant. Given the choice, the shooter wants to get the best break from one point to another. While this will be explained in greater detail as we go on, keep in mind the most important factor in deciding how to address this (and most all moves) is performing *safely*. If possible, the shooter will blend the next move into the last motion of the previous action in order to increase the fluid motion of the overall engagement.

Even if the firearm sequence presents a problem that does not allow a shooter the preferred moves at each critical point of transition, anticipating what moves will be made is important. These are the keys to use when deciding where your best options may be, and making sure the option chosen will pay off in terms of time saved.

Overlooking the importance of correct retrieval and subsequent return of the long guns can be a costly error for many shooters. Staged long guns are found leaning against (or set in) many different vertical positions. They can be laid flat on different surfaces, or found slung inside a scabbard.

Very often the shooter will have some kind of a choice as to exactly how these long guns can be placed in or around these varied positions. If the choice is not yours, as when someone else must stage your gun (to expedite posse movement for example), make sure you let that person know how you want the gun positioned. The right-handed shooter will usually prefer the opposite of the left-handed shooter. The same lesson applies to handguns as well.

Regardless of who placed which long gun where, the shooter should know beforehand exactly how he wants to make contact with it, and how he will bring it up to the ready position. A hasty or poorly thought out maneuver with the lever gun can result in fingers outside the

Photo 6.2B - *A poor set-up can lead to unnatural body positioning for each subsequent move.*

lever as it is racked, a misplaced off-hand on the forend that cannot perform properly, a misguided buttstock into the shoulder or the awkward feeling of not having your cheek on the sweet spot of the lever gun's comb. Any or all of these little mishaps can lead the shooter to a poor stage run. At best, the shooter will have enough control to recognize and re-adjust as needed to regain primary control. This may well result in little time lost. Or it may be significant. But more common and far worse is the shooter who does not adjust and compounds the problem by trying to continue at the normal pace and ends up missing, *and* going slower than usual.

Photo 6.2C - *Speed is less important than being smooth and deliberate in the pick-up and return of these long guns.*

First of all, know exactly where you want each hand to make initial contact. Do not make the moves with undue haste. Be quick, but be deliberate and sure in this handling. The amount of time it takes to perform this transition in a smooth manner versus one that appears fast is most often less than 3/10ths of a second slower. Yes, you have indeed heard this before, and will likely hear it again.

The shooter should watch or "eyeball" the staged gun, get the good grip and bring it into the ready position as a carefully laid out plan. Whether you are standing in front of the staged gun or running to it, know where you want your feet to be. Diverting your attention to a perceived problem ahead of you can produce

the glitches igniting a fuse for failure. To engage targets at the highest speeds your skill level allows will require (at least) the best efforts of contact, hold and address of which you are capable.

Remember to get that good "break" after the last shot by instantly opening the action and knowing (because you planned ahead) exactly how and where that long gun will be set back down after use. A hastily returned long gun that falls over (regardless if its action is open and safe) may well result in a costly penalty. Think about being deliberate, smooth and sure in all of these moves. Part of obtaining a quick break comes from counting the rounds fired. All too often shooters lose track and cannot come off the gun quickly or on time.

One way to know when the last round is out of the rifle is to set a pattern. For example: You have three targets downrange, and nine rounds to fire at them. The instructions say to double tap each target from left to right (six rounds), and then to single tap the same three targets again from left to right. A shooter studying the rifle engagement part of the stage can think: "double, double, double" then "single, single, single." Whatever way is used, it is important to have an effective way to count the rounds in order to obtain the good break.

A few other tips about staged guns include making sure any gun placed in a scabbard or holster is easily withdrawn. Check to insure a lever gun placed in a scabbard is not in so deep as to hinder its withdrawal. If possible, check that a piece of leather fuzz is not attached to the front sight of a long gun when it is pulled from a scabbard. If the stage places a '97 pump shotgun flat on a surface right in front of you and the lever gun is used first from the same position, consider laying the open breech of the shotgun so that there is no chance of an empty rifle case falling into it. You may think this rare, but when it happens to you someday you won't think so anymore.

Correct lateral or forward movement with any long gun must first be learned as part of our conscious safety efforts and hopefully become so ingrained it becomes an instinctive part of our subconscious actions. I have (as many other shooters moving at top speed) tripped, slipped or fallen down while moving with a long gun. The instinctively safe shooter will put all else aside when something like this happens to insure no part of that long gun's muzzle comes close to breaking the safety plane. Because shooters will eventually be faced with moving with a loaded long gun (though more often an unloaded one), it is imperative to perform this action safely no matter how fast it is attempted.

Forward movement with any long gun is basically the same for either the left- or right-handed shooter. Understanding and staying within the confines of the declared safety plane with the long gun's muzzle will keep you in good form. Applying the knowledge of a few other techniques used in effective forward transitions with any of the long guns will help you achieve excellent form.

Photo 6.2D - *Learning to move safely and quickly with the long guns is an important part of getting the most out of your stage runs.*

Photo 6.2E - *Magnum Quigley has learned that lateral movement brings slightly different problems and advantages depending on the direction of travel and the shooter's strong side.*

Naturally, shooters will find moving laterally to their strong side easier than moving to the weak side. The initial "break" will start a fraction quicker, and maintaining safe control of the long gun is equally more natural. The right-handed shooter in photo 6.2E is seen moving to his right, just after the initial "break" was made. Note how little change in the handling of the long gun is required to keep the muzzle safely downrange. It's a natural move. It is the same for a left-handed shooter if the opposite lateral direction is required. Hopefully, stage designers favoring lateral moves such as these will be ambidextrous in thought as they lay out their wily plans for a match.

Moving toward the weak side, the opposite of a shooter's strong side, requires reasonable skill and uncompromisingly safe handling of the long guns. The speed or effort put forth by a shooter executing these moves should be directly related to experience and ability. Your cowboy action shooting compatriots and peers have a lot more respect for a shooter who moves no faster than his or her current skill level safely permits.

Photo 6.2F provides a point of view close to that of the imaginary 180-degree safety plane the shooter operates within. This is a left-handed shooter who must move laterally to the right (the weak side) with the lever gun kept safe. It is not really seen as a natural move, and some may feel it is awkward. This will require a concentrated focus and effort to produce the results a good shooter strives for. The technique shown here has the shooter with both hands on the long gun, maintaining horizontal control of the muzzle and (equally important) the vertical angle of the muzzle as well.

Regardless of the speed at which the shooter shown in photo 6.2F makes this move, part of the initial "break right" process with the long gun is that the strong hand has moved the long gun part way across the body in the same direction as the lateral move dictated. The weak hand (on the fore stock) has changed position by rolling the wrist over and is now somewhat on top of the long gun's barrel. Speed not withstanding, the strong hand has provided two things: Initial momentum towards the desired direction and continued

Photo 6.2F - *Keeping that muzzle safe is of the utmost importance, here is one method of safe, lateral movement toward the weak side for this left-handed shooter.*

maintenance of safe, horizontal muzzle direction. The off (or weak) hand will naturally be turned over by the wrist and provide safe vertical muzzle direction. This method is one effective way to get the job done safely and at a reasonably fast pace for most shooters.

Not recommended for the cowboy action shooter of average skill, photo 6.2G shows a left-handed shooter moving again towards his right or weak side while maintaining control of the gun

Photo 6.2G - *One-hand control requires higher skill and increases safety responsibility.*

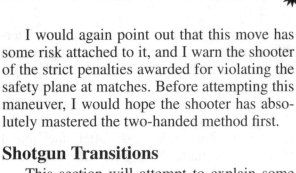

with one hand only. This is usually done with a shotgun with the action open as the absence of an operating lever on a shotgun makes it easier. This move requires some strength and practiced dexterity. The advantage in attaining this skill lies in that the shooter can free one hand to perform the task of round retrieval off the belt while in motion rather than reaching for the rounds upon arrival at the next firing position. It may also provide a slight increase of "break" speed by eliminating the motion of the firearm crossing to the other side of the shooter's chest or body.

I would again point out that this move has some risk attached to it, and I warn the shooter of the strict penalties awarded for violating the safety plane at matches. Before attempting this maneuver, I would hope the shooter has absolutely mastered the two-handed method first.

Shotgun Transitions

This section will attempt to explain some of the shotgun transitions besides those related to the actual loading and firing techniques found in the chapter entitled "Working the Shotguns of Cowboy Action Shooting. " There is much to consider and understand for optimum shotgun work besides the loading and/or firing that will add to the efficiency of a shooter's transitions.

The caption under photo 6.3A asks the question, "Do you know what might go wrong when these shooters touch these shotguns?" I hope you didn't simply think about poor loading, incorrect sighting or other problems subsequent to actually making contact with the shotgun. What about that first contact made with the hand(s)? What you should know about executing this properly must be addressed and correctly planned. Some considerations include other problems the shotgun presents as you attempt to bring it to bear.

Each of the two shotguns pre-staged here vertically may be lying in wait with a built-in handling glitch for the shooter to encounter. A problem common to the double-barrel shotgun, when leaned in this or a similar manner, is that the action often closes as the shooter raises it up to begin the loading process. Not only is the shooter attempting to make contact and raise it up quickly, but is likely to bend at the waist and raise it up by the barrel. Doing this without contemplating an accidental closure of the action can often compel a shooter to go through the motions of re-opening the action, This costs precious time. This can frustrate a shooter and may well cause a string of problems to follow.

There is probably not a single best way to make the desired pick-up of a double-barrel shotgun from this position. If there is any, it would most likely be developed by a shooter who understood the problem and practiced

Photo 6.3A - *Do you know what might go wrong when these shooters touch these shotguns?*

should make sure it is heading in the right direction. As it becomes possible, the other hand should take control of the shotgun and hold the shotgun with its muzzle down, chambers up, ready to load. The other hand, having completed its first task, goes directly to the first two rounds and will bring them to the exposed chambers of the double to load. Much longer in description, this formula for success is fast, smooth and requires little effort when done correctly.

The shooter is less likely to find it effective to bend down at the knees, make contact and raise the shotgun by holding it around the trigger guard area. Not only is this farther in distance and more difficult for most shooters to perform easily, the shooter is encumbered with a fair amount of equipment as well. The shooter must also be aware of the possible loss of shotgun rounds that may fall from the loops during this (and any other) action, especially when bending or stooping. It is fair to note that such stooping over may also put the shooter at risk of a falling handgun, incurring a stage (or even possibly a match) disqualification.

The Winchester '97 pump shotgun is less problematic from this position, but can be a bit tricky for the unwary and/or unprepared shooter. A hasty grab that finds the hand raising the '97 by the wooden forearm instead of a portion of the barrel or magazine can produce two mishaps. The '97's action may actually be closed if the pump travels too far upward as the gun is raised. This can pro-

picking up their shotgun from similar positions to develop their own successful technique. This shooter will become reasonably skilled in both the safe, successful raising of the double and will also find the same skill in handling the inevitable (but hopefully only occasional) closing of the action in a swift and unhindered manner.

A shooter should make the initial contact with the hand that controls the direction and angle of the shotgun. As it begins to rise up he duce varied degrees of problems for shooters to contend with. The least of these problems will be the simple and quick re-opening of the breech to receive rounds by a shooter who has prepared to react correctly when it happens. The worst problem will be the frustrated efforts of a shooter struggling with an apparently locked up receiver. Partial closure of the '97's pump action can occur and shooters often are seen fighting with the unlocking button, bringing the hammer back with their thumb and pulling the trigger in order for the breech to become unlocked. When this happens to a shooter and there has been little or no preparation learned or practiced, significant time can be lost. Some shooters will have to stop their attempts to open the shotgun, surrender it safely to an attending Range Officer or set it down (as instructed) and continue on with the stage. This happens mostly at major annual events where re-shoots are not awarded for gun malfunctions. Besides the time loss incurred here, each of the targets not addressed becomes a five-second penalty as well.

Photo 6.3B - *Wafer-thin, this cartridge guide is not in a user-friendly position.*

Another problem that occurs with the '97 is the unfriendly cartridge guide. This can be present prior to the shooter's initial handling of the gun, may be induced by the contact made by the shooter and may occur regardless if the gun is placed in a vertical or horizontal pre-staged position. The culprit, shown in photo 6.3B, is the flat, thin piece of metal seen partially obstructing the open breech of this '97.

The '97 shotgun's cartridge guide is designed to guide, or keep in place, the shotgun round as it normally comes out of the magazine and upwards into the breech. To accomplish this the guide must be sensitive to any movement of the action as it begins to close. This thin, wafer-looking little piece of metal has gotten in the way of many shooters' attempts to feed directly into the side breech of their '97. The shooter who understands what can happen, when it can happen and how to avoid it, is one more step closer to improved performance.

This premature movement of the cartridge guide is almost always a result of some kind of movement made by the forearm of the '97. This condition may occur in both the tighter '97s or those guns referred to by shooters as loose or "rackety." When the cartridge guide has risen to this position prematurely, the shooter must move the pump handle (forearm) toward the butt of the shotgun, as if re-opening the action.

Photo 6.3C - *Re-open the action to correctly position the cartridge guide.*

The causes of this particular "glitch" of the '97 are handling errors so subtle in nature that it is very easy to overlook or to fail to recognize them. The shooter, a firing line support person, or anyone who handles the '97 with the action opened, is at risk of causing this. Primarily, it is the shooter who grasps the '97 by its forearm in order to raise and bring the shotgun to bear who will most often commit this error. By grasping the forearm of the shotgun, the pumping mechanism can begin the closing process of the action simply because of the weight of the gun as it is lifted. While this is most often not enough pressure to completely close the action, it is more than enough to bring the light, wafer-thin cartridge guide up into this undesired position or (although less often) enough to close the action halfway.

The shooter should also be aware that mishandling a flat or horizontally staged '97 by the forearm could bring about this problem. Anytime a '97 is brought to bear, carried from one point to another, pre-staged or handled by anyone else, there exists a chance the action has moved to start the closing process. The hard working posse member pre-staging a shooter's '97 may be moving with the shotgun in a safe manner, but unaware that the action may have moved into a compromising position. The shooter can also do this inadvertently. It takes very little momentum in the wrong direction for this to happen. The situation warrants an automatic check during, or prior to, actual engagement.

Pre-staging of the '97 should include insuring that the action is completely open and the cartridge guide is in the down (unseen) position. Just prior to setting the '97 down in its final position, make sure you completely open the action. If the shooter cannot pre-stage the firearm without assistance, he should not hesitate to remind the RO or line support person who is doing the pre-staging to pay attention to this.

Whoever handles the firearm while pre-staging it should take care to move the pump or forearm towards the stock of the shotgun and then hold the gun in such a way so as not to partially close the action. It is essential to automatically make sure that the shotgun action is open and clear, even when picking up

Photo 6.3D - *Lamar Shelnut, a.k.a. "Coyote Calhoun," SASS® #4864, knows that grasping the pump forearm like this to raise the '97 may cause the cartridge guide to shift or may even close the action altogether. (Robin Wilson (middle), a.k.a. "San Quinton," SASS® #4818 and Eric Kahmann, a.k.a. "Smokewagon Skinner," SASS® #9233 look on.)*

the gun from a pre-staged position. Here's an example: Upon reaching the shotgun, the shooter grabs it by the pump or forearm and begins to bring the gun into a loading position. At some point prior to the first round going into the breech or side action of the shotgun the shooter will have exerted rearward pressure on the pump to insure the cartridge guide is correctly positioned. This can be done at one of several points during the initial handling, but must occur prior to round feeding. It is an easy technique, one that requires the shooter to recognize the probability of the problem occurring, when to expect it and the proper action to take to prevent or adapt quickly to it. It is part of a smooth transition while using the '97 pump shotgun.

The cowboy action shooter who employs the magazine and the slide action or breech in order to load two rounds (yet to be described to the reader) is also subject to the same possible problems of premature cartridge guide movement.

The lesson for the shooter here is to be aware of where to best make contact with your shotguns to engage effectively from any pre-staged position and to prepare for the occasional mishap when it happens ... and it will happen.

Photo 6.3E - *After firing the last round, it should become instinct to open the action, secure the firearm, and go to the next position.*

An important transition with either style of shotgun used in CAS is the quick, automatic motion of opening (therefore clearing) the action as the shotgun is placed in the required position before continuing a stage run.

Part of the shooter's pre-stage preparation should include a study of what to do with the firearms after they have been used in the stage. Attention to safety is always paramount in these actions. A shooter who has not thought out the "last round fired, return to station, and move out" part of any scenario may have less balance, less correct momentum in the desired direction. Failure to think this through can lead to mishandling errors. On the other hand, a shooter who understands the importance of this "pre-prepping" process will know beforehand exactly how to get through each maneuver. This understanding will lead to better times.

Another common transition involving either style of shotgun is some kind of forward or lateral movement by the shooter. This move-ment is often referred to by shooters as "point A to point B" movement, and relates to any or all such motion. What we will examine is what other actions may be accomplished while moving.

As individual stage scenarios permit, or written instructions demand, the shooter can determine the most effective and time-saving techniques to employ. Movement with a shotgun may require one or more pre-determined positions at which one must stop and engage targets. Or, it may simply require movement while carrying the shotgun to another position without engagement along the way. Other scenarios may include move-ment while requiring a shooter to engage at the same time. Still others will find shooters moving while carrying a prop item (like a moneybag or saddle-bag, etc.) in one hand and the long gun in the other.

Photo 6.3F - *Bounty Hunter seen moving to his weak side with the double, keeping the muzzle safe while two new rounds are being taken out during movement to the next position.*

Photo 6.3G - *Magnum Quigley arriving at a secondary firing position with the shotgun going down while the revolver is being safely brought to bear at the same time.*

Again, the first concern of the shooter as he decides on how the stage can best be engaged is safety. Whatever the shooter decides will work best and what exactly he or she plans to do during the run must be within the prescribed limits of SASS® safety specifications and the requirements of those hosting the match. Learned shooters will not attempt techniques that are beyond their own current skill levels and, therefore, place themselves, the shooters around them and everyone else in jeopardy.

The two photos (6.3F and G) show two shooters in motion with shotguns at different points during their travel from one position to another. The shooter with the '97 pump shotgun is shown at an earlier point of travel than the double shooter. Each of these photos depicts only one action (besides that of actual forward movement) that will aid in their quest to reduce the overall time of the stage run. We will go over these actions as illustrated plus one or two that are less apparent.

After firing the last required shotgun round from the first position, the stage requires the shooter move laterally to the right while carrying his double to a secondary, predetermined spot to again engage with the shotgun. Simplistic as it seems, this shooter's technique of removing new rounds from his belt during movement can either improve or impede his run. How or why depends on when this and other actions are actually performed. The right idea at the wrong time will work opposite of what was desired. Simply being correct in the analytical sense does not insure successful, physical implementation will be automatic. The shooter must think about those important actions.

First of all, realize that the goal of the shooter after the last round is fired from the first position is to reach the next firing position as quickly as possible; the shooter must try to achieve the quickest "break" after the last round is fired. No hesitation should be apparent as the shooter does this. The opening of the shotgun's action expelling the last round(s) should occur at the exact moment that the shooter begins the break to the next position. Opening an action of a shotgun to expel one or more empty hulls before you start moving will

add about one second to the run. If there happens to be three similar positions like this in one stage, that can mean three full additional seconds of wasted time. I say wasted time because there is no reason or value in doing so. A shotgun's action can easily open within a small fraction of a second and few (I doubt any) shooters can over react or out-move this particular action. Even though each shooter will react at varied degrees of speed when initiating motion, any shooter will impede his performance by remaining stationary when he should be moving. One key here is to know beforehand what you will do as the last round is discharged. Think and react as if the two actions are not separate, but are one in the same. As the last shot is fired the shotgun's action is opened at the same time the shooter initiates movement.

Looking again at the shooter in full flight, the additional action being taken is removing new rounds while moving. Besides the obvious advantage of executing two separate actions to eliminate wasted time, it is the timing and consequent effectiveness of these actions that bears examination. Taking the correct action at the right time here includes the initial break, a clean pick-up or removal from your belt of one or more rounds to load into the shotgun as soon as possible and, finally, reaching the next position with all due haste. The better shooters will not forget that they must arrive at the next position and obtain a steady platform to load, bring to bear, and shoot the firearm effectively.

The shooter will want to accomplish all of the above as quickly as all surrounding conditions permit. Stage props, movement requirements, distance moved (which could include thoughts about fitness), even the weather and ground conditions are part of what the shooter should consider in contemplating the engagement.

After making the initial break when the last round is fired, the shooter maintains focus on reaching the secondary firing position. Maintaining safe muzzle control, the shooter should not deviate, nor hesitate. He should engage in no action that will slow or impede this progress. Any new rounds taken out during this movement should be retrieved at such time as there is no interruption in getting to that next position. Mishandled or dropped rounds should be totally ignored. Done correctly, the shooter will have anticipated, executed, and, therefore, adjusted as well as possible to arrive at the new shooting position with optimum stance, firearm positioning and correct positioning of the rounds.

As clinical sounding as that last paragraph is, what it really says or amounts to is somewhat akin to what the late General Bedford Forrest once said. Though only taken in part, the gist of his words meant whoever would "Get there the fastest … with the mostest" was most likely to be the winner of the battle.

Looking at the shooter in photo 6.3F, the reader will see that it is a double-barrel shotgun being carried from one position to another. In this case, the shooter has just about arrived to a new position from which to engage. This particular part of the engagement requires the shooter to move with the double-barrel (action open and safe muzzle direction) and, upon reaching the next position, set the shotgun down safely, and engage designated targets with one (or both) revolvers. For this example there is a horizontal surface for the shotgun to rest on at the new firing position. This should be of keen interest to the alert shooter, for it remedies the often difficult task of finding and using safe, vertical placement of a double-barrel shotgun with the action open. Had the stage required a vertical placement instead of horizontal it may well change the shooter's decisions in the approach.

The shooter in this example is right-handed, but notice that at this point of engagement the shotgun is held in the left hand. You are right if you decided this was done to expedite the execution of his next task: bringing to bear the revolver. The decision to employ this technique was made correctly, and arose simply from one existing condition. This condition was the horizontal prop. It provided a safe, sure and easy place to set the shotgun down with one hand. This in turn provides the shooter an opportunity to make early contact with his revolver.

Again, the advantage of executing transitions during required movement is important. Besides the basic economy of movement, the shooter has two other excellent reasons for this move. The first is to obtain a firm, controlled master grip on the revolver prior to where it will be drawn and discharged from. The second reason is his confidence factor. Who wouldn't be more confident after making these correct moves?

The reader should understand something the photo for the above lesson does not show, but does indicate. There is one more reason for transferring the shotgun to the left hand, as it applies to the right-handed, traditional class shooter. The vast majority of traditional shooter class styles (women, seniors, juniors, black powder and frontiersman) will be using a cross-draw style of holster on one side. While this example is that of a right-handed shooter, the same decision applies to the left-hander taken and executed in the opposite manner. By choosing the strong-side holster from which to draw the revolver, the shooter was mindful of the existing safety plane operating limits.

Avoiding the efforts of turning or twisting the torso for a safe cross draw is not to be overlooked.

Shotguns in scabbards are worth the shooter's attention in both staging and engagement transitions requiring removal and replacement of the scabbard. There may lurk more problems than a little piece of fuzz on a front sight.

The shooter should always check the shotgun's positioning within a scabbard prior to the start of the stage. Is the scabbard tight? If

Photo 6.3H - *Bob Schumacher, a.k.a. "Ned Buntline," SASS®
#14077, knows not to overlook the problems encountered with scab-
bard props.*

so, how much effort will be required to withdraw the gun when needed? Is there a better
depth or position in which the shooter can
arrange the shotgun in order to facilitate an
effective withdrawal? Is the action of the '97
correctly and fully open after final placement
… or has the cartridge guide crept up to block
your efforts? Can the shooter manage
withdrawal that does not promote premature closing of the '97's action altogether? Will the butt of a double-barrel
impede withdrawal or replacement
because of the strong angle presented
with its action open? Are the scabbards

angled in such a way that the shooter will need to withdraw or replace the shotgun in an awkward manner? Does the shooter know beforehand just where the best position is for loading rounds into the chambers of a muzzle-down double? Is the shooter faced with both long guns in scabbards, one on each side of the wooden steed? If so, the order of firearm use and consequent return to the scabbard may have impact worth considering.

Successful withdrawal is one thing, but it is no less important than the transition of returning a shotgun to its scabbard without problems. Again, when checking these conditions look at the mouth of a scabbard's entry end. Does the leather tend to close when empty? Will this cause the leather flaps to close and somehow impede the return when done at speed?

Understanding what to look for, the shooter will need little time in which to include this preparation of the scabbard for use during engagement. Making it part of the normal pre-stage routine is easy and paramount to increasing the chances of a problem-free encounter of this kind.

Two last bits of advice come with this lesson. The first is to remember to check the shotgun rounds on your belt after climbing up on a horse. If you do not check, you may find your rounds have sunk too deeply in the loops for easy retrieval. Or worse still, they may have fallen out. The last bit of advice is to avoid high-speed movements when making these transitions. Accurate, glitch-free motions made at a modest speed will often produce a smooth, trouble-free encounter with the gremlins lurking within a scabbard. The normally fast shooter who does not check speed here, but instead employs the same speed used for other shotgun transitions, will often end up fighting both the shotgun and the scabbard.

Combined Firearm Transitions

Any shooter can improve his or her timed runs during engagement by planning the effective use of combined firearm transitions. This depends on each shooter's skill level, and there is value in any of its applications. As it is with almost every technique, it is not so much the speed used to execute a particular move that will reduce the overall time as much as it is the reduction of movement that contributes to the smoothness of a stage run. These are the actions that add dimension to the shooter's knowledge and applied execution of CAS tactics.

Combining two separate actions, namely those that are ending the use of one firearm while beginning the use of another, requires little more than some planning and safe execution on the shooter's part. There are almost always points during a stage engagement that

Photo 6.4A - *Bob Stutler, a.k.a. "The Major," SASS® #342, making the right moves during a combined firearms transition at the Winter Range Nationals 2000.*

will provide shooters with opportunities to streamline movements. Part of the pre-stage address that each shooter must (to some degree) decide in order to engage at all, is the place from which to initiate each move. The very best shooters in the sport will plan any such move while keeping in mind what all shooters (no matter their skill level) should also be thinking about. They will first ask, can I perform this safely and without serious risk to others or myself? Secondly, there is the factor of "ease of accomplishment" to consider. Can the shooter be assured that the two different transitions done at the same time are such that can be done easily, with little or no chance of one causing problems with the other? If there is doubt in the shooter's analysis of these points, the answer becomes an absolute "no" to the move. One should not risk the possibility of a negative outcome.

There are also other points to ponder before making a decision of this kind. Do the existing stage conditions promote or retard the chances of success? Will a combined move of this sort really offer a significant advantage in terms of time reduction or, more importantly, will it make the run smoother? This is an important one: Can I trust myself insofar as my skills at present allow me to execute this move with confidence? Another important call the shooter must make concerns the other effects the move can produce. Will attempting this move take too much of my focus away from the other parts of the stage that are not yet completed? Finally, if the shooter does decide to implement any combined handling of the firearms as part of his transitions, he must weigh all the preceding information before making a commitment to execute. Doing this in the field is far less difficult than this explanation may appear. Still, you may find yourself coming back here from time to time to review the basics.

One basic combination move that many shooters do regularly is seen in photo 6.4 B. The shooter here is shown setting down a long gun with its action open after completing that part of a pre-scribed shooting scenario. The shooter is experienced enough to understand and execute the act of setting down the long gun in such a manner that the strong hand and arm are free, and can at the same time begin the act of drawing the next gun needed, in this case a revolver. It is a combination firearms transition at one of the more basic levels. It is a very valuable move; one that is used constantly by shooters at all but the lowest levels of competition. The shooter here is gaining momentum towards the direction of the next task while completing the action of another. The strong hand making contact with the revolver, and making a solid master grip from which to start the next engagement problem, best highlights this advantageous move.

Photo 6.4B - *Looks like a simple move ... and it is ... except for what?*

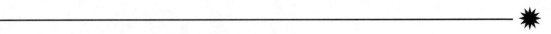

Photos 6.4C, D and E - *A few examples of effective combined firearms transitions.*

The reader may wonder about the "except" part of the caption under photo 6.4B. This exception relates to part of the pre-stage prep thoughts a shooter should consider. The shooter seems to be executing this simple maneuver perfectly, without any risk. Look again. This shooter either began the move a little bit too far from the position to re-stage the long gun as he moved from a previous spot, or he did not think to position himself correctly before the start. Failing to recognize the need for correct distance may well have resulted in the over-extension shown in the photo. Under pressure, don't always count on an automatic correction. A shooter will often react with the more awkward way of turning or stretching the body to complete the task. Whatever the cause, the effect of poor technique can create serious problems. The least of which would be correcting for an awkward move and a small loss of time. If (in this case), the shooter is wearing a cross-draw holster while bending over to complete the re-staging of the long gun, the unattended revolver may be at risk of falling out of the holster as the bending angle increases. Moreover, the shooter is often not thinking of this revolver, the focus is more on a quick move to return the long gun and the simultaneous move to begin the draw of the other revolver. The point here is to recognize all parts of an anticipated move, and to avoid the ramifications of possible errors by pre-stage prep.

I hope this basic exercise has helped the reader to better judge what will work and what may not work in this or similar applications of engagement. Remember, if there are any doubts in your deliberations regarding one move or another, go to the firmest platform of safety and execution.

Non-Shooting Transitions

Few things the cowboy action shooter is compelled to deal with will cause more frustration, or provide more humor to those watching, than those little acts of prop manipulation that are non-shooting but required tasks of design. If there were no tasks of this nature for the cowboy action shooter to perform from time to time, the sport would not be as fun (or as challenging) as it is today. In contrast, there are limits to these little bits of spicing up a stage that should not be exceeded. Hopefully, the thoughtful match designer will understand that it is first a shooting competition that brings speed and action to the forefront, and will add only a proverbial pinch of seasoning for all to enjoy insofar as working the props goes.

The seasoned shooter will come to realize that no matter what kind of non-shooting tasks are placed before them, it

Photo 6.5A - *Magnum Quigley and Island Girl in different roles of prop handling.*

is better to adjust and address the problem than it is to fret, complain and let the task ruin the day. You *will* run into these nightmares. Expect it and plan for it. When it does happen, it won't seem quite as big a problem, and will become easier to overcome. Besides, it is for all competitors to face, not just you. Let it be someone else's nightmare, not yours.

The average non-shooting tasks found in CAS stage events are most often those of simple prop manipulation and/or movement. Sitting at a poker table, holding a "dead-man's hand" just prior to the start of the stage is one example. The list goes on, limited only by the designer's imagination and, of course, sanity and good taste. Some of the cuter little episodes encountered may include handling dynamite, roping a steer or other kind of Western varmint, or sitting in the outhouse while peace-fully reading the local paper. You might be rolling a wheelbarrow along just before "all hell breaks loose" … you just never know what to expect. So, expect just that.

There will be times that the use of seemingly innocent tools such as a safety pin, or, a few feet of rope attached to a bucket you will crank up from a well, will cause you trouble. Even using a key to unlock handcuffs is not unusual. Most of the more problem-prone chores will be judged "not equal" for the field of shooters and in that interest will be performed prior to the actual sound of the timer's starting beep or signal. Some of these chores and others similar in nature are not so easily squared away, and will require your attention and clever abilities if you are to get through "alive" or at least to get through mostly unscathed. The starting position, as shown in photo 6.5B, was seen as a little maca-bre to some, but it was the closing of the lid of this casket just prior to the start of the stage that really found some shooters getting a bit edgy.

Photo 6.5B - *A Whiskey Creek posse looks on as they receive instructions to begin a stage from inside a pine box (far right).*

It is interesting to observe what happens to those charged with completing an apparently simple little chore after the pressure cooking sound of the "Beeeeeeeep." Anxious to get on with the run, many shooters will find they have lost any semblance of normal dexterity as they fail to perform a simple task. Others will try so hard it becomes an exercise in futility instead of the easy fix it really is. Still others are unwise in their hasty attempts to whip through a problem that is best done in a calm, slow manner. These speed runs raise havoc for most, but do provide a certain amount of entertainment for those looking on.

Some more examples of approach in this area are the ones that require an honest effort (usually *two* honest efforts) to be made by the shooter in order to continue the run with no procedural penalty. I more admire a designer whose intent is not to defeat the shooter (and award a penalty), but instead offers a passing grade for a second honest effort that still fails. The shooter is usually so stricken by the first failing attempt, and then even more in the second try as applied in these instances, that there is penalty enough paid in this way alone.

Photo 6.5C - *Mike Barr, a.k.a. "Stoney Burke," SASS® #5500, thought shooting was the only hard part of this stage.*

Besides performing while the clock is running, it is probably the unfamiliar territory of these little chores that breeds the most mistakes. Over-confidence and not paying attention to detail may also attribute to mistakes here. There are a couple of "golden rules" that can often help a shooter get through these non-shooting tasks in better shape than most.

First, the shooter should really pay attention to what it is the stage requires. If, for example, a safety pin must be used to hold two pieces of material together before going on, understand what must be done to complete this operation. Sound too simple to worry about? Well, I've seen 100 shooters red-faced and grief-stricken as their efforts to complete that stupid little pinning exercise cost them an extra 10 seconds of pure anxiety. The seasoned shooter will approach all moves of the stage run with the same interest and attention to details. Can you hold the prop (or safety pin) before you must use it? If so, make sure the action of thrusting it through the material is planned for, and that you have closed the safety pin once or twice

and have the hang of the old, mostly forgotten way that they work. Hold that prop (or pin) in such a manner that you can make it work right the first time. Look closely at what each step of the operation requires for completion the first time. Let's see … how do I hold that darn dress now? Will it be best to go through one piece of material first … or both at the same time?

It does sound a little silly, doesn't it? But I swear to you, the shooters I have seen struggle with this and other little chores like it are far more silly in their ill-fated efforts.

Finally, any task outside that of firearm handling or related transitions is best solved by understanding it first, watching others do it if possible, deciding which actions will produce completion the first time you attempt it and then figuring out the speed at which you are confident will not hinder your efforts. Getting through in reasonable time with no mistakes can be related to the way you will shoot and transition through the rest of the stage. Fighting your way through with frustration will very often cost you any chance of completing a good stage run.

More information along these lines, or principles of engagement, is offered in some later chapters.

Chapter 7

WORKING THE SHOTGUNS OF COWBOY ACTION SHOOTING

Which Shotgun Will You Decide Is Best For You, And Why

How many times has it been argued as to which of the two shotguns can be used the fastest? As long as CAS has existed this topic has been a favorite of both veterans and greenhorns alike. The question never really dies. Regardless of what I offer the reader here, the questions, answers, and friendly skirmishes regarding the '97 or the double will continue around the CAS campfires for many years to come. It would

Photo 7.0A - *End Of Trail 2000 Champion Choctaw and Lefty Longridge stand ready at cowboy port arms, both shooters are focused and ready to go.*

serve no purpose to delve too deeply into this subject, for you will hear it all in time, and will make up your own mind soon enough. The focus of this chapter is to simply provide enough factual information (and some opinions) to help you make a more educated decision. Soon enough, through trial and error, you will find what works best for you.

What I do know is that the shooters in photo 7.0A (Lefty Longridge and Choctaw) can discharge four rounds with their respective shotguns (with respect also to target size and distance), from the cowboy port arms position (both hands on shotgun, rounds on body) in *less than four and three-quarter seconds.* I have timed Lefty personally from this and other positions. Using his '97 he can load and shoot four rounds as fast as *4.33 seconds.* While Choctaw's best time with his double is a foot-dragging *4.67 seconds*; there is no doubt in his mind (or mine) that it can somehow be done quicker. The same opinion holds true for the '97's time as well. Isn't there always going to be someone, somewhere, sometime that is faster? Sure ... it's one of "Murphy's Laws" to the cowboy action shooter. I must tell the reader that these times reflect an all-out effort, more akin to pulling out all the stops one would see at a shotgun speed event or practice session rather than a main match.

What I think the truth is surrounding this tale of two shotguns gets back to the who, what, where and how of using the shotguns. In other words, it is not fair to render simply one final judgment for either of the shotguns. It is more reasonable to look at *who* is shooting which shotgun, *what* and *where* the conditions surrounding the approach and engagement are, and finally *how* well a shooter's technique is executed on a particular run. Neither shotgun is faster than the other, just stand one beside the other and say "go." Hmm ... I'd have to say that was a tie. There is little to be

said regarding which gauge a shooter should consider beyond that of the lighter 12-gauge rounds found in 90 percent of the shotguns. Smaller gauges do not offer an advantage in either recoil or economics, and being smaller in diameter are considered more difficult to manipulate for most shooters than the larger 12-gauge rounds. The 10-gauge is SASS® legal, but I have seen only one, and have no intention of ever getting my old shoulder close to one, let alone taking a crack at shooting one at a CAS match!

The question more valid for this book is: Which of the two styles of shotgun will be best for use in a match? There are other makers of pump shotguns that are legal for the sport (like an old Marlin), and there are many different makes of the external hammer double-barreled shotguns available as well. Mainstream CAS match play shows us, however, that it is the Winchester Model 1897 pump and one of the many hammerless double-barrel shotguns available that get the nod from shooters. Generally, the double is a short barrel (20–22 inches in length) "coach" style shotgun, such as Stoeger offers.

It can hardly be disputed that usually nine out of the top 10 shooters at any national level match will be seen using '97's. On the other hand, we cannot dismiss the fact that Dennis Ming (a.k.a. "China Camp") won five world championship titles in a row ('91 through '95) using a short-barreled double. It would seem though that the odds point in favor of the Model 1897. Why is this? Should you even consider using a double? Will doing so keep the shooter from doing well ... even winning? Let me give you my opinion to the last question first.

Unless there was a perfect match shot by two shooters, each making equal time in every area of total engagement, could we say the double shooter would most likely lose to the flawless use of a '97? No way will the effectively used double barrel keep a shooter from doing well or winning. At the time this was written, Dennis Ming (a.k.a. "China Camp") was battling back from an old injury, starting to shoot again with regularity. He finished third overall in a field of 550 shooters at Winter

Range 2000, the SASS® Nationals of CAS. Of those 550 shooters, there were at least 50 of the sport's finest shooters contending for the top final positions. He used the same old double-barrel 12-gauge to blow all but two of his peers into lower placements.

Should you consider using a double-barrel shotgun? Why wouldn't you? If you dismiss this great gun, you are kidding yourself. There are some very valid reasons to consider their use, not the least of which is simply the fun it can be.

Honestly, there are many points to weigh carefully over both of these shotguns. Let's go over each point of pro and con for the short-barrel, hammerless double and a '97 Winchester pump.

Double-Barrel Shotgun (pro)
- Initial cost may be lower than a '97.
- Fewer moving parts, less chance of breakage.
- Fewer malfunctions compared to the '97.
- Provides average shooters more reliability.
- Is easier to learn how to use than the '97.
- Can perform to high levels of competition with diligent training and modest skill.
- May be used with more success when shooting clay birds in a stage application.
- Has more versatility in class applications.

Double-Barrel Shotgun (con)
- Almost all will require an action job to perform well.
- Requires the shooter to handle and load two shells.
- Requires a lowering of the gun to reload each time.
- Requires the shooter to shift vision to round extraction and loading each time new rounds are needed for engagement.
- Cannot perform through windows or bars as the '97 can.
- Usually cannot perform as fast as the '97 with same skill use after first two rounds.
- Is not as easy to bring to bear from vertical staged positions due to the angle created with the action opened.

- May not use as many different configurations of hull design the '97 will.
- Has more recoil than the '97 (99% moe).
- Is prone to a premature closing of the action when lifted from vertical staging positions.

Okay, that's enough double barrel bashing. I do not want the reader to make a quick judgment without hearing some more about the double and the same pro and con list for the '97. Before I do that, I would offer this in defense of the double. I used one with success for a long time. I found that a practiced shooter with good skill levels can match or exceed 80 percent (or more) of all the '97 shooters. I still have my double and carry it as a back-up. Before I finally began using a '97 almost exclusively, I enjoyed the work of using them both during a match. I hope the reader understands that I have fond memories of using a double-barrel shotgun. They are great guns. So it is with the '97 as well. Here is the same list of pros and cons for the "pumpers" many of us are so keen on.

Winchester Model 1897 Shotgun (pro)
- Provides no less than six different loading techniques for left- and right-handed shooters.
- Offers single round loading when an odd number of targets are engaged.
- Offers the advantage of continued use during engagement while keeping the gun up at the shoulder.
- Offers a large breech opening for round insertion.
- Adapts to lateral movement and firing well and is superior in almost any application requiring moving and firing at the same time.

- Can be loaded with up to five rounds in the magazine when permitted by instruction.
- Allows easy installation of a choke tube system.
- Reduces overall recoil by the partial release of gases to the side of the gun at discharge.
- Allows the shooter to remain focused downrange at targets or other areas during many of the loading techniques used.
- Requires the least amount of loading movement for CAS stage engagements with shotgun applications.
- Is more suited for fast, reliable access when taken from a vertical or horizontal position of pre-staging.
- Feeds almost any hull design without problems.

Winchester Model 1897 Shotgun (con)

- Is many times more likely to break during engagement than the double.
- Is many times more likely to lock-up or jam than the double.
- Is 10 times as likely to induce a "user error" as the double is.
- Average lock-up or jam will cost many more seconds than that of a rare double lock-up.
- Causes more confusion to average shooters during problem moments.
- Is more likely to produce a "slam fire" misfire than the double.

- Needs more attention and maintenance than the double to remain in service.
- Has risen in cost to become 50 percent to 75 percent more expensive than the double.
- Will cost more to fix than the double, and is more likely to require repairs.

There are sure to be a few other pros and cons on both sides of this fence, but most issues are covered for the reader. Regardless of all the information pointed out about the '97 as to its negative points, I would not change today. It provides the quickest and most effective shotgun shooting I've ever found. Part of the challenge in using the '97 for me is that there is some risk. I like this exposed hammer "pumper" because it still rocks after more than a century after its introduction.

There is little left to speak of in terms of comparison of the two types of shotguns we have addressed. There is, however, a whole lot left in all applied tactics of engagement, and that's coming right now.

Photo 7.0B - *The Tortoise and the Hare? ... Too often seen this way, it could not be farther from the truth. (Two former World Champions, Tom Filbeck, a.k.a. "Tutler," SASS® #889 and Mike Schmacher, a.k.a. "Lucky Smucky," SASS® #160.)*

Photo 7.1A - *Four of the South's top shooters show their shotgun leather. From left to right: Dick Hudson, a.k.a. "Doc Dalton," SASS® #12437, Andrea Beale, a.k.a. "Dang It's Darlin'," SASS® #17502, Dan Beale, a.k.a. "Dang It Dan," SASS®#13202, and Randy Jackson, a.k.a. "Single Action Jackson," SASS® #16443 (winner of End Of Trail 2000 Shoot-Off).*

"Hell's Comin' ... And Me And My Double Is Comin' With It!"

There is not much sense in my telling the reader that any shotgun belt will bring the same results. Nor is there any doubt (in my experience) that positioning of any round holder (belt or snap-on style) can make or break the effectiveness of shotgun round retrieval with every single shooter. No matter from where a shooter starts a stage, or where the hands are, or at what point of the stage run the shotgun is called for, the loading process must start with round retrieval.

Quickly, let's just take a look at what is least effective when taking rounds off the body. Rounds kept in the vest pocket are about as effective as if they were in a case marked "break glass in case of emergency." Unless the shooter is brand new and has no belt yet, or simply does not care (and won't be reading this anyway) about shotgun engagement, this method is better left to the sod busters. Use it only when your own round holder cannot exceed the minimum number of required rounds for the stage by two or more. I hope you never need to go there.

The shooter in photo 7.1C is using a very common round holder made for use on the main gunbelt rig. Often called a "snap-on" round holder, the least effective of these carry only four rounds, and the best hold about 12. Taking it from those that are designed with targets that are "shoot until they go down." These are really quite fun stage engagements, all the other shooters will be excited and looking forward to their turn. This shooter may be wondering more about how in the hell he can get through this without trouble. Even if his round holder holds one round per target, he should be thinking about where to put his insurance rounds. When you see this poor comrade of arms next, extend yet another common courtesy often seen in CAS to him. That is, lend him your shotgun belt, or assist him by helping him find another. Now, you shooters who read this and have managed in one way or another to get through a similar stage with the less effective holders, don't get upset with me saying "Ah, I

Photo 7.1B - *James Hammons, a.k.a. "Jesse James," SASS® #1779, knows using a vest pocket for shotgun rounds will cost many seconds.*

the top, even if our shooter did not have to contend with his apparent culinary affluence (another commonly seen tactical condition in CAS), there are other factors to inhibit optimum use of the round holder seen here. One is the distance the hand must travel each time in order to bring rounds out and up to load. Another is the crowding of all this gear so close together. Still another disadvantage of this position is the limited ability to keep the height of the rounds adjusted in the loops or pouches.

Heaven forbid this shooter finds himself addressing one of the stages known as a shotgun assault stage with 12 or more rounds required, let alone

Photo 7.1C - *Jeffrey Sabatini, a.k.a. "Cash Dollar," SASS® #19514, could be much more ready than he is here.*

know how to work those stages." That's okay pards, I'm sure you can. But, you're thinking about the wrong things as you get ready to go. Instead of addressing the stage in terms of the best ways to be fast and furious (to the best of your ability), you will be thinking more about the rounds you must carry and be working on ways to not lose any.

Photo 7.1D shows the same shooter as did 7.1C, except the shooter in the first photo is no longer the greenhorn his appearance betrayed. Looking more like a seasoned hombre to be reckoned with, he even has his shotgun at the ready. And well he should. Check the distance he has eliminated for hand-to-round travel. He may even have been doing a little practicing on the side with some dummy rounds from this newly positioned shotgun belt. As a result, he may not have to look down when obtaining two new rounds from the loops. Keep looking and you'll notice a marked improvement in

how the rounds are better adjusted in the loops by their height. Not only will the rounds continue to remain adjusted as desired (no longer impaired from above by clothing or good eating), they are also set apart from the other equipment, namely the holsters, butts of revolvers, etc. He looks set, and will no doubt be much improved in his address this time. What else must this emerging gunman of today's Old West do to be as fast as he looks? To start with, let's help him get two rounds out of his belt and into the chambers of his double quickly, surely and accurately. None of this "oops" stuff 'round heah!

The techniques described to the reader are parts of the basic foundation of every great double shooter. You only

Photo 7.1D - *Already faster without even touching a round, Cash Dollar is ready to get his money's worth.*

Photo 7.1E - *Frank Holder, a.k.a. "Bull," SASS® #1081, is in the top one percent of shooters using double-barrel shotguns.*

think you're farther away from engaging with your shotgun at the speeds guys (and many gals) like this can. Well, think again amigo, a little bit of work and understanding will find you running in the same neighborhood. A little more work, with no more regularity than most use to water their garden each week, will find you can play in the same league. Okay, so maybe you won't be one of the starting line-up, but you can still make the team and be damn good!

Most, but not all, of the best shotgunners wear a full-loop, separate belt as their round holder. Some of these belts will have about 10 additional loops made for revolver or rifle reloads that may be encountered in main-stage or shoot-off events. This "full-looped" system seems to offer the best for competition and is often pretty close to being historically correct. The one I use was copied from a late 1890s Sears & Roebuck mail-order catalog. Canvas looped belts are also used, but don't quite seem to deliver the service many gun hands of today demand.

I find that being able to shift the belt around my waist to some degree is comfortable, yet I also want it to be tight enough not to shift by itself. I would warn shooters that a belt worn too loosely may shift upwards as the rounds are pulled out of the loops. Tightening it just one more notch will solve this problem. Even a separate belt can encounter or be subject to other pieces of the shooter's equipment. If you are at least aware of the potential conflicts that may occur during a run, you are much more likely to first adjust properly to reduce or eliminate those that you can. You are also just as likely to tread lightly around those you cannot.

Watch out for loose clothing, especially your shirt and (if you are wearing one) a vest. Make what efforts you can to tuck in any loose folds of your shirt (or blouse) that are bunching around the top of the shotgun belt. Make sure you know how the vest may interfere with round extraction, and that you are well prepared to deal with it. I am careful to notice the proximity of the butts or tops of both revolvers as they sit in their holsters as to the distance to where, exactly, the shotgun rounds are staged in the belt. This is for two reasons. One is that I do not want to upset in any way the rounds held in the loops by coming into contact with them while returning a revolver to leather (usually the cross-draw is my concern). If contact is made, there is a chance of the rounds being knocked out of the loops or driven down into the loops. The second reason is no less important and the more likely of the two reasons to cause a miscue. That is, I strive for the clean touch. Any contact made with an outside piece of equipment not part of each independent move is a distraction. This is especially true with shotgun round extraction. A shooter making each move with precision during a stage run has the clean touch. This is not easy, and at speed is accomplished rarely. Add no target misses and it may better be described as the "Midas" touch.

The shooter in photo 7.1E is in good form. There is obviously no loose clothing above or around the tops of those rounds. The suspenders are tight. Many a shooter has hooked a thumb or finger into a suspender that hung slightly open. Note, too, that no watch chain or fob is hanging in the vicinity of where his hand will work those rounds out of the loops. I can attest to having more than one skirmish with my watch and chain in this manner. I have lost more than just time on each occasion; once breaking my good watch, chain and heart in one fatal swoop. Since then (some several seasons back) I either take the watch and chain off to shoot, or slip the whole kit and caboodle into a safe pocket before I do.

Each shooter getting set to engage with a shotgun (regardless of which point during the engagement it is) should have a favorite side or area from which they will begin to extract shotgun rounds off of their belts. This favorite spot will hopefully become part of the shooter's automatic or sub-conscious tools. The rounds taken from this area are best removed with the least amount of outside interference of any kind (as covered above), including the loop leather from which they exit.

There are a couple of ways to assist the shooter in picking the rounds cleanly off or out of the shotgun belt's loops. The height of these rounds in any belt or carrier can be of importance. First off, shotgun rounds left too deeply in the loop can cause problems. Watch a shooter who is actually pushing the rounds upward from the bottom of the loops each time before they can be pulled out of the top. To reposition four rounds this way to then extract them easily costs three or more extra seconds. Pre-setting round height can improve the round extraction process tremendously. As I set up for a stage run, the final check I perform is shotgun round height. Doing this has become part of my overall focus and readiness. It is almost a procedure providing calmness before the storm of engagement.

This routine of pre-setting round height is different for each shooter, and understanding what is most effective, and why, will help you determine how you develop your own technique. Rounds coming out of the loops are taken more easily with the least amount of retention or friction. The farther inside the loop, the more retention and friction is felt during extraction, and the more effort is required by the shooter. The higher the round rests in the loop, the better. I set up for each situation differently. For example, if the stage starts with the shotgun and the very first move is to take out rounds for loading, I will set those rounds right at the top of the loop. Those rounds will fly up and out without the slightest feeling of having been in leather. This ability to "hang 'em high" diminishes quickly with any

Photo 7.1F - *These familiar shooters make shotgun round set-up a personal, final touch of their pre-stage readiness routine.*

WORKING THE SHOTGUNS OF COWBOY ACTION SHOOTING   141

movement. Noting this by each situation presented, I will attempt to set height accordingly for assured retention first, and ease of extraction second. The amount of movement, the speed and even distance traveled will all play a part in my decision(s). The goal here is to reduce as much as possible any time spent at the belt bringing the rounds to bear. The fastest, most effective shotgun work seen will appear as if the rounds came up and out of the loops by themselves. Contrary to some comments occasionally heard around the range, there is no magic involved.

Knowing where to start taking the rounds from and continuing in a predetermined direction best suited for your style is very important and should become instinctual. A shooter demonstrating this will not have to look where each round is as the hand goes precisely to where the rounds are located. The rounds are cleanly picked out of the loops in such a way that the loading or feeding to chambers or breech is not impeded. Many shooters find that by having one empty loop between each set of two rounds assists in making the clean purchase, further reducing the

chances of outside interference. Again, having no contact with any other piece of equipment (like the butts of the revolvers) when taking out those shotgun rounds is important.

The last bit of advice about the rounds carried during engagement is heard all the time at matches. Do not, however, take it lightly. The rule is to always carry at least two and more (often four rounds more) than the engagement calls for. Live rounds, once dropped, cannot be picked up from the ground while engaging. Stages are often seen littered with these unfired, hopefully extra, rounds many shooters dropped. There is also the sheepish look of a shooter who stops firing with shotgun targets still left to look at others and exclaim, "Dang, I'm outta ammo." By the way, when this happens to you, it's best just to keep on going and save the comments for later.

Now that we have the rounds out of the loops and up to the chambers of the doubles, we can complete the loading process. A little thought and practice has produced a skilled hold and positioning of the rounds to be guided and slipped into the shotgun's two chambers with speed and ease. Held correctly from the initial contact will help eliminate fumbling with and/or ending up with rounds being held at different or awkward angles that often end up having to be loaded one at a time.

Photo 7.1G - *Two of the most effective ways used to take rounds out of the loops.*

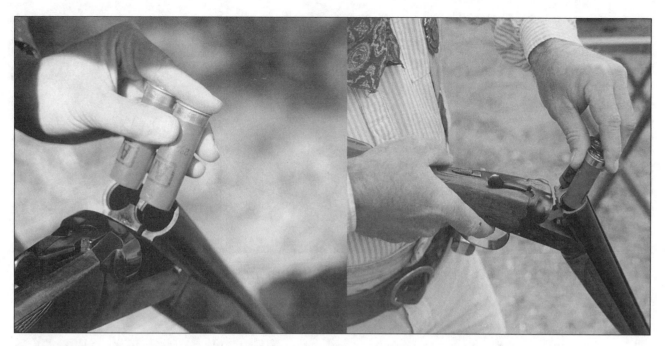

Photo 7.1H - *Here is the view at the chamber's mouth with both holding methods ready to tilt, drop and rock with the double.*

As seen in photo 7.1H, the rounds are brought to the chambers in such a way that they are held parallel with one another, even (or as close to even as you can get) at the ends and with enough space in between to be easily dropped in the chambers at the same time. Yes, I said "easily" and "dropped." This is the real secret behind quick loading of the double. It is important to understand that once the rounds are at the points shown in the photo (poised for insertion), the shooter need only to tilt and drop them as the ends begin their final descent into each chamber. Gravity performs this task far better than the shooter who seeks to assist their fall. Too often this assistance will become an act of force, one that will bring any number of difficulties. It will *not* make the rounds go in faster and it will keep the shooter from making the next move (closing the action and starting to raise the shotgun) at the correct moment. It is important for each shooter to determine the positioning of the open chambers and the entire shotgun in terms of where it will be brought for the loading process. The proximity of the shotgun to the shooter's body should be such that the chambers (and barrels) are even with or slightly below the height of the rounds

in the belt. The distance from the body should also be such that it does not impede the process in either direction, not too far away and not too close. The opened action with its chambers will most often be held pointing downwards. A shooter who takes the rounds out of the loops and raises the hand upward to find the shotguns chambers is most often increasing the distance and difficulty of the task at hand.

Two different positions for the fingers and hand are shown for the tilt, drop and rock method of getting the shotgun into quick action. Both of these ways in which to manipulate the rounds from loops to chambers allow the shooter to maintain control of alignment and distance in between the rounds for simultaneous insertion into the chambers. Photo 7.1I shows the entire process.

Either way of holding will bring the rounds up and tilted for alignment into the chambers as the first step shows. Step two shows the rounds just after they were dropped into the chambers,

Photo 7.1I - *Once the rounds are in the chambers, close the action and fire.*

and how the hand goes right to the fore stock to begin closing the action. Step three is the closing of the shotgun's action as it begins to ascend into the shooter's shoulder for final address and firing. Once a shooter has performed this maneuver in this manner, there will forever remain no doubt of the easy, smooth and effortless feeling it produces. Again, if there was any secret to this technique, it would be the "patience under fire" required to be accurate and deliberate in the entire delivery.

One problem for shooters to overcome as they finally decide to make better use of their doubles is learning to load with the weak hand. For a right-handed shooter, this means using the left hand to load. The reasons to learn to work the weak hand during this operation are worth the trouble to most shooters. If this alternating of strong to weak hand for loading two

into the double just won't do, let's look at Choctaw and his way of loading the double with the strong hand.

Coming directly from the cowboy port arms starting position, Choctaw first moves to remove two rounds with his strong hand. His weak hand holds the shotgun and posi-

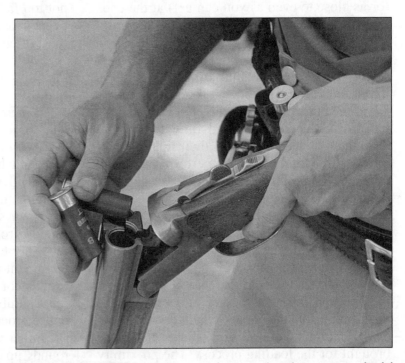

Photo 7.1J - *Trying to go too fast, or having a poor hold on the round, is prone to produce an end result that looks like this.*

rounds are held, with the middle finger doing the job of separating the two for clean insertion into the chambers.

There is no doubt that loading with the strong hand while controlling the double with the weak can be effective. Not only Choctaw, but China Camp also makes good use of the same general technique. Most shooters will not find this strong-hand method as reliable as the tilt and drop when using the weak hand to manipulate the rounds into the chambers. Either way, it will take practice and patience on the shooter's part to develop one technique or the other.

Most often, stage instructions involving movement to one or more positions for shotgun engagement do not allow shooters the challenge of loading and/or shooting during their flight. Thought to be unsafe, I

Photo 7.1K - *Choctaw demonstrating the first step of loading the double with the strong hand.*

tions the chambers for round insertion. Instead of having the chambers slightly lower (as positioned for a tilt-and-drop round insertion), notice how the shotgun is held higher, above the belt. This is because the rounds will be inserted into the chambers straight, perhaps even at a slight upward angle.

Step two of the process shows Choctaw presenting the two rounds to the open chambers for insertion. As stated, there are two ways in which the chambers may be angled to do this. One way is shown here, with the chambers angled slightly downward. Choctaw is quick to tell us that this angle can change to a more level, even slightly upward angle as the rounds go into the chambers. Notice the way in which the two

Photo 7.1L - *Choctaw aligning two rounds for insertion into this double's open chambers.*

Photo 7.1M - *With the ends of the two rounds started into the chambers, Choctaw will complete the insertion, move the strong hand to its primary position of control and close the action as he brings the shotgun to bear.*

will not argue the merits one way or another. I would point out that you may still expect to encounter these stages someday, somewhere, and that the variations presented by these "shotgun assault" stage designs are one heck of a lot of fun. I have participated in no less than 50 of these stages from time to time and have yet to see a shooter or designer present any more than the normal safety problems that must be addressed on all stages.

Perhaps it is the growth of cowboy action shooting and the introduction of more and more competitors along with a like amount of opinions that offers less opportunity for the shooters to engage in this manner. It is worth noting though, that the home range of SASS® (where the End of Trail World Championships of CAS takes place) will often host a

stage permitting all or part of this style of stage design. The SASS® home range club (Coto Cowboys) will often provide their monthly match shooters a great run of shooting and moving up the streets of "Hell Town." As it should be, and as it is, sometimes you can run and shoot, sometimes you cannot. Be able to address whatever problem is presented, that's part of the fun.

The cowboy action shooters using the double-barrel are faced with a more difficult task than those using the '97 when presented with the opportunity to insert rounds under movement. Again, it is the severe angle of the double along with the accuracy needed to effectively insert two rounds into the open

Photo 7.1N - *Danny Moore, a.k.a. "Sparks," SASS® #1412, seen breaking forward during the shotgun assault stage at Stampede 2000.*

Photo 7.1O - *Besides stage instructions, distance and speed can also affect a shooter's decision to load while moving. (This is Choctaw moving with his rifle.)*

chambers that caused these problems. The '97 (yet to be covered) presents its open breech and magazine at a more desired level, determined most often by what the shooter decides is best.

So, how does the double user cope under these conditions? How and what is the best way to go? The first (and most important) decision should be based upon the confidence and knowledge of your skills. Do not attempt what you are not fully confident of achieving safely and correctly. The second decision can be related to the overall scope of the match. How much will this really benefit (or cost) in terms of seconds, rank points or total time? Finally, how will it affect your overall performance? The answer to this one can be key. Even if you are well seasoned and able to perform these moves safely, could a fumble or bobble hurt your run more than if you simply omitted the move and stayed focused on completing a successful (albeit slower) stage run? Often the

answer is yes, but more often we want to "go for the gold" so to speak, and take the risks.

Since we are going for it here, part of the pre-stage planning should include the distance from one firing point to another. The primary goal of the shooter is to reach the next firing point as quickly as possible. Any action impeding this speed (like loading on the run) becomes of no value. If the distance is too short for the shooter to extract and load while moving at their top speed (as Choctaw in photo 7.1O), prior to arriving at a firing point, don't try. If the shooter is confident of successful completion within the distance presented, there is a technique that can assist the double shooter in loading those chambers at top speed while focusing on the path of travel.

One way to get the rounds into the chambers when moving is one at a time. Taking two from the loops, the shooter is *feeling* first one, then the other into each chamber at separate times. Do not forget that the first concern of the shooter must still be the speed and direction of travel as this loading process takes place.

At the very least, shooters should try to get those rounds out of the belt, into their hand, and have them ready for insertion into breech or chambers, if at all possible, during movement. I do know that most stages will not allow loading on the move, but I've yet to see one where a shooter could not at least get ready to do so.

If presented with a stage involving forward movement and shotgun targets that may be engaged while moving, most shooters will move only to gain target acquisition, and fire when in a stationary position. Loading while in motion is one thing. Shooting is yet another. Even when allowable, to truly be on the move while discharging a round (let alone hit the target) is one tough maneuver. If you see a shooter moving at top speed, loading and shooting without any slowing down as the targets are engaged … let me know. I have no knowledge of one so skilled. Even the most skilled will slow down and almost stop to insure target hits for all but the closest and largest targets offered.

Many good shooters will find that walking, loading and shooting can be done successfully. What these shooters are doing well is controlling the upper portion of the body while moving. The shoulders are probably even, and no bobbing or height change is seen by either the shoulders or head. Stay even and level from the waist up while moving and shooting. This technique is applicable to the use of all three categories of firearms used in the sport. Most often shooters will find that shooting while moving will involve a revolver and that lateral movement will be made in about one-step increments (five shots, five steps). Remember not to bob your head here, keep the shoulders even, and don't move so quickly that you get ahead of each target. Move only fast enough to engage as each target presents itself to your zero-degree heading of downrange.

Since it is the responsibility of each shooter to know his limits, it is important not to attempt engagement in such a manner that exceeds that level. I have more respect and admiration for those

Photo 7.1Q - *Dixie Bell (left) and Lusty Lil' sighting their shotguns.*

shooters I see engaging at a pace that reflects all the good aspects of technique rather than those who engage at breakneck speed, with poor technique and consequential results.

Many beginning (even some intermediate) shooters will find themselves missing shotgun targets too often. This is often due to poor sighting technique. Applicable to both the double and the '97, it is the apparent lack of a rear sight that seems to fool the shooters. All these shotguns have a real nice bead out front, but "where's the beef" in back? There is almost none. Hardly designed for precision shooting, a shotgun is built to allow the shooter to get the weapon up and sighted with speed that is paramount to hunting small animals with any success. Hence, there is little more than a slight curve on the top of each shotgun's breech. This curve (or notch) is the rear sight appendage. It is in the middle and will align directly to the front sight.

The shooter's alignment must be a direct line from the top of the breech (through the curve or notch) to the bead out front. The most common mistake is to see any portion of the barrel while putting the front sight on the target. The shot will invariably go high over the target, resulting in a frustrating miss. The shooter should see *no* part of the shotgun's barrel as they sight targets. As with all firearms, it is the *front* sight that should be in focus, both the rear sight and target are blurred. It is impossible for the human eye to focus on more than one precise point at a time. Try using the shotgun a few times as if it were a rifle. Take a little more time sighting and don't let the round go off until you see the front bead on the target. You should soon regain the confidence once lost with your shotgun.

Part of the problem for some shooters who see the barrel while sighting is how and where they bring the shotgun up to their head and into their shoulder. It is an absolute must for the shooter to understand and execute properly the act of bringing a long gun to bear. I say long gun because it is the same for either the shotgun or the rifle. The key

word for success is "up." The shooter *must* bring the long gun *up* to their head, *not* their head down to the gun. To feel just how awkward and wrong this is, take any of your long guns (safe and empty) and start at the cowboy port arms position. Now change hands so you will be taking it up to your weak or unnatural side. Unless you are practiced at this (which is a valid technique to learn) many shooters will experience a pronounced tendency to bring their head down and meet the firearm at some point to obtain the sights. Make sure your strong side has no tendency to do this at all, and practice keeping your head still while bringing the long gun up, into the shoulder and the cheek in one move. This is called a shooter's "sweet spot." Know where yours is and learn to hit it every time.

Shotgun work is much more pleasant when the shooter remembers the importance of keeping the shotgun tight, well into the shoulder during discharge.

Photo 7.1R - *"Correct sight alignment includes no portion of the shotgun's barrel."*

Photo 7.1S - *Ladies Traditional Class shooter Terri Holder, "Prairie Fire," SASS® #2066, shows how to bring the gun up to your head and into your shoulder…*

Photo 7.1T - *…and not your head down to the gun.*

To a new shooter and especially to the ladies (in my experience) the roar of a shotgun along with its promised recoil is intimidating. Beyond any recoil pads (on or off the shotgun), the new shooter who learns correctly and applies a forward posture along with holding the shotgun into the shoulder correctly, will soon find it is *he* who is intimidating with the shotgun. I would hope also that these shooters are taught to use the lighter shotgun rounds and also hope that no one, as a joke, hands a rookie shooter a shotgun with a high-brass or magnum load in it. This can cause a flinch that will take years to cure.

Another common miss to occur with the double barrel is the second shot. The double triggers of the shotgun are best operated when the index finger goes to the forward most trigger to engage the first shot (discharging the right barrel), and moves to the rear trigger immediately to fire the second shot (discharging the left barrel). The second shot is the one to watch out for. It soon becomes of relative ease (and fun) to let loose with that second shot real fast. BoBoom… This is fine for real big targets, top and bottom swingers close in, but beware of those knock-downs requiring good hits and the smaller targets often seen on tougher courses. Many shooters, who do not recognize these design challenges for what they are and adjust to them, will find the "slap" shot (the second round) missing too often.

Posture plays an important role in shooting any shotgun. The slightly aggressive stance, slightly forward or into the target area is one that will promote balance, act against forces that might rock the shooter back on the heels and provide a better all-around platform from which to engage. Setting up or planting the feet as desired, about shoulder's width apart, is a good place to start. Just as with any firearm, set up relative to the target radius to be addressed. The torso should be able to traverse whatever path the target order requires while remaining comfortable. Failure to do this can cause the body to twist, strain or otherwise become out of shape and cause misses or other problems. A baseball, tennis or other athletic stance showing readiness reveals a slight flexing or bending of the knees. This too will lend support to the overall posture from which to engage. All transitions, breaks and other moves during engagement are better executed and developed from a similar position of readiness. I do not mean that the shooter should look as though he is about to start a race at a track meet. I do mean looking sharp, flexible and ready to do business. The reader will see examples of what I mean throughout this book. Feel free to compare and develop your own effective stance or shooting posture.

The goal of the shooter after firing the double is to begin opening the action during the end of the recoil from the second shot. The action must be opened

before any other task can be performed. Stock springs on doubles are often pretty stiff, but an action job of merit will include the reduction of force required in order for the thumb to operate the spring lever. Be cautious in how much the spring is lightened. Too much and you'll need to start all over again.

The astute shooter will make the move to open the action an instinctual one, so automatic that it will occur at the end of the recoil without much thought at all. The quicker the action is opened, the quicker the empty hulls can exit the chambers. Whether the next step is to secure the shotgun, or to load two more rounds and engage again… get that action opened quickly.

Although a double-barrel's action does not lock up and refuse to open very often, there is reason to prepare for this occasional mishap. When this happens, most veterans will waste no time in

Photo 7.1U - *Three-time Ladies Champion of CAS, Island Girl, shows what needs to be done to the double a split-second after the second round is discharged.*

making a second effort with the use of one knee. Keeping the muzzle safely pointed downrange, the thumb will engage the release lever while the action is forced open on top of a knee or thigh. The shooter will have turned in such a way to execute this method safely. If the shotgun action refuses to open, a second attempt is made the same way. Failing to open after this, the shooter can almost always secure the firearm safely (even with the closed action) by stage instructions or handing it off to an attentive Range Officer close by. It is often the more powerful loads (providing greater hull expansion in the chambers) that are blamed for a problem like this.

Spit em' out, shuck them hulls, or dump those rounds. Whatever the term used, it means the same thing. The empty hulls within the shotgun's chambers are best removed by one or more techniques that *do not* require the use of the fingers. It's that single motion made by shooters sending the empties flying out of those chambers that is essential for success.

Besides developing an effective means to dump those hulls, a few other factors will play a part in your success. The low-base round is better suited for easy ejection than the high-base round. While thought by many shooters another cause for extraction problems, the ribbed hull round may not always be the culprit once so blamed.

Bojack, (president of the Cajon Cowboys Club in California) found that the expansion of these ribbed hulls after discharge and subsequent refusal to exit the chambers as desired may also stem from the crimp. This observation found that the rounds divided into six portions of crimp seem to exit with more difficulty then those divided with eight. Except for the obvious conclusion that more expansion occurs due to this type of hull design or crimp, I cannot answer what causes this. To a shooter, that is pretty much moot. To best *engineer* what I

Photo 7.1V - *Each shooter has the shotgun in a favorite position to shuck out the empty hulls.*

want to happen during engagement, and what will or won't work in the dirt, is the shooters' business. Again, it is the more powerful rounds that will expand more in the chambers of your double (and cause you grief) than the less powerful ones.

If it is not the rounds causing the empty hulls to stick, either the chambers need to be honed and polished, or they are too dirty. If it is the latter, consider carrying a long, soft brush to clean those chambers a few times during a match.

Final Notes On Match Shooting The Double

Many times the double-barrel shooter is faced with the prospect of working a double in and around various prop conditions. This seems to be more so at annual matches than during practice ones, chiefly due to the time, trouble, and good intentions of a club putting out their finest efforts to please the guest shooters. Engaging from positions requiring the use of the double through windows (with and without bars on them), over a bar, and even through a hole in the wall are some of the more difficult problems for many using the double. Any horizontal plane crossing perpendicular to the barrel pointed downrange much higher than the shooter's knees can come into play.

As it is with all firearms on any stage, simply recognizing the conditions and planning your engagement accordingly is most of the battle. This can require a little extra thought and solid footwork at times for the double user. It is the severe change of the double-barrel shotgun's downward angle when the action is opened that must be worked with here.

Avoid contact with any prop while loading and positioning yourself in such a way that loading, shooting, and loading again cleanly is the goal. It is a common sight to watch a double-barrel bang against a windowsill, a table or bar top, or one of many other props

that are below the barrel. These encounters between a shooter's double and a stage prop can happen at more than one point during the process. Listed below are some of the more common problems or faults to avoid, and then a list of what a shooter may do to avoid making mistakes.

These mishaps are what you *don't* want to happen on your stage run:

- **Right after round insertion, the shooter goes to close the action and engage … when bang, the barrels smack something on the way up. This can happen as the action is being closed, as well as after it is**

Photo 7.2A - *Approach these engagements with care and understanding.*

closed. The least problem is the interference, readjustment, and continued engagement.

- Making contact with a prop as the action is closing and the shotgun is rising has caused one or both of the fresh rounds to fall out of the chambers, requiring an additional reload.

- Loading and closing the action successfully, the shotgun is held in a "ready to fire" manner as it is raised up and brought to bear. On the way up, the barrel comes into contact with a portion of the prop in such a manner that it causes an accidental discharge. Premature discharge, or in this case a slam-fire of sorts, is most likely the worst consequence of poor planning.

- Upon discharging the second (final) round, the shotgun is lowered without thought of avoiding a portion of a prop below. The contact can occur as the action is coming open, after it is opened, or before it is open. This is another basic interference problem causing readjustment problems at best, and continued loss of focus at worst.

- Standing too close to the prop, the shooter does not move to lower the shotgun for insertion of new rounds into the chamber. Instead, the shotgun stays up while the shooter makes an attempt to insert rounds into chambers that are level with the shooter instead of at the usual angle to accept the rounds. The shooter keeps the shotgun up after expelling the empty hulls, brings two fresh rounds out and up, making the attempt to insert them. Insertion is difficult, but this effort is defeated further when (at this position) the front portion of the shotgun (forearm and barrel) is raised to close the action. The level and height of the chambers cause the fresh rounds to start a premature exiting of the chambers, and either fall out or block the action from closing.

- Any one of the problems encountered may cause the shooter to lose focus to such a degree that the reaction(s) to correct them cause serious mishandling of the shotgun. This mishandling results in a muzzle sweep or safety violation.

- Prop contact inhibits the shooter' s initial arrival or the start of the engagement from this kind of "double vs prop" collision.

- Prop contact inhibits the shooter's efforts to move cleanly to the next required task or position of the stage.

Any or all of these problems encountered by the unknowing or unprepared cowboy action shooter can happen. These are nasty little surprises but there is no need to let them get the better of you, even if one or more occurs after careful plans are laid to avoid them. As you read the next list, remember that rehearsing how you will react to a problem will assist greatly in overcoming it with the least amount of consequence. Win the battle of your "double vs props" encounter by:

- Recognizing the distance required between you, your shotgun, and the vertical/horizontal surfaces that represent potential problems, and making this part of your pre-stage address.

- Knowing beforehand the best starting point and/or where you will advance and be positioning for the best address. These pre-determined spots (exact or approximate) help insure none of the normal engagement actions you must execute with the double will be infringed upon by the prop(s).

- Planning exactly how you will withdraw the barrel and open the action through the opening in the same way other distance considerations are anticipated. The same is true for closing the action and bringing the shotgun up to bear.

- Checking the line of sight to targets best suited for your address at each position, and what (if any) part of the opening will give you the best opportunity through which to engage.

- Knowing the actions and moves that will permit clean removal of fired rounds and clean movement to the next stage position.

- Finally, to rehearse what may go wrong during your engagement and how best to react to each instance. (An example: If you find yourself too close, deciding to take one step or more away before the stage starts will allow you to react as planned during the actual run.)

A shooter's size can make a difference, being right or left-handed may also come into play. The importance lies mainly in understanding and planning accordingly.

Advance And Be Recognized With The Model '97 Shotgun

The Winchester Model '97 shotgun has to be the most successful of its kind produced in two centuries. First offered in June of 1897, over a million were manufactured up until 1958. Designed with an improved action, this shotgun would replace and silence the complaints made about the actions of the Winchester Model 1893.

The '97's combat worthiness was proven as early as the Spanish-American War, and kept pace with the fighting soldier for another 70 or so years. Later

Photo 7.3A - *High strung and a little temperamental at times, the '97 is still the greyhound of CAS shotguns. (Lefty Wright gets a little help from his friends.)*

in its illustrious career it was chosen rather than issued. That's a strong argument in favor of a gun that was used by more than a few troops fighting during the Vietnam War.

It is probably fair to say that never in the '97's long history has this shotgun been used at speeds approached by some of the cowboy action shooters today. As I stated before, going from open and empty with both hands on (or even off) the gun to loading and shooting four rounds accurately in 4.33 seconds is amazing. I would hazard a guess that few of today's state-of-the-art combat shotguns could match that feat as described. The '97's versatility seems only as limited in application as the shooter's imaginations. Though the Model '97 was never intended to be a single-shot, load-and-shoot firearm, the technique of engaging a cowboy combat scenario

by single loading into the open breech and firing is a natural act for both the shooter and the Model 1897.

After such a heralded introduction, and as the cowboy action shooting sport takes the Model '97 pump shotgun into its third century of promised virtue, let's take a closer look at *all* of what it brings the cowboy action shooter.

There is not a single experienced shooter I know who does not understand just how easily the '97 can revoke their license to engage in the wink of an eye. Sometimes the Model '97 will throw a tantrum when you least expect it. Accept that these little outbursts will be your fault 95 percent of the time. The other five percent will most likely be due to the strain of field performance and the equipment failure that is fair to expect along the way.

More often than not, the severity of the fine a shooter pays for mishandling the '97 can be as little as a few tenths of one second. But it goes up from there. The shooter who does not correct a problem quickly, or fails to recognize a problem that cannot be resolved during engagement, is in big trouble. Add the seconds of futile efforts to correct, plus those seconds for each missed target and each one not engaged, and you are indeed up that proverbial creek so familiar to us all. Safety penalties are not part of the mishandling referred to here, but the frantic efforts to correct a problem have caused more than one shooter to lapse in this, the foremost area of responsibility. Adding something like this to a fouled up '97 run would *really* put the icing on the cake.

As we look at many of the common handling errors, it is only fair to point out that the '97's value far outweighs any risk in the eyes of those who love them. Below are two lists of common errors. The first list is

Photo 7.3B - *Even the most skilled will experience the wrath of a '97 problem now and again. (Lou Taub, a.k.a. "Longshot," SASS® #747, having a tough time of it.)*

about some common shooter mistakes. The second is a list of possible equipment failures. Both lists will include the resulting problem(s) and some solutions after the fact. Don't forget that even the most minor problem for one shooter can become a major incident for another. It depends on well you know your '97. Knowing how to get past those little handling glitches is the key to success.

Common Shooter Errors
Resulting Problems / Probable Solutions

- Failure to check or notice cartridge guide riding high, obscuring open breech (remember that one?)

    Result: First round attempted to load in the open breech will be blocked.

    Solution: Apply rearward pressure (complete the opening action cycle) with the hand controlling the forearm of the '97. Failing that, physically move the cartridge guide back down into place.

- Accidental or premature closing of the breech action, with *no* live round inserted into breech or chamber.

    Result: Immediate reaction to attempt to reopen the action by racking the forearm to the rear, meeting only resistance. Subsequent attempts have the same effects.

    Breech or action release button on right side of case is pressed while shooter again attempts to re-rack the forearm rearward meeting same resistance and no success.

    Shooter lowers the exposed hammer with thumb, continuing futile attempts to re-open the action.

    Solution: Knowing *no* live round insertion has been made, the shooter simply engages the trigger, and the hammer *falls* on an empty chamber. The action will now respond instantly to the first attempt at re-opening the breech for loading.

Again, *no* live round insertion is made and the shooter engages the trigger. The release button may be used at this time if so desired, but is not usually mandatory for the slide action to commence.

- Single-style of loading one round into breech produces odd angle of round in breech (usually pointed downward, not fully lowered into the breech).

    Result: First attempt to close action (rack forearm forward) fails, and second attempt is required to complete task.

    Odd positioning of round in breech causes racking motion to throw live round out of breech completely.

    Solution: Shooter needs to change from *dropping* new round into breech gently to a direct, and more positive insertion force *into* breech with each round.

- After single-round insertion in breech, shooter does not rack forward with the forearm (slide or pump) to a true or fully closed action position.

    Result: Trigger will not engage hammer due to unclosed action or hammer falls but no discharge occurs due to unclosed action.

    Solution: Use as much forward force as needed to complete closing of action with forearm or slide. Attempt to engage again.

    Open action completely, insert new round into breech and re-close to engage.

    Check overall fit and length of '97 butt stock to individual shooter. Too long will promote this difficulty.

- While shooter is speed-loading he fumbles with rounds and inserts new round into breech backwards.

  Result: Action will not close, round stays in breech.

  Solution: Open action, use hand to extract round or open action and tilt open breech downward, shake shotgun until round falls out.

  Slow the hell down.

- Right-handed shooter finds '97 slipping down, out of shoulder each time the left hand is used to purchase and load new round from belt.

  Result: Shooter fumbles reloads, round to breech task is impeded reacquiring butt of '97 in shoulder for every shot, poor placement of butt in shoulder.

  Solution: Check and insure off-hand is correctly performing the continued rearward force or pressure needed to hold shotgun in shoulder.

  Try the slight lowering of '97 from level to a more comfortable angle to assist the weak hand and arm task of continued force rearward to keep butt in shoulder.

  Check to see if shooter is twisting the butt of '97 out of shoulder as he moves head to see the round extraction from belt. If so, train to extract rounds from belt without changing head position.

  Check the overall butt length and correct fit to individual shooter. If the butt of a '97 is too long it will cause difficulties for the weak hand and arm to exert enough rearward force for needed stability.

- Shooter has continued problems with accurate round insertion into breech. Misses breech completely or cannot insert rounds cleanly without apparent mishandling of some kind.

  Result: Additional round must be drawn from belt due to loading problems.

  Subsequent attempts to extract and insert new round into breech breeds more problems and errors.

  '97 starts to come out of shoulder as shooter is having these problems.

  Solution: Insure shooter is keeping '97 butt stock into shoulder during re-loading.

  Check overall fit of the '97's length to the individual shooter.

  Check method by which hand is holding new round, and how the attempt at round insertion is made into breech. Correct as needed to insert smoothly. (Shown later in photo 7.4A of this chapter.)

  Insure the shooter is picking up round with eye as it comes into view and watches round go into breech. This should be done until problem ceases.

- Shooter is using method of one round into breech (closing action) and one round into magazine and cannot improve, or is continually fumbling.

  Result: Continual lack of improved performance, multiple errors and problems resulting from same.

  Solution: Dry-fire training with dummy rounds.

  Check '97's loading platform stability. Is shooter pinning butt to body properly to allow first round and action rack forward without the '97 losing purchase as held by shooter?

  Try different methods of loading.

- Shooter experiences any or all problems associated with loading or shooting '97 after fourth reload, or as main match stage engagement continues during the day.

Result: Technique and effectiveness deteriorates because of shooter fatigue causing multiple problems with stage runs.

Solution: If shooter is using a long barrel '97 for engagement, fatigue may result from the over-exertion of one arm over time. Consider using a Model '97 with a shorter barrel.

- Action of the '97 is closing prematurely as shooter brings the gun up from a vertically staged position.

Result: One or more problems associated with empty, closed action '97.

Solution: More attention to point of contact on '97 to raise up. Initial contact made at the barrel rather than the forearm will prevent this.

- Knockdown targets missed with regularity, even with apparent good shot hit on targets.

Result: Missed targets, shooter frustration.

Solution: Try an increased dram equivalent and shot weight. One or 1-1/8 ounces of shot (heavy target load) may solve problem.

Check shot pattern on paper at different distances to insure shot is not overly spread due to open bore.

- Missing large percentage of all shotgun targets.

Result: Penalty seconds for misses, shooter frustration.

Solution: Check sighting technique, proper head and cheek placement, and finger position on trigger. Check for abnormal shooter flinch.

- Rounds do not easily feed into chamber of '97.

Result: Cannot complete action closure with new round in chamber.

Solution: If rounds are used-hull reloads, check crimp, etc. If problem is still evident, seek advice from gunsmith.

- Empty hull does not exit breech after action is opened.

Result: Empty hull is hung up either all the way in action, or hangs out part of the way, causing shooter to take steps to remove empty hull prior to next reload.

Solution: Time of engagement correction requires hand to extract empty hull or tilting breech downwards and shaking unwanted hull out.

Check that the technique of opening the action (rearward slide motion) is done with enough force to fully expel the empty hull.

Check technique area of where shotgun's breech angle is at during slide action to open and eject round. If the shooter is tilting the breech (shotgun) upward (skyward) during this move to open and eject, the round will often not be easily ejected. Keep breech level or tilt slightly downward during rearward slide action.

- '97 shooter slam fires rounds at exact moment action is brought to the fully closed position with new round in chamber.

Result: Missed target(s), focus interrupted, possible safety violation incurred.

Solution: Shooter is not removing finger from trigger as slide action closure occurs. Train to be aware of this problem and correct it.

Hopefully the reader may refer to the above for all but the most uncommon ailments of shooter errors associated with the Model 1897 shotgun. Below is a list of the more commonly experienced component failures of the 97 in CAS match play.

**More Common Failures
Of The Model 1897 Shotgun**

- Empty hulls will not eject properly and this does not seem to be an operator error.

    Result: Each round is taken out of breech by hand or is shaken out by the shooter.

    Solution: Check tail of ejector spring inside breech action, insure that it has not broken off.

    Ejector spring replacement should be carried in the field. Inexpensive, it is a one-screw, simple operation to repair. The ejector spring is located on the upper part of the breech, on the opposite side of the breech opening. One screw holds the small, flat piece of metal on a plate. The tail is inside the breech.

    Check the extractor inside the breech action to insure it has not broken. This usually requires gunsmithing services to replace and repair. The extractor is located on the forward end of the bolt, closest to the open side of breech. You can see it with the action halfway open.

- Action will not close or open easily, or at all. Rounds are not thought to be the problem.

    Solution: Check for a loose action slide hook screw, located forward of the cartridge guide with the action in closed position.

- Model 1897 shotgun's slide action not functioning well or as easily as operator knows to be normal.

    Result: Slide is dry. An absence of oil lubrication is evident.

    Solution: Apply gun oil to upper and lower parts of the slide, around edge of both ends of forearm, and work action several times back and forth.

- Action is sticky, hard to operate smoothly.

    Solution: Action gummed up and dirty. It requires cleaning and correct lubrication.

    Actions vary insofar as the amount of lubricant needed for peak performance. One action may prefer a more dry condition, another may require more lubricant to work well. Determine what is the correct amount of lubrication for your '97.

The items listed above are the most common equipment failures seen during match competition.

As I said, problems with the Model 1897 shotguns in cowboy action shooting are about 95 percent shooter error, and five percent equipment failure. Now let's get into the field techniques of loading and shooting the '97 in match play.

Both shooters in photo 7.4A are right-handed and have just begun two methods of loading the Model 1897. The shooter on the right is using the more common method of extracting, loading, and firing each round separately. This is the right-handed shooter's most reliable technique, one that should be learned prior to attempting the more advanced systems. Part of the reason I recommend this is to build a strong basic foundation that will allow a shooter to choose, adapt, and even reassign methods learned for a myriad of conditions. Not only may certain field conditions be a factor at times, there is also your skill level to consider. Perhaps you are not quite as sharp at the moment and want to be confident of success by using the more reliable method. Perhaps on a previous

Photo 7.4A - *The shooter on the right is executing the start of single-round extraction and loading with the strong hand. The shooter on the left is initiating the weak-hand, double-round, over-the-top feed method of loading one round and palming the other. (Magnum Quigley and Madre Kid.)*

stage you had some problems attempting to engage with multiple-round extraction methods. Instead of continuing with a technique presenting problems, you can choose to go back to an easier (yet still effective) method you are very comfortable with. The successful shooter of a Model '97 will exhibit versatility in both technique and judgment.

The three basic steps to single-loading the '97 as a right-handed shooter are shown in photos 7.4A and 7.4B. Step one is taking one round from the belt with the weak hand, preparing to insert it into the breech. Step two is the insertion of that round. Step three is closing the slide action while the strong hand moves to

primary control position to discharge the round. To repeat, open the slide action (expel empty hull) and begin again.

I think it important to note here that this basic, yet reliable method is capable of great speed and success. Many of the sport's more notable shooters have used this exact way of working the Model '97. Tom Filbeck, a.k.a. "Tutler," uses this method and, as he is seen in the video *Top Shooter's Guide to Cowboy Action Shooting Part I, Approach and Technique*, can rival the speed of any other method. Tutler used this method in 1998 to win the SASS® World Champi-

Photo 7.4B - *On the left, Earl Stafford, a.k.a. "Ignatious Guns," SASS® #16097, and Dane Price, a.k.a. "Lefty Wright," SASS® #9157, show the basic right-handed single-loading steps two and three for a Model '97.*

onships of Cowboy Action Shooting at End Of Trail. It is only sensible that any right-handed shooter become proficient with this method before any other more advanced techniques are attempted.

To complete the two-round, over-the-top method of loading, let's start again. As photo 7.4A shows, the right-handed shooter uses the weak hand to take and feed rounds into the '97's breech. Photo 7.4C (bottom shooter) shows the second step as the weak hand goes over the right side of the '97 and feeds *one* round into the open breech from the top. The middle shooter in photo 7.4C shows step two as he continues to hold (or palm) the second round in the weak hand, and closes the slide

action of the '97. The shooter at the top of photo 7.4C shows step three of the process by opening the breech and inserting the second round into the open breech in the same manner as before. Upon insertion, the weak hand goes directly to the slide action, closes and discharges this round. By opening the action, the process is repeated as needed.

This two-round, single-loading technique can be exceptionally quick. The perceived advantage is the reduced number of times the shooter must extract rounds from the belt, and the reduction of time that this brings to the stage run. The shooter must realize that to be successful at this, there can be little or no bobbling of the rounds or other glitches. If more than one is dropped, or the weak hand does not close the slide action completely while palm-

Photo 7.4C - *From bottom to top: steps two, three, and four of loading two rounds over the top are shown by Madre Kid, Lefty Longridge, and Magnum Quigley.*

ing another round, or any other miscue causes additional actions or moves that must be corrected, the advantage turns into a disadvantage. Most shooters will find they can perform this technique with a little work but should not forget that they will be faster and more efficient with an easier one.

The reader should consider that to be effective while using this technique two other factors most come into play. The Model '97 must stay up in the shoulder while the strong hand is maintaining complete control of the firearm, while the weak hand is taking rounds off the belt and feeding these rounds over the top of and into the breech. This is done with the strong hand supporting from its primary firing position, and requires some strength to do cor-

rectly. If the shotgun is lowered from the ready (or level) position, the technique is lost. Model '97s with a longer barrel become the most difficult to wield like this because of the added weight. A short-barrel '97 is the one to use here.

Worth knowing about: photo 7.4D shows one more way in which some right-handed shooters bring the two-round hold, single-loading technique to the '97's workplace. Obtaining optimum support with the weak hand and arm, the shooter takes two rounds out of the belt, and feeds one into the open breech while keeping the other in the strong hand as it goes to the primary firing position. Upon discharge and re-opening of the breech,

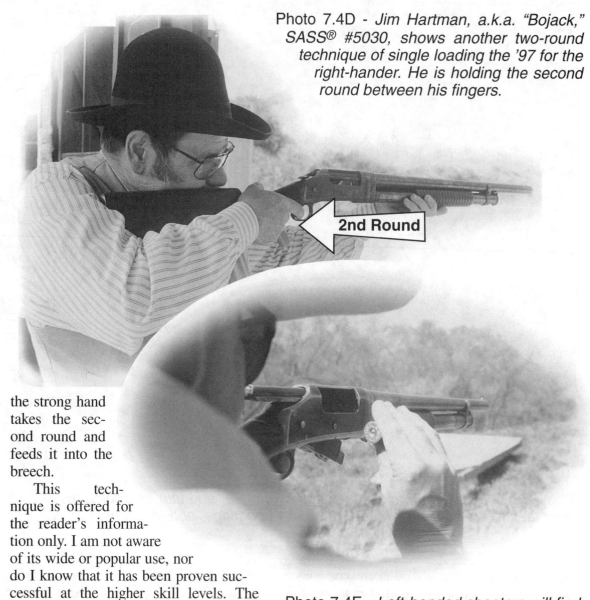

Photo 7.4D - *Jim Hartman, a.k.a. "Bojack," SASS® #5030, shows another two-round technique of single loading the '97 for the right-hander. He is holding the second round between his fingers.*

2nd Round

the strong hand takes the second round and feeds it into the breech.

This technique is offered for the reader's information only. I am not aware of its wide or popular use, nor do I know that it has been proven successful at the higher skill levels. The shooter must be able to perform some tricky round manipulation with the strong hand, and do so while engaging the trigger and maintaining control of the firearm. To the author this does not appear as one of the best moves with the '97, but that does not invalidate that some shooters may find it can work for them.

While any of the techniques requiring a shooter's weak hand and arm (the supporting members) to come off the slide action of the '97 in order to extract and feed rounds may not be easy, the left-handed shooter may be the first to decide in favor of learning one's use. As the

Photo 7.4E - *Left-handed shooters will find that the open breech of the '97 on their strong side is easy to see.*

photo 7.4E reveals, the open breech of a '97, as seen by the left-hander, looms as one big target, naturally positioned for a maneuver of this kind.

Looking at photo 7.4F, the steps for single-loading the '97 by a left-handed shooter do not change whether one or two rounds are taken from the belt. With step one not shown (the initial round extraction from belt), steps two, three, and four are seen demonstrated by three different shooters.

Photo 7.4F - *Here are some single-loading techniques holding one or two rounds for the left-handed shooter (steps two, three and four seen from top to bottom).*

While supporting the short-barrel '97 with the strong hand and arm, step two shows this shooter presenting the first round into the open breech with the weak hand. Step three shows another shooter with the closed action and in position from which to engage the trigger. The last shooter in the photo shows step four as it occurs for a two-round, single-loading technique. The second round is shown being inserted into the breech right after the slide action has re-opened the breech. If the shooter was using the single-round and single-load method, the action would be open as seen but the hand would go back to the belt to retrieve another round for insertion instead of a palmed second-round insertion as depicted here.

Regardless of which particular technique is being used by either a right- or left-handed shooter, the handling of more than one round in the hand is a critical part of the single-load and fire operation of the '97. My personal method of single-round loading of the '97 is that of the left-handed shooter as mentioned above. Most often I take two rounds off the belt when using the multiple rounds in hand, sin-gle-load-and-shoot technique. I am not alone in having taken up to four rounds off the belt at the same time and proceed to load one, close the action and engage the trigger while holding the unfired rounds in my weak hand. The reliability factor of this many rounds being successfully manipulated is very low. Three rounds are manageable, but do offer a significant rise in the percentages of failure at one point of the maneuver or another. I believe that most of the top shooters in their respective classes have found that a maximum of two rounds taken at one time provides them with the best overall performance in any of these applications with the '97.

As the close-up of the initial contact made by the weak hand of either a left- or right-handed shooter to extract rounds off the belt shows in photo 7.4G, the correct technique for multiple rounds in hand starts here. The rounds must be taken out and held in such a manner that will offer quick, accurate

Photo 7.4G - *Holding a second round, or palming of the second round prior to inserting it into the breech, requires the shooter's attention.*

Photo 7.4H - *The hand is at a natural angle for each round insertion into the open breech of these '97s.*

insertion for each round taken off the belt. Taking these two rounds off the belt by this method does allow the hand to insert the first of the two at a natural angle.

Shooters will pinch, throw, slip, roll or slap these rounds off their fingers into the open breech of the Model '97. Each has developed a way that will accurately deliver one round into the breech, and will allow correct retention of any others as the hand turns over and closes the slide action forward for engagement.

Shooters will find that working the slide action to either close or open the '97's breech with a hand having a less than normal purchase on the forearm or pump requires additional force and concentration. Attention must also be given during these moves that will not change the position and/or hinder the subsequent insertion of any palmed rounds.

Load-Two, Shoot-Two Techniques For The '97

While many adaptations will vary today in loading the first round into the open breech, closing the action and inserting

Photo 7.4I and J - *Closing or re-opening the Model '97's slide action should not be impeded by the presence of the palmed round as it is held by the weak hand, nor should the round's position for re-insertion be hindered in any way.*

the second round into the '97's magazine before firing the two rounds, there is only one other technique besides the original method that reflects a noteworthy character change. It probably is best to note here that to the author's knowledge, there is no viable system of the load-two, shoot-two techniques for the left-handed shooter. There are, however, ways to do this, and any left-handed shooter with the desire to figure one out will surely do so.

Credited to both Doc Holiday and "The Durango Kid" (Larry Cohen, SASS® #8), this method is primarily for a right-handed shooter. Photo 7.5A shows Doc Holiday as he begins

the maneuver. Taking two rounds from his shotgun belt, he will insert the first round into the open breech of a '97 (photo 7.5B). It is important to note the way the Model '97 is secured by pinning the butt stock between his body and a portion of his right arm. The technique depends on this anchoring of the shotgun to prevent unwanted motion when the shooter racks forward the slide action to close the breech after the first round is inserted.

As photo 7.5C reveals, the remaining two steps after the first round has been put through the '97's breech open-

Photo 7.5A - *Brett Meinhart, a.k.a. "Doc Holiday," SASS® #419, shows step one of double loading into both breech and magazine of the Model 97 shotgun.*

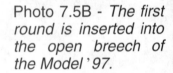

Photo 7.5B - *The first round is inserted into the open breech of the Model '97.*

Photo 7.5C - *After inserting the first round into the breech and closing the action, the second round is seen going into the '97's tube magazine.*

Photo 7.5D - *Completing the loading of two rounds, the shotgun comes up and is ready to fire the first of two rounds.*

ing is to then close the breech and insert the second round into the magazine. All that is left for the shooter to do at that point is to bring the shotgun to bear and engage with the two rounds. The '97 would then be taken to the initial point as shown in photo 7.5A, and the process repeated.

The real basis of change in the technique shown in photos 7.5E is twofold. The Model 1897 is held away from the body with the strong hand controlling the angle and acting as the anchor point when needed. The weak hand loads the first round, and palms the second round as the slide action closes the breech. The instant the breech is closed, the weak hand will go back to the magazine feeding tube and insert the second round.

While the following opinion will not be held by some, I am in the vast majority of experienced cowboy action shooters who feel the double-load and shoot technique cannot match the double-round, single-load and shoot

technique when shooters of equal skill are pitted against one another.

I would be doing an injustice to some other top shooters in the sport (such as San Juan, SASS® #1776) if I did not specify that some of them use a double-load and shoot technique at *different, chosen* points of engagement. While this is highly effective for *them,* the other 98 percent of the shooters will find it is the double- or single-round method of load one, shoot one that is far and away faster and more reliable. This especially applies to those shooters who have attained a reasonable measure of skill with the load-two, shoot-two techniques. The last comment worth mentioning about this topic is this: If the shooter finds it more *fun* to engage with one technique over another, then the obvious choice is have the most *fun* possible.

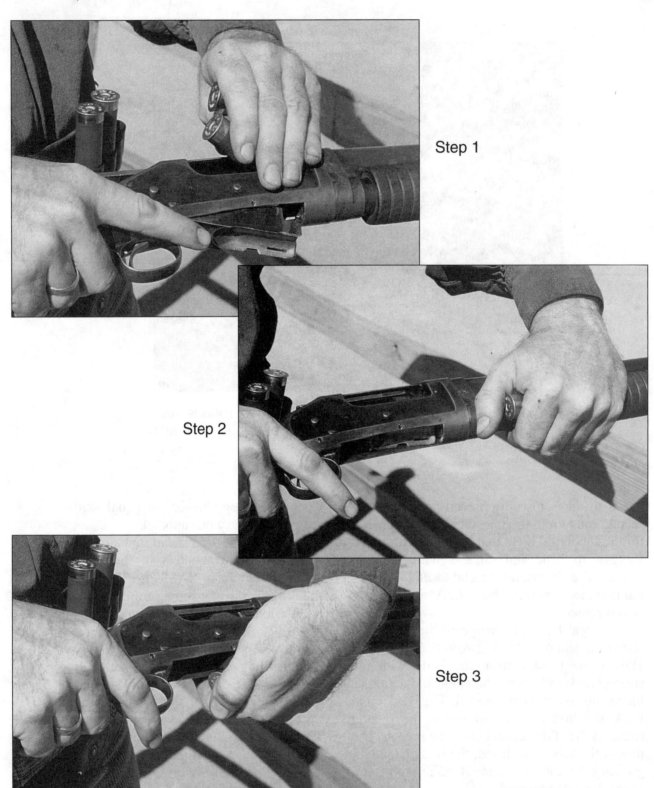

Step 1

Step 2

Step 3

Photo 7.5E - *Another method shows the Model '97 held by the strong hand as the weak hand does the other steps of the "load-two, shoot-two" technique.*

More On The Shotguns

Approaching a '97 staged flat or in a horizontal position which permits the shooter to raise from about waist level provides some options that should not be overlooked. This is mainly a right-handed shooter's option, as the natural pick-up points for a '97 lying horizontally will almost always be one where the open breech is facing upwards. Left-handed pick-up is usually done with the '97's open breech facing down.

The choice is whether or not to place the first round into the open breech just as the initial contact is made with the '97, but prior to the act of raising the shotgun. There are two schools of thought about this subject, and I would recommend that a shooter try both ways before deciding which is best.

Looking at the decision to make the insertion of a round at precisely the moment of contact offers a totally stable shotgun, and one with an open, motionless breech to feed into. The consideration is that there will still occur a space in time when the shooter is loading, and *not* raising the shotgun. This moment of time is shorter for some shooters than it is for others. It does, however, provide a nice, big target that is not moving.

The other side of the coin advocates that the shooter (with round or rounds in hand) makes the approach and with no hesitation, raises the shotgun up. The loading of the first round into the breech is made either *during* this move, or when the shotgun is up in the shoulder and presented to engage targets. The

Photo 7.6A - *Approaching with rounds in hand, is the shooter better off to load one before or after the '97 is up and off the table?*

Photos 7.6B and 7.6C- *Bob Silverman, a.k.a. " Marshal Law," SASS® #854, shows one way to cock each hammer while another action is being performed during the loading process of an exposed hammer shotgun.*

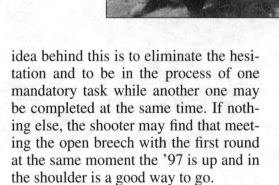

idea behind this is to eliminate the hesitation and to be in the process of one mandatory task while another one may be completed at the same time. If nothing else, the shooter may find that meeting the open breech with the first round at the same moment the '97 is up and in the shoulder is a good way to go.

The external-hammer shotguns need not be handled any more slowly than those with internal hammers in CAS. Many shooters have learned to cock those hammers during the loading process in a way that no extra time results from doing so.

Besides starting with both hammers cocked when the shotgun is empty and has a broken or open action, the shooter can learn the other clever ways in which each hammer is cocked while loading and closing for renewed engagement takes place. An action job here will include the "lightening up" of the springs that allow the cocking of each external hammer to be done with relative ease.

One common method of cocking each hammer separately in photos 7.6B and 7.6C shows the shooter after firing the last of two rounds, breaking open the action and expelling the empty hulls as normally done. What is shown, is that as the weak hand moves to extract two new rounds from the belt, the *thumb of the strong hand controlling the shotgun* will be seen cocking the hammer located towards the *outside* of the shooter as the other action takes place.

The loading process continues with the weak hand using a tilt-and-drop insertion technique into the double's chambers. As the new rounds are in the chambers, the weak hand goes to the forearm of the double to assist closing and begins to raise the shotgun up for engagement. It is during this time of *closing and raising the action* that the strong hand thumb will again be used to cock the second hammer.

Practice prevails here. The need for dry-fire practice with dummy rounds is paramount to obtaining desired results. It is, however, quite a sight to watch a practiced shooter use this technique with the external hammer shotguns, one that I hope you will soon be doing yourself.

This chapter on shotguns is perhaps best closed with the conviction of the author that more time is lost on stage runs by ineffective shotgun work than any other firearm. Cowboy action shooters know that to miss a shotgun target is a cardinal sin in the game, as the targets are largely seen as the easiest to address. This notion leads to mischief and missed targets as a result. The stage traps laid by the clever designer will temp the shooter, and more often will lull the shooter into a false sense of security. Not recognizing the size, distance, or need to place shot impact for knockdown or show color targets have long been some of the causes for a cowboy's lamenting over these shotgun misses.

Even greater than missed shotgun targets are the mishandling or poor techniques of loading or operating the shotguns, and the time loss this brings the shooter. There is more movement, more repeated manipulation, and more chances to bring about failure during shotgun engagements than *any other of the firearms used!* Sure, many of us say shotgun work is a "no-brainer" factor but only in the sense that to perform correctly with one or the other is taken for granted.

Chapter 8

ENGAGING WITH THE MAIN STAGE RIFLES AND CARBINES

Understanding The Differences

Even after the first lever gun for main stage engagement has been purchased, many a cowboy action shooter has (for one or more reasons) decided a change must be made. This is often a dilemma in the mind of a shooter who feels a change in the main match lever gun is needed, but does not fully understand or anticipate which carbine or rifle will provide the best field performance, and why.

There are some basic characteristics of the most popular lever guns used in the sport today to consider before making another choice (or guess). These differences are often subtle and are related not only to a particular characteristic

Photo 8.0A - *Here, mine is best. No! Mine is. No, no, this is really the best one.*

of one gun or another, but also to a shooter's style. It is *you* who is the most important part of the equation. It is how a shooter strokes or levers these firearms; how one reacts to a particular barrel length or the weight of a lever gun that counts. The shooter's natural moves and personal tendencies play a big part in whether one lever gun or another is right for him.

Understanding there are two parts to this puzzle leaves the shooter one more avenue to consider before changing the main match lever gun. That would be *not* to change before all of the possibilities are considered, some field observations are conducted, and (if possible) a field test or two is performed. The information that follows is based on the combined field observations, personal field performances, and the resulting opinions of many of the sport's most experienced shooters. My own experience includes having owned and tried just about every main match lever gun that could be called common to CAS competition. I will also relate my experiences and conclusions after two separate tries with the less common Colt Lightning (a pump-action CAS rifle).

After the reader has digested the information presented here there may well be a chance for reconciliation between the shooter and his lever gun. If not, at least there will be a good chance that the next decision to purchase will be a more informed one, and ultimately be more successful.

The three most commonly used styles of lever guns in the sport today are the Winchester Model 1892, Marlin's Model 1894 Cowboy and the earlier model carbines, and the Winchester Model 1873 (whose elevator actions include the 1866 Yellowboy). While each group here does have original, older models that fall within it, mostly it is the reproductions and the later Winchester and Marlin models that are specifically addressed.

It should be made clear to the reader that these lever guns are all excellent firearms, each of which can be attached to one or more of the sport's top competitors at one time or another. Each of the three groups has a different nomenclature (within the basic lever-action), and, therefore, is credited with different attributes or

Photo 8.0B - *The lever gun can create one of the sport's more common love/hate relationships.*

characteristics. Action jobs or "slick-ups" performed by gunsmiths may or may not affect some of what is to be described, and may or may not improve or correct some of the problems a shooter may encounter.

The manner in which a shooter handles some of these lever guns during the speed levering and firing of rounds in main stage engagement is critical. There are shooters who use a certain "finesse" or lighter touch during levering than others. These are the shooters who will find the Model 1892 less troublesome than those who are perhaps heavier handed in the levering motions. The Model 1873 and 1866 are known to be more forgiving and less apt to act finicky with their link and toggle elevator actions. The Marlin '94 needs to be worked with a certain amount of finesse as well.

So, it boils down to the individual shooter and to which of these lever-actions they seem best suited. A shooter can develop and adapt their style to some extent, and the lever-actions of these firearms can also be worked on to some extent as well. It's not easy to discern, nor is it easy to put it in terms that will not upset or anger some manufacturers. Be this as it may, an attempt to provide the reader with as much knowledge and understanding of these lever guns is necessary.

These observations of field performance take for granted that the ammunition used is conducive in terms of projectile configuration, length of cartridge and other similar considerations. Literally, on a "gun-to-gun" basis, the .38 Special cartridge may or may not work as desired. Two possible solutions include additional gunsmithing work, or using the longer case of the .357 Magnum. Remember too, that the operating speed of these lever guns during engagement is a factor not to be overlooked.

Winchester Model 1892
(Reproductions Or Winchester Originals)

The ramp delivery system from magazine to breech to chamber may prove sensitive at times for some shooters. Look at the shooter's lever (or stroke) technique if problems are occurring. If no operator error can be discerned and problems of light taps or live round ejection do not appear to be from short-stroking the lever-action, consult a qualified gunsmith for possible solutions. This rifle

Photo 8.0C - *Levering when the action is tilted to one side or the other may produce feeding problems with the Marlins.*

may also experience problems due to over-working the action at times of extreme, high-speed levering.

Marlin
(1894 Cowboy And earlier Carbines)

The ramp delivery system and side ejection may prove sensitive for some shooters. Look at lever or stroke technique as with the Model '92. This rifle may also be inclined to have feeding problems if the racking or levering action is done when the firearm is not in a level position (photo 8.0C). The Marlin may also experience problems by over-working the action known to occur at times of extreme, high-speed levering. If no operator error can be attributed to problems, consult a gunsmith for possible mechanical solutions.

Model 1873 And 1866
(Reproductions And Winchester
Factory Models)

The elevator delivery systems may feel clunky to some shooters, or may seem to require a longer lever stroke when compared to a ramp delivery system. A high degree of feeding reliability is given to the elevator action, credited with being far less sensitive to angle presentations and other problems associated with the ramp delivery systems. Action problems are usually correctable with competent gunsmith work. These are considered by many to be the workhorse lever guns of cowboy action shooting.

Note: The Winchester Model 1894 has not been known for outstanding success in cowboy action shooting, but will be seen on the range. The "drop down" action of this ramp delivery system has not performed as well as the other models at the same speed of engagement. Action work has not (for the vast majority) provided a solution. Not to be discarded totally, the Model '94 Winchester is still a viable lever gun for some in the sport.

Only originals, no reproductions, of the Colt Lightning pump-action are available at the time this information is written. These carbines and rifles are seen used by shooters from time to time.

Well-maintained versions are known to provide reasonable success and reliability up to a point. The Lightning is expensive and somewhat unusual. Normal action work and repair requires more than average expertise on the part of the gunsmith. Versions that have been highly modified for competition have proven to lose effectiveness when the pump-actions are used at the same lever-action engagement speeds attained by the fastest group of shooters. One model that I gave considerable time and effort towards developing was a 38-40 carbine. This carbine was action slick and the bottleneck cartridges of the 38-40 caliber were also part of "the right stuff." Ultimately, what happened was that the pump action of the Colt Lightning could not keep up. It proved to be that the lever-action could be worked faster than the pump-action without failure at top speed. A known tendency for stovepiping rounds during main stage use is the common ailment for the Lightning. While this was indeed the problem we had, understand that this particular carbine would have worked for all but the top five percent or 10 percent of shooters. Our modified version performed flawlessly up to 85 percent of normal match speed in varying conditions of target address. Once considered the possible "ultimate" long gun for cowboy action shooting, our efforts found that in the end, the right shooter with the right lever-action is significantly faster and more reliable.

Now that many of the attributes of those lever guns are out in the open, let's look at some of the shooter's operating techniques that may induce problems and influence those actions which are more sensitive than others. Again, remember that this sport finds these firearms performing at a higher rate of fire than ever before. The top shooters in the sport will routinely fire 10 rounds out of a lever-action rifle in less than five seconds when presented with the appropri-

Photo 8.1A - *Ralph Fendley, a.k.a. "Cliffhanger," SASS® #3720, racks the lever as the gun is on the way up to the shoulder. (Mike Wallace, a.k.a. "Mustang Mike," SASS® #4105, looks on.)*

Photo 8.1A - *Champion shooters Jim Lincoln (EOT Senior Class Champion), a.k.a. "Jim Bowie," SASS® #4775, (on left) and Danny Moore, a.k.a. "Sparks," SASS® #1412, seen racking the lever from positions some may find more stable.*

ate target size and distance. Average main match target size and distance will produce average times of around seven to 10 seconds for a 10-round lever gun engagement.

This chapter will provide instruction for effective technique(s) of lever gun application later on. The following are specific things that may cause problems to occur in the aforementioned category of lever-action firearms.

Common Operator Errors To Recognize And Correct

Operator Error #1

Levering the action prior to setting the firearm firmly in the shoulder may be the cause of repeated short-stroking related problems. The motion of levering made at this time (while the firearm is moving upwards) may not be obtaining the full or complete cycling action because of a lack of a stable platform. While commonly done without problems by many shooters, some may find that the final position of ready to engage (that is when the gun is up and held firmly into the shoulder) will provide an excellent, stable platform. This position may assist the shooter to more often successfully complete the cycle of working the action, and possibly eliminate some of the problems attributed to short-stroking. There is also a possibility that the shooter may not have to change the technique, if after the realization of *why* this is occurring he develops a more positive motion to complete the levering cycle.

Operator Error #2

Levering (or racking) the action quickly but not completing the full cycle of delivery to move the round into the chamber or fully cock the hammer. If the shooter is not extending the lever during the racking action to the fullest forward position, short-stroking by this manner can cause one of two problems. Either no round was cycled into the chamber or, while a new round did cycle in, the bolt was not successful in fully cocking the hammer. The hammer will often look as if all is well, but when the shooter engages the trigger nothing will happen. The other problem is to react correctly. Often, a new round is in the cham-

ber and a shooter will be seen bringing back the hammer with their thumb and discharging the round. More often a shooter will be seen making an automatic re-racking motion which will eject any live round in the chamber, causing either a re-load or one missed-target penalty. If this is happening with regularity, concentrate on a full extension of the lever to complete a successful cycling action. It should be noted that rounds with high primers can be part of the problem. The first time the hammer falls, the primer is seated. The next time the hammer falls, the round will discharge as normally expected.

Operator Error #3

Some lever guns will respond differently to how one or another particular racking motion is made. If the racking (levering) motion is too slow, some actions will glitch (hiccup, hang-up, etc.). If the shooter racks the lever in some way that finds a slight hitch midway through the motion, and has to coax or work through this little hang-up, it may mean the action needs work, or it may not. The shooter may not be racking with the crisp, smooth and fluid motion needed to finesse a particular style or make of lever gun. I know this sounds a little odd, but it is true. Start looking at the rest of the shooter's motions. Is the head still? Is the cheek staying in the sweet spot on the comb of the stock? Is the angle of the elbow and arm of the shooter correctly aligned to promote as perfectly forward a motion as possible? Is the shooter using the weak hand and arm to support and retain stability properly? These are many of the more subtle techniques that can affect both equipment and competitor alike.

Operator Error #4

The final ready position attained to engage the lever is awkward or feels unnatural. The error or technique flaw is a poor or incorrect final address position. Not corrected, it can have a negative impact on all actions with the lever gun from that point on.

Operator Error #5
Completing the racking motion of the lever, the shooter begins engaging the trigger with the index finger *not* resting on the trigger. The rearward motion of the finger actually starts with air between the finger and the trigger. This can cause accuracy problems.

Operator Error #6
The shooter's index finger is not extending straight, and is not *outside* the lever during the racking motion.

Operator Error #7
The shooter is not keeping the gun still during lever gun engagement. The worst technique will find the shooter lowering the lever gun each time a new round is racked into the chamber. Unless this is done on purpose (it is okay to impersonate the Duke if that's what

turns you on), the shooter will, in effect, be re-acquiring both the ready to address position and sighting for target acquisition for each round fired.

Operator Error #8
The shooter's body position does not take target radius or direction of target acquisition into consideration. This will usually result in straining of the upper torso (and affect the normal address) or cause the shooter to re-position by moving the feet and body during the stage run.

Operator Error #9
Incorrect or poor sight alignment techniques are used. Failing to focus on the front sight is common, but don't discount or fail to recognize that poor sighting techniques may stem from improper set-ups within the ready to address position.

Old West Lever-Action Tactics
Main stage competition in cowboy action shooting will find the shooter firing at least six rifle rounds, and more often nine to 10. Less often will competitors find more than 10 rounds in the design, with the occasional exception of reloading more during a stage run.

Photo 8.2C - *Blackjack McGinnis knows well that racking the lever is not quite as open and shut as one may think.*

Consideration to barrel length may be limited to personal preference, but only insofar as that a 10-round minimum will fit in the tube magazines. Most of the top competitors prefer a shorter barrel main-stage lever gun. The size and distance of the targets in CAS allow for very fast address, and the shorter barrel seems to assist the swinging or movement made for quickest target acquisition. That is not to say other barrel lengths are not used effectively. They are. They are simply not usually the choice for many shooters to work with in the "close in" designs found in cowboy combat. One reason I have come to prefer the carbine's shorter length is the reduction of forward weight. Whether an octagon barrel or not, a lever gun that seems to favor my own center of gravity feels quick and crisp as it acquires targets and fires rounds at an average of one every 3/4 of a second, must be one that feels just right. For me, the Navy Arms 1866 Yellowboy carbine does just that, and provides a high degree of reliability.

Regardless of which firearm (revolver, shotgun or lever gun) we speak of, one interesting point remains. Each firearm should bring the shooter confidence enough that no thoughts of possible malfunction(s), different sight alignments or any other equipment concern should distract from the focus of engagement. Needless to say, equipment problems will tear you up in the field.

I don't think all that much has to be said (as it has *all* been said before by many) about which caliber to use. Yes, the .38 and the .357 are used extensively, but so are the .45 Colt, 44-40, and many others. Loading to the cowboy action shooting criteria for main stage

Photo 8.2D - *The arm with the elbow pointed outward will promote unwanted motion. The arm with the elbow in a downward angle will assist to isolate and reduce sideways motion. (Left to right: Jeff Taverner, a.k.a. "Hud," SASS® #16409, and California State Champion Doug Bleek, a.k.a. "Smoke Parnell," SASS® #5494.)*

ENGAGING WITH THE MAIN STAGE RIFLES AND CARBINES   181

Photo 82.E - *Rowdy Yates (foreground) shows incorrect space or "air" between the trigger finger and the trigger before engaging.*

competition, the recoil becomes less of a factor than many would have you believe.

Thinking along the lines of muzzle movement, it is the operator's physical act of *racking* open and closed the lever-action that can create the most movement off of desired sight alignment to target. Any of the subtle glitches that occur during this process, as well as many of the other associated problems, will directly affect the muzzle.

This seemingly simple act of racking forward (to open), then rearwards (to close) the action by using the lever is critical. To begin with, 95 percent of all shooters will (or should) be using the three fingers (excluding the index finger) of their strong hand to operate the lever. These three fingers are the final extension of the shooter's arm and hand that control the racking motion.

The anchor, or attachment point of the three fingers to the firearm, lies within the lever itself. There is more to this particular point as to both the width and length of the lever to that of the fingers. Photo 8.2C shows how the three fingers form a thin, broad band. The length of this band of fingers does not (in most cases) fill the entire length of the lever. The shooter will find that by applying rearward pressure with the strong hand, the three fingers will find reasonable stability at the rear or bottom of the lever, from which to operate.

The average width of a shooter's finger is about 3/4 inches for a male and less for a female. The average width of the lever is around 1 1/8 inches. This can leave between 3/8 and 5/8 of an inch of open space between lever and fingers. For some shooters this may pose problems of both control and comfort (even pain). As chapter five mentions, one way to assist or eliminate these problems is by using a leather wrap to reduce the excess room, and make it more comfortable to rack the lever.

Many shooters find they don't need (or care) to wrap the lever. I have found that the anchor point at the rear of the lever allows pressure to control in both directions. This holds true for the lever-action carbine I am presently using. It may not be the same with a different firearm. Notice the positioning of the three fingers in photo 8.2B and where the anchor (or control) points are in either the open or closed position of the lever.

Although the video *Top Shooter's Guide to Cowboy Action Shooting, Part II; Quicken the Pace* provides a visual examination and demonstration of what is called a "flicking" motion used to rack the lever guns, I can only try to explain it to the reader here. Correctly done, the action should be opened and closed in around 10 to 15 hundredths of a second. Described as "flicking," it is hoped to portray how one move is made in two directions (forward and back) while at the same time having the least amount of movement to either side of the firearm. This is also done in such a manner that no motion is transferred to the shooter's shoulders or head.

The overall reduction of movement here includes other techniques to further isolate the racking action taking place at high speed. Some shooters appear to somehow loosen or hinge the wrist. Still others (although very few) have hands and fingers so shaped that from their anchor point they are flicking the lever open and closed with merely their fingers. This is a rare technique, one that most of us are not equipped for. I must say though, the sight of a shooter racking multiple times with the fingers only and no movement in the wrist back is quite a sight.

The vast majority of shooters must move the arm (and in turn the elbow and shoulder) in order to achieve complete

cycling of the lever. The angle of the arm must be such that it is conducive to a stable presentation position and will in turn assist in the reduction of motion during racking. Photo 8.2D shows two shooters with their elbows pointed in two different directions while at the same midway point of racking their lever guns. The shooter's elbow on the left is outward, pointed at 90 degrees or so from the ground. This may well be an excellent technique for a military application, but not here. To rack with the arm and elbow held this way produces a sideways motion that leads to less isolation and more movement. The shooter on the right is racking open the lever-action with the elbow at more of a downward angle that allows both the forward and backward motion to be executed in more of a parallel direction with the firearm. It is kind of an under-

Photo 8.2F - *Barbara Ormond, a.k.a. "Cat Ballou," SASS®, #51, racks her lever gun while keeping her cheek properly positioned on the comb on the stock.*

hand move, straight out and straight back. Shooters will find slight differences in the exact angle that the arm will work best. Do not get so close in, or have the elbow pointed at such an angle, that the head and/or rest of the body start to compensate in order to accommodate this. Just understand what it is you are after, and use these basic techniques to find your own way.

Checking back to photo 8.2C, the reader can see how the index (trigger) finger becomes extended and kept outside the trigger guard area during the racking open motion. This should become a natural method, one that the finger is reacting to in two ways. Racking open, the finger is straight out and off the trigger. Racking closed, the finger comes right back to and on the trigger. As the action closes, the shooter should find that the index finger does fall or return to the trigger quite naturally as a resting point. No forced move here is required, just let it happen.

Some shooters may be having problems associated with where the finger is located as they start to engage the trigger. Photo 8.2E shows how a shooter who may be afraid of an accidental discharge has adopted a return spot for the index finger *in front* of the trigger instead of lightly on it after the racking motion. Too often, the shooter will begin the trigger pull from this position with air between the finger and the trigger. This will cause any number of pulled or errant shots due to the totally ineffective trigger press. Work on returning that finger directly to and on the trigger after completing each racking motion. A correct anchor point here will assist obtaining the same return point.

Both shooters in photo 8.2E are demonstrating good positions of final address or "ready" positions (except the trigger finger of one). Part of the overall stability of any shooter

Photo 8.2G - *Cheryl Lincoln, a.k.a. "Sassy Lassy," SASS® #4776, (on left) and Cheryl Beesley, a.k.a. "Ella Watson," SASS® #4552, show the "ready …. or not?" positions of cowboy port arms.*

to accomplish what we have discussed is found here too. The weak hand and arm is an important part of this, providing rearward pressure to better anchor the lever-action firearm into the shoulder. This pressure must be kept constant, otherwise the lever-action is subject to react (move) when the lever is operated. The other task the weak hand and arm are charged with here is to support the lever-action firearm's weight and assist in controlling movements when acquiring targets. Each shooter should experiment to find where the weak hand will hold the forearm to perform both of these tasks. If the arm is extended too far, the shooter will feel fatigue at some point, and lose part of the effective support. Not extending far enough will often create an unstable situation and lack of good control with the front portion of the lever-action. This will often end up with a pronounced increase in forward muzzle movement. Look where each of the shooters in photo 8.2E has placed their weak hands on the forearms. Each is on a different portion of the forearm yes, but each has a similar angle of support seen almost as a "V" from each side of the elbow. As the shooter becomes more familiar with where on the forearm he wants the weak hand to be, an effort should be made to go to that same spot each time the lever is brought to bear. Doing this will soon make it part of the subconscious and the shooter will find the right position automatically.

Obtaining the individual shooter's perfect "sweet spot" where the cheek rests on the comb of a long gun's stock is important. It is a position that when found presents the shooter with a comfortable feel and excellent sight alignment. As described, each shooter will instinctively know when his or her cheek has found this place. The trick is to obtain the position quickly, without adding time while adjusting or sliding along the top of the lever-action's stock.

A shooter may best do this by understanding how the length of a long gun can affect this positioning, and how to fit either a lever-action or a shotgun.

Each shooter should experiment to find where the weak hand will hold the forearm.

To check the length in a general manner, place the unloaded long gun in the crook of the arm with the muzzle pointed upwards. See where the shooter's trigger finger falls in relationship to the trigger. Too long, too short, or just right, there is a difference in how the long gun will feel to each shooter. The shooter, who finds a closer, correct fit will find it more natural for them to bring a long gun up into the shoulder and hit their "sweet spot" ready to engage. The ones whose fingers end up shorter or longer than right on the trigger will find that most often a slight adjustment or sliding along the stock's comb must be made to hit the right spot. Many shooters aware of this will make the adjustment an automatic part of their actions without a problem. The key is to be aware of what is happening and why, and to then adjust to correct. It is easier to shorten than to add length to a stock, but most shooters will find a stock too long for them. Failing to adjust will simply compel the shooter to engage from a less advantageous ready position, and have an adverse affect on the shooter's overall technique.

As with each firearm used in cowboy action shooting, body posture is an important part of the rifle shooter's address. The lever-action is no exception. Again, the upper torso should be set to radius comfortably along the target line(s), and (if possible) require the lower part of the body to remain firmly anchored in one place. The forward (slightly aggressive) attitude of leaning in, towards the targets will prevent any tendency to be rocked back onto the heels, and will assist in target acquisition. The similar stance to that of an athlete, feet at shoulder-width apart, knees slightly flexed, will add more control. Having obtained an effective set-up in these areas will find the shooter in comfortable command of all the elements of firearm handling.

The speed of engaging a lever-action is perhaps better described as a shooter's own rhythm. This rhythm is directly related to each shooter's ability to rack, acquire the target, engage and repeat the process. As the shooter develops and improves the lever-action techniques, it will become apparent that an inner rhythm develops. This is the time it takes between each shot to do the steps just mentioned.

More time spent behind the trigger will improve the shooter's rhythm accordingly. Adjustment and control factors are the target size, distance and sequence of hit order. These are key elements for the shooter to recognize and to then engage as appropriate for his skill level. To correctly apply your own rhythm to each set of targets for 10 separate events takes considerable effort. "Correctly applying" does not mean simply hitting the target (although that is a good start). It means that the shooter has adjusted his rhythm and controlled his shots to hit the targets at between 80 and 90 percent of his top speed. This is again relative to

the shooter's skill and field conditions. The overall time (whether fast or slow) is *not* the important part of this lesson. What is important is the individual shooter's time and the application of the above for that shooter.

The two shooters in photo 8.2G may appear similar, but there are differences that by now the reader should see immediately. The cowboy port arms standing start position is the same only in name here. One shooter has assumed a ready position with the strong hand in the lever and comfortably anchored. The weak hand is on the forearm where the shooter will gain stability and support. The stance of this shooter is that of truly ready, one that will see only arm movement as the lever-action gun comes up to bear on that first target, and no change in body height.

The other shooter's position of readiness could use a little work. The strong hand must be moved to operate the lever, the weak hand is supporting from a less than desirable position, and the stance will most likely see the shooter move his feet, his torso, and height change before the first round is fired (and likely will miss).

If you were not ready before, and began your stages looking too much like the shooter shown here, I hope that now you look more like the one who we know is ready to "rock and roll" with the lever-action long gun.

Chapter 9

PROBLEMS, MALFUNCTIONS AND OTHER NUISANCES

Recognize Your Own Problems And Correct Them

Of course Buffalo Chip posed for this photo, but any cowboy action shooter has seen this kind of thing time and again. We don't even need to get into all the problems shown here, but don't you wish this poor fellow would at least get some decent glasses?

Every shooter knows when something is going wrong. Some problems are very recog-nizable while others are not. Let's look a little more closely at some problems the shooter may be having, and discuss how to help recognize and correct them.

A good place to start with is the shooter's flinch level. Although flinch-ing is most often associated with the handgun, it can occur in either of the long guns as well. The term "flinch-ing" means that the shooter is applying

Photo 9.0A - "… Pssst! It's the same old thing pard, he'll finish and wonder what he did wrong …. again!" (Shooter John Beck, a.k.a. "Buffalo Chip," SASS® #793, timer Scott McCoid, a.k.a. "Hondo," SASS® #21, Tex and Prairie Fire are doing the whispering.

a slight forward motion to the firearm as the trigger is engaged. It is often said this is done subconsciously in anticipation of the recoil. This may be partly true, but flinching may also stem from simply not isolating the index finger from the rest of the strong hand as the trigger press occurs. The resulting action from flinching (also called "milking the shot") will cause the round to impact low, due to the forward motion and consequent lowering of the muzzle.

all shooters flinch at times, sometimes more and sometimes less. A good exercise to check how much a shooter is flinching, and correct this problem, is by dry firing an *empty* and *safe* handgun. Just get into your ready to engage position, cock and engage the trigger. If you flinched, there will be no doubt. It is usually an obvious feeling and can be seen as well. No flinch or very little flinching will be just as apparent; the handgun will not be felt or seen as having moved. As you dry fire and notice how your flinch is that day, continue trying to eliminate more and more of whatever movement outside of the perfect trigger press you feel. A few minutes of dry firing will find you can reduce your flinch significantly just by being more aware of the condition.

The amount of flinch can change from one day to the next. I have found that checking my flinch before I shoot helps me to focus and use my best techniques. Going through this check I have found that the arm extension and lock-out method is one of the keys to help me reduce my flinch. Whatever system of check you use, the days you are flinching less are the days you will shoot well.

If the shooter has the opportunity to practice fire in the field, there is another exercise to help recognize and reduce flinching. It is a live-fire exercise, one that should be done only by a safe, competent and experienced shooter. Best done with a partner, it is sometimes called "skip loading." This method will utilize two or three rounds in the six chambers of the single-action revolver. Doing this in a *safe* area with safe handling techniques is mandatory (this must be said). A shooter will load one (or two) rounds, skip a chamber, and repeat until the order of loaded and unloaded chambers is random. The cylinder is spun or turned at this point. The shooter will then cock and engage the trigger without attempting to know which chamber is hot. Little doubt will be left as to the amount of flinching a shooter may or may not have as the hot and then cold chambers are gone through.

Missing targets is certainly an easy way to see a problem.

It is easy for a shooter to recognize a problem. Missing targets is certainly an easy way to see a problem. Other problems like fumbling or poor course and prop management are also easily recognized. These examples are more the *results* of the problems, *not* the cause. To get beyond simply knowing you are doing something wrong, and that *something* must change, is difficult if you fail to look in the right places.

The finest shooters in cowboy action shooting use the same basic techniques that any shooter does. Their secret (for lack of a better word) is that they have refined these basic tactics and are using them a higher percentage of the time than most others. When a top shooter is having problems he will most often go back to the basics and begin a check of each move. While perhaps not as quickly as these top shooters, any shooter can solve most problems in much the same way.

With few exceptions, shooters will find that "going back to the basics" will often provide the remedies they are looking for. Below is another list for the shooter to check when problems occur, but may be having trouble putting their finger on what exactly they are doing wrong. These items are more physical techniques than the mental ones we will address later.

If the revolver is giving you problems, you might ask:

- Is the revolver sighted in properly with the loads you will use in competition?
- Are your master grip and trigger finger finding the correct position to hold the revolver?
- Is your weak hand correctly supporting your technique?
- Is the weak hand's thumb being brought to the best position from which to re-cock the hammer?
- If the thumb goes to the rear (on the web of the strong hand), is it too close to the hammer? Could it possibly be interfering with the hammer as it falls forward?
- Is the strong hand creeping up the back strap of the revolver during round discharge?
- Are you getting full-arm extension and lock-out when bringing the revolver to bear?
- Are you focusing on the front sight?
- Are your head and shoulders being kept as level as possible during engagement?
- Have you positioned yourself so the upper torso can move comfortably along the path of target radius?
- Is your initial stance and body posture in the "ready to engage" position?
- Are you "milking the shots" or flinching?
- Is your trigger press or squeeze correct?

If the lever-action long gun is giving you problems you might ask:

- Is it properly sighted in with the rounds you are using for competition?
- Does the long gun fit you correctly?
- Is the long gun's action one that you normally have no problems with?
- Does the long gun's weight and barrel length feel comfortable?
- Are the weak and strong hands making correct contact for optimum support and levering operations?

- Is the weak arm both supporting the long gun, and exerting rearward pressure into the shoulder for stability?
- Is your strong arm angled to reduce sideways motion during the action of racking the lever?
- Are you attempting to isolate the motion of "flicking the lever" as much as possible?
- Are you bringing the gun *up* to the head, and *not* the head down to the gun during the initial move of bringing it to bear?
- Are you short stroking or having feeding problems due to positioning of the long gun, and not mechanical problems?
- Is the long gun correctly anchored during engagement?
- Are your head and shoulders as level as possible?
- Is your stance and body posture correct and set for correct target acquisition?

If the shotgun is giving you problems you might ask:

- Is round retrieval hindered by belt and loop location?
- Are the rounds too deep in the loop for easy removal?
- Are you making contact with, and holding, the round(s) correctly for easy insertion into the breech or chambers?
- Are you sighting correctly, and seeing no barrel when discharging rounds?
- Are you keeping the '97 *up*, and into the shoulder during the "shoot one, load one round" techniques?
- Are you bringing the open chambers of your double to an effective position for accurate, error free round insertion?
- Is your stance and other points of address being done correctly?

In addition to these above problems, there is another that applies to almost any of those listed, and may well be the cause of the entire problem. That is the speed the shooter is attempting to attain while going through all these actions. Could your problems be caused by too hasty an engagement speed? Are your misses due to simply going beyond your current ability to deliver accurate shots?

I think it safe to say that virtually all competitors will attempt to go faster than they can perform correctly. Recognize when you have gone too fast and force yourself to slow down enough to perform the basic techniques correctly first. Then try to add more speed to your run. The smoother and more accurate all the aspects of total delivery become, the faster the shooter's overall time will become as well.

Target Acquisition Problems

There are two problems (at least) that can appear as the shooter moves the firearm's muzzle from one target to another. Make sure that you are not doing one or the other as you contemplate why there seems to be so many missed targets in your runs.

The first of these is what I call "scalloping." It is defined as the act of dipping down, or making an upside down arc with the muzzle of either handgun or lever gun while moving from target to target. Move and acquire new targets with a direct or straight-line movement only. "Scalloping" from one target to another will add many additional movements during the address that will hinder the shooter.

The other problem encountered is that of over- or under-swinging to a target. Swinging too quickly can easily produce impacts that are indicative of a muzzle having gone past the target. Swinging too quickly and then trying to stop and engage the target may find the rounds are short, indicative of stopping the muzzle swing too quickly before

engaging. Move the muzzle from target to target no faster than you can operate either the hammer on the revolver or the lever on your long gun. First make sure you are not swinging improperly or "scalloping," then you will get back to hitting targets. Then begin to pick up a little more speed only when it feels natural to do so.

Malfunctions

All that I can really tell you about malfunctions is to expect them. Then you need to know what you can and must do to reduce the amount of time they will add to your run. Well, that's not *all* I can tell you, but those are the two main things you want to keep in mind.

As far as equipment goes, the shooter should try to field firearms that have been checked and cleaned prior to match use. Tighten those ejector rod screws, check the screws on those '97's. Check everything in order to insure nothing is loose and ready to fall off.

Match ammo should be checked as well. High primers, split cases, and other little things that may cause you grief can often be eliminated simply by handling and taking a good look at the 220 or so rounds you will be shooting during a 10-stage match.

Malfunctions can be lumped into two categories. Ones that you can overcome quickly and those that cannot be corrected. You must learn to recognize both kinds instantly. A shooter must learn to stop any futile efforts. If you break, you break. Render that firearm safe and continue the stage. If you have another kind of malfunction (something more minor in nature) like a short stroke, a stove-piped round, an empty hull not ejected properly or something that *can* be sorted out during engagement, fix it and keep going. The best way to do this is to rehearse what you will do in the event of malfunction. Try to anticipate what might go wrong and what actions you will take if something happens.

The shooter who planned ahead will not find it too difficult to get past a problem during the heat of battle. Nor will the prepared shooter be so surprised and unprepared when a malfunction occurs that he is at a total loss as to

Photo 9.2A - *Few shooters misunderstand the meaning of the saying, "never did see a target so big or so close... I couldn't figure out a way to miss it!"*

the best way to cope. Even if you don't have any idea of what to do, at least render the firearm safe somehow, and complete the course as best you can. That seems better (and safer) than having the line support personnel shout out directions from all sides. That is really tough on some shooters.

Other Nuisances....

The "action" in cowboy action shooting means pretty much what you'd think. The fantasy gun battles of the American Frontier that are played out on today's CAS ranges are more akin to what we have all seen on the silver screen and read about in countless books, both fiction and non-fiction. They are fast, furious

and see shooters unloading a lot of lead on steel targets. These targets are usually fairly big and reasonably close. However, no cowboy action shooter of any experience will fail to understand the saying, "Never did see a target so big or so close that I couldn't figure out a way to miss it." Some shooters see more humor in that than others, and at different times.

There will be a few frustrating moments for most all shooters as they find the above statement a very true one. But not to worry, this is again just part of the game.

Five shots on one big target (about 18 inches by 18 inches), or five shots on a medium sized target (about 12 by 12) will often be one of the little nuisances that will make shooters shake their heads and wonder how they could miss a target so close. Often, the targets are even larger.

It is most often the manipulating of the firearm (either the lever of the long gun, or the hammer of the handgun) at too high a speed that produces these misses. The motions of racking or cocking these firearms for *each* shot at the high speed is probably what needs to be considered here. Do judge correctly how fast *you* can do this and stay on target, and remember that being locked on target during successive shots is paramount for success.

Also consider the time difference between five controlled shots and five that are not. Using one 18-inch by 18-inch target at seven yards for this example, let's say that a top shooter can bust five caps with hits in right around 2.5 seconds or a little less. The average shooter who can muster reasonable technique here should be able to maintain speeds of four seconds on the same target. Even though these times are simply to illustrate a point, the time difference is the key. One second or so slower is not the place to worry about keeping up or going that fast. Besides, much of the total time will be related to how well a shooter makes the transition to the move.

The lost time of approximately one-second per revolver is not (in all likelihood) going to make the difference one may think. A shooter using correct control and obtaining all five hits, versus one who runs on the ragged edge, is a much better approach. If the match is one scored with rank points (individual ranking on each stage), the risk of running at an all-out speed becomes even higher. One example of this is the top shooter who happens to miss one shot on a bank of targets that the whole field of shooters are addressing at fairly high speeds. That one miss (adding five seconds to the time) will very often put a large amount of other shooters (who slowed down a little and got all hits) ahead of that top shooter in the final ranking of that stage. Many stages have found me watching some of the younger top guns really smoking a five-shot string at speeds I *know* better than to try. If the target configuration allows one of these talented lads to get five rounds out in two seconds or *faster*, I will settle for 2.5 or even 3.0 seconds. To compete at all in the overall scope of the event, it is better to slow down and be as consistently clean as possible.

In other words, if one shooter engages one or more targets in three seconds and *misses* one of them, while many other shooters engage the same targets in around four or five seconds with *no misses*, that first shooter's time is now eight seconds. Believe me, I *know* just how much fun it is to really "whup" or bust five caps out as fast as possible but, under match conditions like this, it is far more prudent to go only as quickly as will produce solid hits and *no* misses. It is like this: WOW! That guy was unbelievably fast… too bad he missed one. If you were slower but clean, it is fine to snicker to yourself here because you beat this fast hombre fair and square!

Shooting scenarios have many of what we might call "design traps" within them. Some are intentional, but probably most are not. The "trap" or particular area of a stage that finds a large number of shooters having trouble comes in all kinds of shapes. A bank of revolver targets where four are big and one is small is not to be overlooked. Double taps on big targets with a single shot on a smaller one is another. Small targets that are set out at only seven yards *appear* so close, yet can be easily missed. This type of tar-

Photo 9.2B - *Engaging the MGM style of reactive target encountered in cowboy action shooting matches.*

get is a trap. Look for these target traps, recognize them for what problems they offer, and adjust accordingly.

Other "traps" may include shooting a small or medium sized target at the very end of a stage that the shooter faces after running hard or exerting a lot of energy. The shooter may be somewhat out of breath, and (if not mindful of this) will not take enough time with the shot.

The small shotgun target is another common stage trap shooters will encounter. Remember the double's second shot? Knockdown targets require decent hits, not just a few pellets, in order to react. The MGM style of shotgun reactive targets is a very good example. Often, the small target will be required to rock or move rearward enough to show the color painted on the underside of the target. Shooters should not take for granted that their "scatter guns" will produce enough energy needed to rock or knock over a target. Sometimes a shotgun needs to be used more like a rifle with some of these targets, meaning the shooter gets good front sight acquisition before letting the round go off.

Knowing the shot pattern of your shotgun at different distances can be helpful. Using some pieces of cardboard (about 18 inches by 18 inches), mark the center of each with a marking pen. Set these cardboard targets up at seven, 10, 12 and 15 yards. Aiming at the center of each target, fire a controlled shot at each one to find out how much shot is concentrated on each target at what distance. Consider different dram equivalents and amounts of shot to improve hits that seem weak at the longer distances. Screw-in chokes can sometimes help with this.

Stage props are the last of these little traps to remember. Get through them by not being too hasty and by paying attention to what the other shooters are dealing with. Try not to let that set of saddlebags that must be carried during the run, or the bars you must shoot through, be your nemesis.

Another of the nuisances we face as outdoor shooters are the many field conditions encountered. Extreme heat, cold, wind, rain, even snow won't always cancel a major cowboy action shooting match. I've seen many

dust-caked faces of both men and women toughing out a match. More than once mud has created havoc on a field of fire that shooters were still required to negotiate. Many shooters know what high humidity and cowboy gear feels like. Such weather conditions can take their toll.

To overcome, even prevail during these monster matches is not easy. I try to do two things to help me. First, I try my best to prepare for what is both expected and unexpected. The other thing I do is to kid myself a little. If it is raining, I am *the best* rain shooter I know. If it is hot, cold, whatever the case may be, I do not want to be thinking negative about how something may affect me. I do want to believe that there is something positive to be found, even if it is only the way I choose to *see* it. Remember *every* shooter must deal with the same conditions as you. Why not be the one who deals with those conditions better?

Some shooters may well consider it a nuisance when the occasional hip-shooting requirement presents itself. I can relate. The first few times I was faced with having to hold a revolver or rifle waist-high and fire it, I ended up with more misses than hits.

All I can do is tell the reader about what works for me, as there are, no doubt, many techniques out there. Larry Darr, a.k.a. "Canyon Kid," SASS® #xxx was one of the original horseback riders, stuntmen, and cowboys on some of the 1950s TV series like: *Gunsmoke*, *Tombstone*, and *Bat Masterson*. Larry's love of the Old West has endowed him with a tremendous knowledge of many things related, not the least of which is shooting. Maybe the hip-shooting technique Larry taught me will work as well for you as it does for me.

First of all, most any stage in a match that requires either a revolver or rifle to be fired from the waist will present a *big* target at close range. This

Photos 9.2C - *Bounty Hunter hip-shooting… cowboy style.*

(as many shooters will attest to) is not enough, and too many misses still occur. Even if the shooter has some idea of how to do this, it is something most people don't do often enough to do it well.

Stand to face the target as much as possible, with both feet pointed directly downrange. If the revolver is being used, center it directly with your own line of sight to the target. The backstrap should be in line with the center of your body, held waist high. With your eyes centered on the target, the revolver's muzzle will be aligned much the same way. Before the first shot is fired, lower the revolver's barrel just a little bit, as the natural tendency is for the barrel to start high. The shooter should be able to see where the first round goes (high or low), and adjust accordingly.

The only difference with the lever gun is that it is easier for the shooter to center. The butt of the lever gun can be placed directly on (or near) to the shooter's belt buckle (as worn in front), providing somewhat of a platform from which to engage.

It is the centering of both firearms to the shooter's eyes, or direct line of sight to the target, that makes this technique a good one. Also, don't try to be like the old TV star and bang those rounds out there too quickly. Just like learning to shoot with the weak hand or weak shoulder, occasional practice here will pay dividends someday.

What Goes In Your War Bag?

If you've never competed as a cowboy action shooter or are just getting started, you probably do not yet (but soon will) appreciate just how much gear is taken along to attend a major match. Careful preparations insure the firearms are in peak condition and that the ammunition is checked and rechecked. These are certainly things almost any shooter can do with relative ease. It is the same with all the clothes, leather and accouterments as well. You would think there would be no problem… right?

Some years back I wrote an article on getting all the gear ready for a big match. It included all the various items we all take, and some of the steps one can take to make sure they are well prepared. This gear was (and still

Photo 9.3A - *Larry Darr, a.k.a. "Canyon Kid," SASS® #2116.*

is) part of the fun of cowboy action shooting, and I hoped readers would benefit from some of the experiences I and other compatriots had gone through.

I told a story Rowdy Yates had once related to me of when, after packing all the gear to travel from California to Oklahoma for a shoot, he had remembered everything but two little items. The items were his main match revolvers. I wrote about a couple other instances of how we had all forgotten our gun rigs, hats, shotguns, ammo and other things a time or two, and (while it was humorous to write about) it was *not* very funny to realize our mistakes in the field. I remember pointing out that to

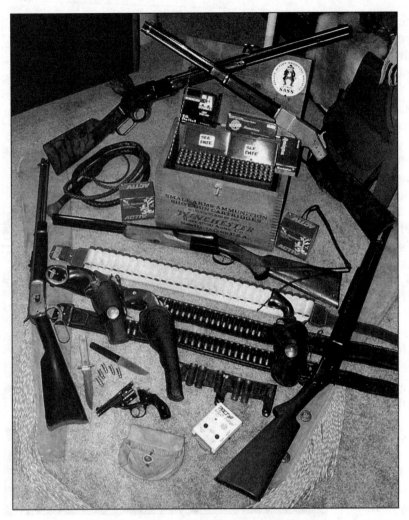

Photo 9.3B - *"Tools of the Trade."*

leave a favorite piece of equipment at home was like forgetting your wallet or purse… except worse. Too many times during the match the thought of having forgotten something would pop into our heads. A milder quote of mine at the time might have been, "dang it, what a dumb thing to forget!"

Worst of all were the results of our blunders. Borrowing an unfamiliar firearm, even someone's extra gun rig, is usually not going to improve your day. Most would agree that is an understatement. Nevertheless, the best thing to do is to just roll with it… and vow, "that's the *last time* I ever do that!" Yeah, sure it is.

The bottom line of that old article was to prepare your war bag in advance. That part of the fun was to lay out all those great cowboy duds and Old West smoke wagons, and have a good look at them before packing. A checklist including all the articles of clothing, the cowboy accouterments, firearms, ammo and any other things (like your wallet) you may want with you was heartily endorsed.

Chapter 10

PRACTICE... HARDLY A DIRTY WORD

Don't ask me why practicing in this sport is sometimes seen as a negative act by some shooters. Perhaps it is because many shooters do not feel they get the same chance, or that to practice is not part of a level playing field. I really am at a loss over some of what has been expressed over the years by some, and hope that most will see practicing as no more than one's desire to improve and enjoy the sport more. I am also not going to tell you that practicing is something you must do in order to have fun and enjoy this sport. I will say, however, that the effort will pay off in terms of personal performance, and that most shooters have more fun as they get better.

Practicing, that is *real* practicing, becomes less fun to most shooters as they do more of it. Plinking at a range is not really practicing, so if you go to a range to plink and call it fun, you are right. If you plink and call it practicing you may be kidding yourself. Sure, it may be better than not shooting at all, but plinking away without knowing what or why you are doing something will severely limit the ways you improve your game, and might even hinder it.

Don't be discouraged if you cannot find the time or do not have the place to practice live firing at a range. Much of what cowboy action shooters need to develop and improve can be done at home. All those positions of address, the actions of levering and cocking the firearms correctly, and the all-important firearm transitions can be honed with *unloaded* and *safe guns* in your house or garage. Not knowing your neighbors, I'd exclude the backyard.

I like to call the repetition of practice (either dry or live-fire) the development of a shooter's muscle memory. Certain transitions done many times become an automatic response after a

while and, in turn, are part of the shooter's muscle memory or subconscious tools. A good example that shooters will come to understand illustrates this well. Have you ever seen or had the first pistol shot going off sooner than the shooter really intended, but *still* hitting the target. Yes, it was an accidental discharge in a way, and will surprise the shooter in most cases. But because the shooter had become so ingrained with the correct techniques of address (that the pistol was brought to bear automatically on the target), that muscle memory and subconscious skills made the difference. Now I am not saying this is what you want to do, for it is not. I am simply giving one example of how a well-developed muscle memory can be recognized (and even save your butt someday). By the way, an accidental discharge of this kind does *not* constitute one deserved of a safety penalty.

There is more than one source of study that tells us the difference between the conscious and subconscious. I agree with the experts that say the human can only have one truly conscious thought at any one moment. Try looking at a target and thinking of both hitting and missing it at the exact same time. You can't really. You are either thinking of hitting it or thinking of missing it. Perhaps the best thing to be conscious of here is that the *front* sight is aligned on that target.

So, with only a single thought available to us at any one time insofar as our conscious mind permits, what about our

Photo 10.0A (left) and 10.0B (below) - *Madre Kid practices outside, while Ned Buntline practices at the office.*

subconscious? That is the key for so much of what we do well in our whole lives. Our subconscious is the part of our minds that allow us to perform literally dozens of actions without conscious thought or action. We do these things automatically; usually much faster than if we had given them any thought. We are not born with most of these subconscious skills; we *developed* them through repetition. Yes, the hand is *quicker* than the eye, but only if the hand knows well what it's supposed to be doing… *without being told.*

The cowboy action shooter can use dry-fire exercises to develop subconscious shooting skills. As little as 10 minutes a day on one of the areas that needs improvement will produce positive results in a short time. The imaginary targets used in dry-fire practice may be paper ones placed on the walls, objects already handy, whatever the shooter decides. The distance can vary, it is not that important for these drills.

Taking these skills to the range as developed subconscious tools (ones that no longer need conscious thought to perform) is one of the most beneficial things a shooter can do to improve performance. Below are some of the dry-fire exercises you may want to try at home. If you have a timer available, using it on delay can be very helpful. Please, remember to check and insure that *any* firearm you use is totally *safe* and *unloaded* before you ever begin. Check and re-check that only *dummy* rounds or snap caps are used in these exercises. One more thing that must never be forgotten is to *never* point any firearm at anyone regardless of its supposedly safe condition.

Dry-Fire Exercises For Revolvers

* Total position of address, readiness and focus.
* Drawing from each side separately, the three main starting positions:

    -Hands flat

    -Hands close, but not touching

    -Hands above shoulders

* Obtaining the correct master grip and weak hand position during the draw.
* Gaining good arm extension and lock.

* Developing a comfortable and consistent method of thumb-cocking the hammer.
* Controlling and reducing the shooter's flinch.
* Sight alignment to target, focusing on front sight.
* Transition from target to target smoothly, while cocking the hammer.
* Re-holstering accurately.
* The snatch-and-grab method of bringing the handgun to bear off of a horizontal surface.
* Two pistol runs, five clicks each with all transitions as related.
* Checking body posture or attitude in a mirror.

The above are some of the things that can be easily done to improve your revolver work. There is one exercise that I found to be interesting and helpful in proving the benefits of dry-firing. It is shown in the video *Top Shooter's Guide to CAS, Part II*, but I will explain it here for the reader.

Standing at the ready with an *unloaded* and *safe* pistol, the shooter is holding the pistol as if to start from the "gun out at 45 degrees downrange" position. Picking any target (picture on the wall, etc.), the shooter works on bringing the gun up, cocking and engaging the target with *one* imaginary round at the beep. Focusing on this presentation of the first round only, the shooter must concentrate on all the correct address techniques each time. After several runs of presenting to the one target, stop a moment. Now, assuming the same stance, readiness and focus, do one thing differently. As you look at the target with the gun out, you are focused and ready… now *close your eyes.* Try to see the target in your "mind's eye." Without moving, begin to do each run off the timer keeping your eyes closed until *after* you have engaged the trigger. Without moving, open your eyes each time to see how close the sight alignment is to the target. Focus on technique, see the target and the front sight as you would normally, and shortly you will find yourself *on* target without looking. Each time you spend a little time dry-firing, include this exercise to assist in the development of your subconscious tools.

Here are some areas you may look to develop as you design your own exercises for the lever-action rifle or carbine.

Dry-Fire Exercises For The Long Guns

- Total position of address and readiness focus.
- Improved methods of racking the lever.
- Positions of the fingers, hands and angle of arm during racking motion.
- Bringing the gun *up* to the head during presentation.
- Practicing from the cowboy "port arms" start position.
- Practice bringing the lever-action firearm to bear from a vertically staged position.
- Practice bringing the lever-action firearm to bear from a horizontally staged position.
- Ingraining the act of automatically opening the action when completing the lever-action's target run.
- Counting number of targets addressed and getting the break to the next task correctly.
- Ingraining the "sweet spot" of cheek on comb and the automatic sight alignment found when applied correctly.
- Sight alignment and target acquisition control as in swinging the muzzle correctly.
- *Dummy* round practice of one or more reloads after initial targets are engaged.
- Correcting a known problem in the field (such as scalloping, etc.).

There are surely more things to practice, but those mentioned above are many of the main lever-action techniques that you may find useful in your dry-fire practice sessions.

Dry-Fire Exercises For The Shotguns

- Total position of address, readiness and focus.
- Positioning of belt and rounds for optimum loading results.
- Insertion of *dummy* rounds into breech or chambers.
- Position of shotgun during loading.
- Sight alignment, cheek on comb, head position.
- Overall dexterity in areas of round manipulation.
- Note: The '97 will not perform the ejection of dummy rounds during dry-fire exercises as it will when used in the field with live rounds. The shooter may find this somewhat annoying at first, but should continue with the idea to improve their loading and address techniques.

Okay, that's a lot of what can be included in a shooter's dry-fire exercises. The additional benefits of this practice can be the shooter's sense of improved safety in terms of muzzle control and awareness. Once again, the repeated actions will soon become automatic responses and part of your subconscious tools. Make sure you practice correct techniques that will improve your game, and not incorrect ones that will not!

Live-fire practice is more or less similar to dry-firing. Presentation (or the first shot) out of each firearm is one good area not to leave out. Movement is another area that may be easier to work on during live-fire practice. Try practicing with targets of different height, ones that compel you to adjust for both horizontal and vertical movements.

Demonstrations and instruction in both dry-fire and live-fire exercises are part of the visual training as presented in the video series, *Top Shooter's Guide to CAS, Parts I and II.*

Chapter 11

YOUR FINAL APPROACH

Develop A Pre-Stage Routine

When it's all said and done, the lone shooter stands at the line. Ahead of the shooter stands between 15 and 60 seconds of real-life blazing gunfire within the fantasy setting of the Old West. The shooter nods when asked about the course of fire and his readiness to engage. "Stand-by" is the last command heard before this shooter is propelled into what many say is the "e-ticket" ride of the cowboy action shooting sport. Nothing matters except what is now in motion, the band is playing and you are doing the dance.

The command to begin a stage in cowboy action shooting creates an adrenaline rush not so dissimilar to those I have felt when just completing the pace lap in a field of race cars as the green flag waves. The pedal is to the metal. The roar and thrust of the car is that of the roar and buck of the guns. The high-speed turns made at the edge of one's envelope are similar to the moves made during a stage engagement. For me, these are both extraordinary experiences. I cannot help but to see the

Photo 11.0A - *Top shooter Fred Ruane, a.k.a. "Calahan," SASS® #12298, knows that having a good plan is part of the pre-stage routine.*

similarities: anticipation, preparation, reactions of both the conscious and sub-conscious minds and the development of skills through practice. These are two environments filled with action, noise, and movement that compel the senses to operate at full speed.

Regardless that the speed of address is relative to many factors, shooters will find that to control their own adrenaline rush is not often easy. To begin with, simply recognizing what's happening is the first step. By establishing and implementing a systematic approach, most of the better shooters will develop what's often referred to as a pre-stage routine. This routine accomplishes many things, not the least of which is one way not to let the heat of engagement overwhelm us with confusion and unwanted results. Remaining focused during a time of action like this does not simply happen because we want it to happen. Focusing, like all the other traits and attributes, requires some work to develop.

To begin a stage with little or no preparation will bring the expected results. Each shooter can develop a pre-stage routine that will help him remain calm, insure successful engagement, and carry through most of the rough spots. Below is a list of different things many shooters do as they ready themselves for actual engagement. It is my hope the reader will take from this list what might work, and begin to develop a pre-stage routine to meet the firing line head-on.

- **Before you go to the loading line visualize yourself shooting and moving through the entire scenario with your eyes closed at least two times.**

- **Listen to the R.O.'s instructions, but learn the stage by working it first, whenever possible, before shooting.**

- **Go to school by watching others. Learn from their mistakes and successes.**

- **Consider all the possibilities and anticipate whatever problems are foreseen.**

- **Look for the stage traps and how to best address them.**

- **Decide at which point you will begin to focus only on the upcoming run, and nothing else.**

- **Learn to relax during the pre-stage routine, taking several deep breaths as you approach the firing line. (More oxygen to the brain will help.)**

- **Go through any prop manipulation prior to engagement if allowable.**

- **Make the final check of ammunition (counting rounds and making visual examination) part of the pre-stage routine.**

- **Try not to ask questions at the line, ask them well before it is your turn to shoot.**

- **Make and stick to your plan of attack.**

- **Look at the targets and apply your own rhythm of engagement to them.**

- **Know all the transitions you will make for the entire stage run, decide which will be the safest first, and then the quickest.**

Adapt, Adjust And Advance

There will be times the cowboy shooter finds himself in unfamiliar territory in one stage or another. Whether it's sitting down at the sewing machine, wearing an apron with shotgun shells in the pocket or some other unusual setting, it *will* happen.

Shooting from the top of a stagecoach, a moving ore cart, even the unsteady raft modeled after the one used by John Wayne and Katherine Hepburn in the movie *Rooster Cogburn* are things you can expect will happen.

The point is that the shooter must adapt well to whatever is presented as a shooting problem. For example, any of shooting positions that offer an unsteady or moving place from which to engage must be recognized and adjusted for by the shooter. Most often, these areas will move only as much as the shooter does. Performing the levering or racking

Photo 11.1A - *Chop that wood, tote them bags; no one is familiar with everything encountered in cowboy action shooting. Here we see National and World Champion Lisa Hancock, a.k.a. "Pearl Hart," SASS® #2766, robbing a bank!?*

motion of a long gun, the transitions and cocking of the revolver, or loading and working a shotgun will have a direct bearing on how much the prop will move and how much it will, in turn, move you.

When faced with this particular problem, it is best to first see what exactly is happening (and to what extent), and plan for it. If possible, feel for yourself what it will be like to engage from. Can you stand or place yourself in a better position to reduce movement?

One common problem is not to first make sure of the line of sight offered to the targets from a required position prior to the run. It is not unusual to find that one or more targets are obscured from view if care is not taken to obtain the best position to shoot from. Failure to do this may cause a shooter to shift unnecessarily while engaging from this position, and end up costing additional time. If the target

placement offers no choice to the shooter but to shift, it is better to anticipate and execute a pre-planned move whenever possible.

The smallest amount of outside motion will greatly affect the overall stability of the front sight. Adapting to the problem through recognition is one thing, adjusting during actual engagement is another. This adjustment is usually best accomplished by slowing down. *Slow down* enough to hit each target and don't worry about your speed. It is best to get through a stage problem like this without attempting your normal rhythm. The speed will take care of itself. You be the one to get through unscathed, and let the others make the mistakes while you adapt, adjust and advance correctly.

Steady Under Fire

Remaining cool, calm and collected during the heated run of a main stage engagement is often not the easiest thing for a shooter to do. As fun as this sport is, there is still a certain amount of stress shooters are subject to as they meet these personal challenges. It's fair to say that there is some amount of stress attached to virtually any sport that challenges our mental and physical abilities to one degree or another. What would be the "sport" of something that did not?

Either by thought or deed, mistakes made while operating in a fast-paced environment will produce stress. The emotional state of feeling stressed is the opposite of that of feeling confident and calm. The more mistakes made during a stage run, the more we become stressed. This can often have a domino-effect on a shooter, resulting in a disastrous stage engagement. On the other hand, the confidence of having prepared properly will most often produce a smooth, clean and efficient stage run.

Fatigue is a factor during match play that should not be ignored. Stress alone can bring on fatigue, but more often it is the way one takes care of himself during the long day. To guard against fatigue, I eat mostly high-protein foods, stay hydrated, and take potassium supplements twice a day. When I'm shooting well, the last thing I want to happen to me as I prepare to engage the final stages is to think of how tired I am, or to wish it were "beer-thirty" time.

No shooter, regardless of experience or expertise, is immune from these problems. To "keep it together" for all of the main stages over a one-, two-, or even three-day major match is one elusive ambition. The top shooters (both in class and overall place of finish), are those who have made the least amount of mistakes. Shooting at 90 percent of one's top speed while holding the misses to a minimum and not committing some other kind of error is truly challenging.

I've made more than my share of mistakes at major matches over the years, and (while not pleased about them) have come to accept that these things do happen. At one recent match I was reminded of how our brains can mix up signals no matter how well we *think* that we are prepared. This particular stage involved four separate firing positions requiring three lateral movements to the shooter's left. Only a few steps separated each firing position. The shooter started at the first position with the rifle at port arms, and engaged four targets twice. Setting down the lever gun upon completion, the shooter was instructed to then carry with him a set of saddlebags for the duration of the stage. This set of saddlebags was then carried while engaging the shotgun and both revolvers, each from its own separate position along the line.

Receiving good instructions from our Posse Leader, this was one of those stages I personally found to my liking, and got right down to my pre-stage thoughts and preparation. I knew exactly each move I wanted to make, how I would pick-up and throw the saddlebags over which shoulder, how my shotgun rounds would best be placed on my belt, and from which side to take them for the most effective engagement. Upon reflection, there were about 12 different transitional moves, not including the levering of the long gun, the cocking of the revolvers, the loading of the shotgun, or the firing of any firearm.

As I said, this stage design was one that especially appealed to me, and I was totally ready (or so I thought). Right on cue, I had my '66 Yellowboy up and on the first rifle target at the beep. The first two shots produced two quick hits. Acquiring the third target brought me to a sudden stop. The target was in my sight, nothing was wrong with the '66, what the heck was I waiting for? C'mon, let's go! I did nothing for about three agonizing seconds. I was frozen with the front sight blade right on the damn target.

Seeming like a lifetime, it took those three full seconds for my mind to escape from the reign of confusion that had taken over. There was a good reason I had not engaged that third target on schedule, I did not know if it was the right one. Since shooting targets out of order will produce a 10-second procedural penalty, the instinct to hold was strong. What *was* wrong?

Finally I realized what had happened. "Omigod" I thought to myself, and continued on with the stage. Before I tell the reader about the rest of the run, this is as near as I can figure out what had happened. The order of target address for the rifle was to sweep twice, from "near to far," or right to left. The four targets angled away to the shooter's left line of vision, each one about two yards farther downrange than the preceding one. Now because I do not shoot with both eyes open, my depth perception is severely limited when addressing targets even at short distances. I never considered that my brain would react to the verbal command "near to far," instead of right to left it had also heard. Failing to set the order firmly as sweeping "right to left" twice, the lack of depth perception prevented me from knowing (at that moment) which was the next *farthest* target away. I can only hazard a guess that the strong signal to halt came from two possible commands, and an instant failure to confirm both were correct. At the time, it was indeed a mind-boggling experience.

The rest of this stage run was (as the reader might expect) hardly memorable. The old saying, "the best plans of

Photo 11.2A - *"Keep your chin up cowboy, you'll get better." (John Saliba, a.k.a. "Har Trigger," SASS® #338, has a bad stage as Scott McCoid, a.k.a. "Hondo," SASS® #21, times and counts along with Jim Hoffbauer, a.k.a. "Jesse Jim," SASS® #1650.)*

man and meeces… often go to pieces" applies. I lost 90 percent of my plan to engage. Instead of throwing the saddlebags over my left shoulder as I had planned, somehow they went over my right. This of course caused the shotgun rounds to become far less accessible than had been planned, and slowed up considerably the six rounds needed at that position. To compound this problem, the transition of movement to the next two positions was far from precise, as I overstepped and was forced to come back in both instances. It was a mess. The only possible redeeming factor of this entire run was that I missed no targets. This little trick my mind played on me caused me to lose at least seven seconds (probably more like nine) on this run after I compared my raw time to that of my contemporaries.

While not finding this episode very humorous at the time, I have to chuckle about yet one more lesson learned. Those among us who strive to do anything well are usually more subject to failures than those who do not. In order to succeed, one must accept the fact that he will fail along the way.

The modest successes I have enjoyed in this sport are strewn with failures. It never fails to amuse me just how quickly one can be humbled. Perhaps seeing Tommy Davis of the Los Angeles Dodgers drop an easy fly ball to lose a National League playoff game against the Giants in 1962 has led me to this conclusion, I don't know for sure. One thing is for sure though, that small 10-year-old (myself) will never forget how *humbling* that looked.

By the same token, at 36 years old I will never forget that night in 1988 when, at Dodger Stadium, I saw Kurt Gibson hit one of the most famous World Series home runs ever, in the bottom of the ninth inning. Injured and swinging badly, Gibson was slumping at the time and all seemed lost. Down by two runs, the count was three balls and two strikes. The Dodgers had two runners on base when this man experienced the greatest success of his career and those of us there that night witnessed a small miracle. How many times would you think men had failed in this same situation? The fact is that *no one* had ever succeeded in a World Series game before Gibson did in this manner. Do you think he was thinking about all the others that failed before him… or was he just thinking of hitting that ball?

Chapter 12

THE LITTLE THINGS

Making The Major Difference

The reader should understand that it is not one single move that will ultimately improve his or her times. You will not instantly approach the times run by those near the top of this sport. It is dozens of small choices, in many areas, that will add up to a significant difference. Each small step will not work every time, either. The smallest "glitch" will cost time. More moves made to save time (as used correctly) will aid in offsetting any penalty loss, or time lost to one glitch.

The shooter who has put to work all the skills he is confident of using, such as pre-approach stage study, correct positioning and movement, coupled with his or her current skill level of transitions and firearm handling, will find progressive improvement in performance. The measure of this improved performance will coincide with the level of skill and knowledge in each one of the areas that the shooter has attained. Like most things, it is the sum of the parts that make up the whole.

At Major Matches

Major matches today rarely have less than 200 competitors. The largest matches will find several hundred shooters in attendance. The average shooter (meaning most all of us) wants to do well, and anticipates giving his best efforts at any of these events. For many shooters, this does not happen nearly as often as they would like it to. I'm not referring simply to where one finishes, but more to one's personal performance. What happens to us at some of these matches? How can I be shooting so well at the local practice matches only to fall down so badly at an annual or trophy event? Oh yes, there is still lots of fun to be had, and I have learned to try to never lose sight of that. The only thing is that when this happens I am not having as much fun as I know I could.

One thing that plagues shooters to this day is the pre-match pot shooting events. Usually held the day before the main match stages begin, these are fun, short, speed shooting events that offer light competition and warm-up shooting for many competitors. What shooters don't always realize is that they can be falling into a trap of sorts. The pot shoots are fun (don't get me wrong), but they are not usually indicative of what you will be facing in the main match in terms of target acquisition and/or speed of engagement. If you continue to shoot the main match scenarios at the breakneck speed of these pot shoots (that have no consequence on the main match), you may well carry this rhythm of total speed into those main stages… and find yourself missing way too often. I try not to overdue the number of pot shooting events, and use them for more of a warm-up than anything else. Sure, I let it hang all the way out sometimes, but not without first reminding myself this is *not* my main match speed.

When other problems of main match engagement occur, is it because we have let ourselves be intimidated? You bet it is! Not only are we excited about shooting at an event of note, we pick up on the electricity of everyone else's feelings. Thinking of nothing else save shooting, some shooters will find it nearly impossible to even get a good night's sleep before the match. I have to laugh at myself here, as it reminds me of

THE LITTLE THINGS   207

those years when the anticipation of Christmas morning and what was under the tree deprived me of sleep the night before. I guess cowboy action shooting really is like Christmas to some of us!

To top off all the anticipation and intimidation factors the really important matches may present to some, have you ever arrived at the first stage in the morning and found a top name shooter on your posse? Does this really get the nerves working overtime? Do you think to yourself, "Oh boy, do I really have to shoot with so-and so?" I hope not, for the shooters who do this will have probably lost any chance of doing well during that match. Too often shooters will make the classic mistakes of trying to run with this top shooter instead of sticking to their own game plans. They will end up trying to chase this shooter, listening or watching a rhythm or pace that is not their own, and then trying to engage with that rhythm. Sadly, all this will end in frustration to those who make these mistakes when, in truth, it could have easily worked in just the opposite way.

Learn to hope for and enjoy shooting with the best competitors you can. Realize that these are opportunities to improve your own skills by observing the non-shooting transitions of a known expert. Understand that this will be of value to you. Go through each of your pre-stage routines thinking only of good technique. You know the speed will take care of itself, just get the front sight on the target for each shot. Be satisfied (even happy) as you make these correct moves and feel the confidence of having prepared well. I know it is hard not to compare times, so if you do this remember, the differences are more in the transitions then in the actual shooting. Many of the better shooters will be happy to answer a question or two if you ask at an appropriate time. Use this opportunity to learn more.

Top shooters who find themselves on the same posse understand fully the ramifications this brings. They do not chase directly, nor feel like they must wind up their speed, in order to keep pace. They will observe each other's run closely, because they know what to look for to improve their own run. Given the many ways a shooter may choose to make transitions, a top shooter will recognize one that is the most effective. Before a top shooter will change his approach in this regard, he will weigh at least four factors. First, does his style allow him to perform this task with a high percentage of success? Second, does this move present a risk equal to the gain? Is the gain so significant that the risk must be taken? Third, is he comfortable with this move? Can he do this automatically, or is it something he is not wholly familiar with? Finally, the fourth factor when considering a significant change in the approach (especially one that has risk attached to it) is to remember this is only one stage of 10 or 12. Weigh carefully the consequences of a costly error on this one stage as compared to a reasonably quick, mistake-free time that keeps you in the hunt.

One thing top shooters do less than others when shooting on the same posse is alter their own rhythm of target engagement. Now, they may not like the fact that their own speed cannot rival that of someone else, but they know to change it here is out of the question. The key is to be only as close to the outer edge of their own speed envelope as they can without going past. This is much easier said than done. Play your own game, play it as well as possible, and let the chips fall where they may.

Top shooters (as most other shooters) know where they are insofar as their current skill levels. The only difference is that the top shooter will be able to recognize and perform to that particular level on that particular day. For example, if little time was spent practicing prior to a match, the top shooter will understand that the chances of performing at his or her personal peak levels are diminished. The speed of engagement will still be effective, and impressive to most, but the top shooter will know it could be better.

I think the evidence of truth to these comments is in the consistency of the finishing places of these shooters. Rarely will these names be seen lower than the top five percent (or 10 percent at worst) of almost every event in which they compete.

There is something else I hope will help shooters start off a match on the right foot every time. Getting through that first stage of the day is often difficult. We are not yet warmed up, and there is some truth to having those first-stage "jitters."

Make the extra effort to engage that first stage more slowly than you know you could go. Taking the speed down a notch or two and insuring a clean run to start the day will help set a precedent for the rest of the match. I can't tell you how many times I've heard shooters complain about the difficulties of that first stage address.

At Speed

I picked up and began using the term "at speed" during the mid 1980s. Probably learned from my father, we used this term frequently during the three seasons of driving an older GT 2 Porsche as a father-and-son team in Regional and National races of the Sports Car Club of America.

Questions about what happened in a race, what the car was doing, and, finally, what one of us was dealing with at any time on the track often included the catch all phrase "at speed." It was one of our (and probably many other drivers) easiest ways of communicating to one another that whatever the incident, it happened at a moment when we were performing on the track at the peak of our individual abilities.

This term has found relevance for me time and time again in cowboy action shooting. I have come to this conclusion partially while observing thousands of shooters as they engage the stage scenarios under time. It matters not at all that the shooter is someone such as China Camp, Tequila, Evil Roy, Columbus D. Shannon, Dang It Dan, Harlan Wolf, Tutler, Choctaw, San Juan, Idaho John or Island Girl. These shooters (whose ages range from 25 to 65 years old) run at or near the top of the heap in cowboy action shooting and each have their own "at speed" pace of engagement. So do shooters like Blackjack, Pecos Pop, Deaf Laws and a score of other, older shooters, whose "at speed" engagement is as fast as their skills allow. Each man, woman, and junior cowboy action shooter has this in common.

This understanding of your own pace, how it is directly related to the current skill level at which you are competing and how it will increase with time, experience, patience and practice is important. If part of the fun of this sport for you is the challenge it presents on a personal level and you find improved personal performance a pleasurable experience, then knowing when you are "at speed" will aid your quest to excel.

As your ability increases to put to use all the tools, so too will the speed at which you will engage. The three-gun combat style of cowboy action shooting is about both shooting and non-shooting tasks. One of the most difficult (if not the most difficult) aspect a shooter with high ambitions must learn is to perform at the top of his or her game with consistency. To engage cleanly (with no misses or procedural penalties) "at speed" requires real effort. Engaging at a pace that exceeds one's ability will most often bring multiple misses. By the same token, engaging at a pace that produces clean runs, but does not challenge the shooter insofar as how fast he is performing will rarely lead to a higher level of performance. In order to raise our skill levels we need to know where and when to draw the line. Admittedly, it is a fine line to draw. At times it is easy to step on or across.

More times than I care to remember, the line for me is the single miss. Running on the edge of my envelope for almost an entire stage, I would sometimes falter by missing one target. I knew then (as I know today) what was happening, but holding back just the

Photo 12.2A - *Shooting on or close to the edge of our envelopes while at speed is a great feeling.*

right amount to achieve a clean run that must be a competitive one amongst those I am contending with is no easy feat. In all probability, it will be no different for you. Try (and continue to try) to slow down and reduce your misses. At first it may be to take off two misses of an average of four. It may be slowing down enough to average only one miss. When you are slowing down enough to run clean, and are just under what you feel is the fastest time you can run, this is running clean and "at speed."

The need to control your speed during a stage run really becomes important after that one miss has occurred. One five-second penalty requires me to come down in terms of how fast I am addressing the rest of the stage, and to try to make sure I do not miss any more targets. No, it does not always work, but surviving five seconds is one thing, taking 10 or 15 seconds feels like the end is near.

The hard work and effort it requires to shoot really well is too often referred to as simply "God-given talent." This could not be farther from the truth. Like most things, we get out of something what we put in. The most satisfying matches for me are those where I made the fewest mistakes and shot as close to my full potential as possible.

Photo 12.2B - *Bounty Hunter, SASS® Regulator #1849.*

Epilogue

I would imagine that most authors have had to deal with some of the same agonizing feelings that I experienced while writing this book. Many a nights I've pondered the accuracy, origins or validity of this point or that. I also fear that I may have left something out. As I write this, I know full well that later I will wish I had not forgotten to tell you about… something. If I think of it, I'll tell you the next time we meet. I may well also regret some of the things I told you. That's because nothing in this sport is constant.

I do not profess that the techniques, opinions, and information provided here are going to be accepted as "the last word." There is not just one right way to do something. I can say, however, that all of what has been offered is worthy of consideration, field tested by the dust and experience of shooters with the combined experience of more than 10,000 cowboy action shooting matches. At the very least, this information is worth knowing about. It is also a place from which a shooter may begin to develop his or her own tactical shooting skills in this discipline.

I found the most difficult aspect of this book was the accompanying photography. In comparison to the audible, visual, and editing abilities (or tools) that producing videos offer, the still photograph and written word was far and away the most difficult of the two media for me to communicate through. Forgive those photographs that appear to be somewhat lacking, they were taken by an amateur… me.

What I found most attractive and satisfying while working on this project is the way our written words allow so much detail in so many areas. I guess that would lend itself to the fact that few people find many films to be nearly as good, or as complete as the book from which the film version was taken. I don't want to cut off my nose to spite my face here, visual and audible instruction has its advantages, too!

With little or no written sources of information about how to actually engage in the mock warfare of CAS, this book may be a bit like *The World According to Garp* in its presentation. I hope (no, I pray) that the explanations offered are clear or at least can be understood. I think I've accomplished that.

My deep, personal interest and love of CAS has taken me down many paths. CAS has prompted me to try my hand at being a writer, producer, director, and now an author. These are all endeavors that, prior to my involvement in the sport, I would have never even thought of attempting.

One thing the reader can depend on while reading this book is that a real competitor wrote all the words. I did not relate information by guessing how it's really done, or after trying it a few times. This is information gathered from experience and hard work. I know I have repeated information in different chapters but repetition is building, and I want to help you build.

It is my sincere desire that as a cowboy shooter you get as much fun out of this great shooting sport as I have. There is little doubt in most quarters that CAS is very likely the best shooting discipline for friends and family ever to come down the pike. It has certainly earned its reputation of being "America's fastest growing shooting sport."

I hope you will find something in this book that will help you to shoot well, feel good about the way you shoot and perhaps even enjoy the sport more than you do right now. I'll leave you with the same final thought my dear friend Red Jones (Deadly Redley) told me so many times, "Remember to see that front sight!"

Good luck, God Bless, and good shootin'…

Your pard,
Hunter Scott Anderson
"Bounty Hunter," SASS® #1849

Directory of Vendors and Services

Firearms

American Arms, Inc.
715 Armour Rd.
N. Kansas City, MO 64116

American Derringer Corp.
127 N. Lacy Drive
Waco, TX 76705

Ballard Rifle & Cartridge, LLC
113 W. Yellowstone Ave.
Cody, WY 82414

Uberti, USA
PO Box 509
Lakeville, CT 06039

Cimarron F.A. Company
105 Winding Oak
Fredericksburg, TX 78624

Colt's Manufacturing Co., Inc.
P.O. Box 1868
Hartford, CT 06144-1868

Dixie Gun Works, Inc.
P.O. Box 130
Union City, TN 38281

E.M.F. Company, Inc.
1900 E. Warner Ave., Suite 1-D
Santa Ana, CA 92705

European American Armory Corp.
P.O. Box 1299
Sharpes, FL 32959

Freedom Arms
P.O. Box 150
Freedom, WY 83120

Guntrader (Lobo, Inc.)
Redmond, OR (541) 923-0686

H&R 1871, Inc. (New England Firearms)
60 Industrial Row
Gardner, MA 01440

Navy Arms Co., Inc.
689 Bergen Road
Ridgefield, NJ 07657

Marlin Firearms Company
100 Kenna Drive
North Haven, CT 06473

Remington Arms Co., Inc.
870 Remington Drive
Madison, NC 27025-0700

Shiloh Rifle Manufacturing
P.O. Box 279
Big Timber, MT 59011

Sturm, Ruger & Company, Inc.
283 Lacey Place
Southport, CT 06490

Taylor's & Company, Inc.
304 Lenoir Drive
Winchester, VA 22603

US Repeating Arms Company, Inc.
275 Winchester Ave.
Morgan, UT 84050

Cowboy Clothing & CAS Leather Products

B-Bar 10
9685 Cty. Rd. B
Amherst, WI 54406
715-824-3750

Redfeather's Leather
Phoenix, AZ (480) 324-1045

Red River Frontier Outfitters
P.O. Box 241
Tujunga, CA 91043

Columbus D. Shannon's Cowboy Leather
Redmont, OR (541) 548-1663

Gunslingers
757 E. Arrow Hwy. #K
Glendora, CA 91740

John Bianchi's Frontier Gunleather
P.O. Box 2038
Rancho Mirage, CA 92270

River Junction Trade Company
312 Main St.
MacGregor, IA 52157

Amazon Drygoods
2218 E. 11th Street
Davenport, IA 52803-3760
(800-798-7979)

Running Iron Outfitters
P.O. Box 205
Sonoita, AZ 85637

Tonto Rim Trading Co.
5028 N. Hwy. 31
Seymour, IN 47274

Trailrider Products
P.O. Box 2284
Littleton, CO 80161

Buckaroo Bobbins
P.O. Box 1168
Chino Valley, AZ 86323-1168

Classic Old West Styles (C.O.W.S.)
1060 Doniphan Pk. Cir., Suite C
El Paso, TX 79922
(800-595-COWS)

Wolf Ears Equipment
702 S. Pine
Laramie, WY 82070

Tucker Custom Leather
2026 Karbach #2
Houston, TX 77092

David Espinoza, Bootmaker
6042 N. 16th Street
Phoenix, AZ 85016

Galco International, Ltd. (Leather)
2019 W. Quail Ave.
Phoenix, AZ 85027
(800-874-2526)

Wild Rose Trading Co.
P.O. Box 5174
Durango, CO 81301

The Old West Mercantile Co.
24445 Sunnymead Blvd
Moreno Valley, CA 92553

Horsefly's Old West Clothing
107 South Bridge Street
Henrietta, TX 76365 (817-538-5301)

Oklahoma Rose (Ladies fancy dress hats)
422 Mendel Rivers Road.
Oceanside, CA 92054 (760-385-4826)

Old West Reproductions, Inc.
446 Florence South Loop
Florence, MT 59833

Tombstone Outfitters
24 Railroad Street, P.O. Box 667
Kingston, GA 30145

Wild West Mercantile
Phoenix, AZ
(800) 596-0444

Gila River Leather Co.
Phoenix, AZ
(623) 587-0936

Victor's Leather
Burbank, CA
(818) 845-4708

Jax Leather Co.
P.O. Box 937
Madera, CA 93639

Kicking Mule Outfitters & Leather Maker
Camp Verde, AZ
(520) 567-2501

Buckles by Mike
1225 Manzanita St.
Los Angeles, CA 90029-2233

Logan Chastain Leather, Etc.
Phelan, CA
(760) 949-7449

Jake Johnson Maker
Glendale, CA
(818) 241-5560

Buffalo Runner Boot Co.
Henrietta, TX 76365

Arizona Stagecoach
Phoenix, AZ
(623) 582-8989

Western Leather Co., Inc.
Chino, CA
(909) 464-9183

Walker '47
Anaheim, CA
(714) 821-6655

Baron California Hats
Mark Mejia
(818) 563-3025

Alphonso's of Hollywood (leather)
North Hollywood, CA
(818) 764-6555

Cowboy Corral
Sedona, AZ
(800) 457-2279

D Bar J Hats
Las Vegas, NV
(702) 362-HATS

Colorado Hat Company
Fairplay, CO
(719) 836-1411

Cowboy's General Store
Lawrenceburg, IN
(812) 537-3030

Heritage Quartermaster
Waterford, MI
(248) 648-90541

1880's Cowboy Mercantile
2563 N. Campbell
Tucson, AZ 85719

Gunsmiths, Guncarts, Parts, Targets, Etc.

Off The Wall Guncarts
224 N. Howard St.,
Greentown IN
(765) 628-2050
www.guncarts.com

Lee's Gunsmithing
Orange, CA (714) 921-9030

E.M. Horton Wagon Co. (guncarts)
Long Beach, CA
(562) 431-2400

James & Guns
Phoenix, AZ (602) 547-1942

DS Welding Steel Targets
Chatsworth, CA
(818) 727-WELD

JMS Enterprises (Har Trigger)
La Palma, CA
(714) 761-2609

The Oak Tree (guncarts)
Los Angeles, CA
(323) 728-0915

Wolff's Custom Gunsmithing
Lexington, NC
(336) 764-5442

Turner's Outdoorsman
Chino, CA
(909) 590-7225

Competition Electronics, Inc.
Rockford, IL (815) 874-8001

Don Busick Scrimshaw, Gunsmithing
N. Hollywood, CA
(818) 761-0512

PACT Timers
Grand Prairie, TX

Shady Lady's (women's clothing, etc.)
(714-998-2106)

Peacemaker Specialists
P.O. Box 157
Whitmore, CA 96096

Colonel Carter's Mercantile
Grayslake, IL

Munden Enterprises
1621 Samson St., Butte, MT 59701

Bill Johns Master Engraver
Cody, WY
(307) 587-5090

Ogelsby & Oglesby
744 W. Andrew Rd.,
Springfield, IL 62707

Smith Enterprise (cowboy gunsmithing)
Tempe, AZ
(480) 964-1818

Trader (Don Walters)
Cypress, CA (714) 827-7360

Dave Smith's Guncraft
Ruskin, FL (813) 645-3828

Jim Martin's Single Action Specialists
Phoenix, AZ
(623) 581-2366

Ammunition, Reloading Equipment.

Ten "X" Ammunition
Ontario, CA
(909) 605-1617

Laser-Cast Bullet Company (Oregon Trail Bullets)
Baker City, Oregon
(800) 811-0548

Hodgen Powder Company
(913) 362-9455

Blackhills Ammunition
Rapid City, South Dakota
(605) 348-5150

Goex, Inc.
(318) 382-9300

Dillon Precision Products
(800) 223-4570

Starline Brass
(800)-280-6660

Lyman Products Corp.
(860) 632-2020

Double A Limited
(612) 522-0306

Alliant Powder Company
(800) 276-9337

Publications, Videos & Membership Organizations

SASS (The Single Action Shooting Society)
Yorba Linda, California (714-694-1800)
(www.sassnet.com)

The Cowboy Chronicle
Membership magazine of SASS (see above)

Bar H Productions (CAS Videos)
www.bar-h.com

Krause Publications (books and videos)
700 E. State St.
Iola, WI 54990
800-258-0929
www.krause.com

Shoot Magazine (CAS publication)
(208-368-9920)

Dixie Gun Works, Inc. (Pioneer Press)
www.dixiegun.com

NCOWS (National Congress of Old West Shootists)
PO Box 221
Cedar Falls, IA 50613

Handmade Sites (web site designs)
www.cowboyactionshooting.com

WASA (Western Action Shooting Association)
PO Box 51983
Palo Alto, Ca 94303-0744
www.wasaranch.com

Independent CAS Instructors

West Coast
Quick Cal: (775) 575-6700
Choctaw: (909) 988-9491
China Camp: d.ming@worldnet.att.net
Columbus D. Shannon: (541) 548-1663
Bounty Hunter: (818) 843-2493
Lefty Longridge: (661) 222-9380

Midwest
San Juan: (970) 249-4227
Blackjack McGinnis: (217) 544-8813
Evil Roy: (970) 247-1234
Tequila: (512) 865-3579

East Coast
Harlan Wolffe: (336) 764-5442
Dang It Dan: (863) 325-8300
Sourdough Joe: (757) 851-0859
Wolf Bait: (706) 276-3363

Books With *FIREPOWER*

Action Shooting Cowboy Style
by John Taffin
Feel the rich gun leather and taste the smoke of America's fastest-growing shooting game. Every aspect is explained for shooters of all levels. Join the fun of cowboy-style shooting. Let John Taffin take you from the general store where he'll show you the latest in old western garb, to the firing line where some of the fastest guns around drop the hammer in search of a winning score.
Hardcover • 8-1/2 x 11 • 320 pages
300 b&w photos
8-page color section
Item# COWAS • $39.95

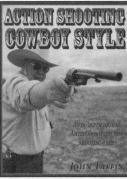

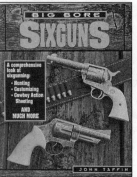

Big Bore Sixguns
by John Taffin
Follow the development of the big bores from model to model in this fascinating study. More than 300 photos provide fine details on the pioneering sixguns, as recognized firearms authority John Taffin relates the influence these guns have had on each other and the field of competitive shooting.
Hardcover • 8-1/2 x 11 • 336 pages
320 b&w photos • 16-page color section
Item# BBSG • $39.95

Black Powder Hobby Gunsmithing
by Sam Fadala and Dale Storey
Keep busy with projects for all levels of competence, from kitchen table through home workshop, all the way to the academic. Step-by-step kit-building tutorials and a resource directory make the grade.
Softcover • 8-1/4 x 10-11/16 • 256 pages
440 b&w photos
Item# BHG • $18.95

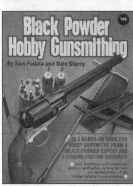

The Complete Blackpowder Handbook
3rd Edition
by Sam Fadala
Indispensable information has been funneled into a huge new edition, completely rewritten and refreshed by Sam Fadala. This textbook for black powder shooters is topped off by a catalog of all currently-manufactured black powder firearms. The ultimate source for black powder.
Softcover • 8-1/4 x 10-11/16 • 400 pages
600 b&w photos
Item# BPH3 • $21.95

Colt's Single Action Army Revolver
by "Doc" O'Meara
Learn more about the Colt Single Action Army Revolver as "Doc" O'Meara guides you through a historical look at the world's most famous revolver. With production figures and serial number ranges for early versions of the gun, this book is a must for any collector. O'Meara also mixes in stories about rare Colts and their owners that will both inform and entertain anyone interested in the gun that has come to symbolize the American cowboy.
Hardcover • 8-1/2 x 11 • 160 pages
250 b&w photos • 16-page color section
Item# CSAAR • $34.95

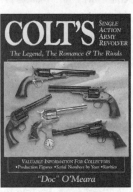

Flayderman's Guide to Antique American Firearms and Their Values
7th Edition
by Norm Flayderman
Dramatic changes in collecting tastes, prices and trends are completely covered in this must-have reference. More than 3,600 models and variants are described with all marks and specs necessary for quick identification. Includes 2,800 individually priced firearms and 1,700 large-scale photographs.
Softcover • 8-1/4 x 10-11/16 • 656 pages
1,700 b&w photos
Item# FLA7 • $32.95

The Gun Digest® Blackpowder Loading Manual
3rd Edition
by Sam Fadala
Worth its price just for the load data on 158 firearms alone, Sam Fadala crafts instructive articles and a loading tutorial into the must-have book blackpowder shooters have been craving. All-new information with expanded sections.
Softcover • 8-1/4 x 10-11/16 • 368 pages
390 b&w photos
Item# BPL3 • $19.95

Collecting the Old West
by Jim and Nancy Schaut
More than "Cowboys and Indians" this book contains a wealth of information on collecting Old West Art, Ephemera, Homestead Items, Military, Mining Mexican, Rodeos, Wild West Shows and Tourist collectibles. Also features a great variety of Cowboy and Cowgirl Gear, as well as Native American items. More than 500 photos and over 1,500 items with current values.
Softcover • 8-1/2 x 11 • 208 pages
500 b&w photos • 32 color photos
Item# WEST • $21.95